CONTEMPORARY VISUAL MERCHANDISING

Jay Diamond

Ellen Diamond

Prentice Hall
Upper Saddle River, NJ 07458

Library of Congress Cataloging-in-Publication Data

Diamond, Jay
  Contemporary visual merchandising / Jay Diamond, Ellen Diamond.
    p. cm.
  Includes index.
  ISBN 0-13-741794-2
  1. Display of merchandise. I. Diamond, Ellen. II. Title.
HF5845.D46   1999
659.1′5—dc21   98-4441
                                                             CIP

Acquisitions Editor: Elizabeth Sugg
Director of Production and Manufacturing: Bruce Johnson
Managing Editor: Mary Carnis
Editorial/production supervision and interior design: Inkwell
    Publishing Services
Cover design: Miguel Ortiz
Manufacturing Buyer: Edward O'Dougherty

 © 1999 by Prentice Hall, Inc.
Simon & Schuster / A Viacom Company
Upper Saddle River, NJ 07458

Formerly published as *Fashion: Contemporary Visual Merchandising,* by Jay Diamond and Ellen Diamond (Mission Hills, CA: Glencoe Publishing Company, 1990).

All rights reserved. No part of this book may be reproduced, in any form or by any means, without permission in writing from the publisher.
Printed in the United States of America

10 9 8 7 6 5 4 3 2 1

ISBN 0-13-741794-2

Prentice-Hall International (UK) Limited, *London*
Prentice-Hall of Australia Pty. Limited, *Sydney*
Prentice-Hall Canada Inc., *Toronto*
Prentice-Hall Hispanoamerica, S.A., *Mexico*
Prentice-Hall of India Private Limited, *New Delhi*
Prentice-Hall of Japan, Inc., *Tokyo*
Simon & Schuster Asia Pte. Ltd., *Singapore*
Editora Prentice-Hall do Brasil, Ltda., *Rio de Janeiro*

Contents

Preface *vii*

Chapter 1
The Visual Merchandising Concept in a Contemporary Environment — *1*

- The Visual Merchandiser's World   *3*
- Creating Effective Visual Presentations   *6*
- Trends   *6*
- Other Factors in Visual Merchandising   *10*
- Careers in Visual Merchandising   *13*

Chapter 2
Planning and Developing Visual Presentations — *19*

- Department Store In-House Visual Departments   *20*
- Centralized Visual Merchandising   *25*
- Freelance Arrangements   *30*

Chapter 3
Facilities Design: Exteriors, Window Structures, Interiors, and Fixturing — *39*

- Exteriors   *41*
- Storefronts and Window Structures   *42*
- Interiors   *45*

Chapter 4
Mannequins and Other Human Forms — *58*

- Types of Mannequins   *60*
- Component Parts of Mannequins   *61*
- Dressing the Mannequin   *64*
- Wigs and Makeup   *66*
- Other Human Forms   *68*
- Purchasing Mannequins and Other Human Forms   *69*
- Creating a Mannequin   *69*

Chapter 5
Materials, Props, and Tools of the Trade — 80

   Materials   *81*
   Props   *85*
   Tools and Accessories   *90*

Chapter 6
Principles of Design — 99

   Balance   *100*
   Emphasis   *103*
   Proportion   *106*
   Rhythm   *108*
   Harmony   *110*

Chapter 7
Color: Fundamental Concepts and Applications — 118

   Dimensions of Color   *119*
   The Color Wheel   *120*
   Color Harmonies   *120*
   The Neutral Ingredients   *124*
   Choosing a Color Scheme   *124*
   Psychology of Color   *125*

Chapter 8
Lighting: Dramatizing the Selling Floor and Display Areas — 136

   Light Sources   *137*
   Lighting Fixtures and Systems   *140*
   Track Lighting   *141*
   Decorative Lighting   *142*
   Lighting with Color   *143*
   Lighting Accessories   *143*
   Light System Acquisition   *147*

Chapter 9
Themes and Settings for Windows and Interiors — 152

   The Permanent Total Environmental Philosophy   *153*
   Types of Themes   *154*
   Institutional Themes   *162*
   Special Events and Promotions   *162*
   Other Themes and Settings   *162*

Chapter 10
Signage and Graphics — 169

   Types of Signs   *170*
   Sign Materials   *174*
   Letter Materials   *175*

In-House Sign Production   *178*
Sign Layout   *179*
Commercial Sign Sources   *180*

Chapter 11
Point of Purchase Display   186

Retail Point of Purchase Users   *187*
Types of Point of Purchase Fixtures   *192*

Chapter 12
Execution of a Visual Presentation   200

Selecting the Merchandise   *201*
Preparing the Merchandise   *202*
Assembling Props and Materials   *203*
Preparing the Display Space   *204*
Selecting Mannequins and Forms   *205*
Preparing the Lighting   *206*
Installing the Display   *206*
Display Sketches   *208*
Graphic Plans   *208*
Developing Specific Displays   *209*

Index   246

PREFACE

The world of visual merchandising continues to provide excitement for today's retailers. With competition at an all-time high, the job of those responsible for visual presentation has taken on greater importance than ever before. The creative accomplishments of the professionals in the field contribute a great deal to the success of the company. While few will argue that the proper merchandise is key to any retailer's success, the manner in which it is featured on the selling floor, in display windows, and in interior arrangements gives it additional interest to motivate shoppers to become customers. With innovation and creativity at their command, visual merchandisers are able to transform the most pedestrian environments into exciting shopping arenas.

In the past, the emphasis of the display person, as visual merchandisers were referred to, was on window display. Today, the scope of activities in this field has been significantly expanded. Visual merchandisers no longer just trim windows, but are involved in store design and layout, fixture selection, lighting design, the direction the store's visual program will take, and the planning and execution of displays.

The second edition of *Contemporary Visual Merchandising* retains all of the important practices and procedures of the field that were in the first edition. There are however, many significant additions to this edition. They include:

- A wealth of step-by-step illustrations depicting exactly how displays are developed, beginning with the basic elements and concluding with the finished presentation.
- A detailed illustrative presentation on how to produce the alternative mannequins that are being used by many contemporary retailers.

- A new chapter on facilities design that features the latest innovations used by retail organizations.
- A new chapter on point of purchase displays.
- A list of important terms of the trade at the end of each chapter, to help the reader develop a visual merchandising vocabulary.
- All new photographs throughout the text.
- Numerous visual projects, complete with the forms necessary to complete them.

The chapter sequence of the first edition has been retained except for the inclusion of the two new chapters. All the materials have been updated to reflect what is happening in today's retail environments. Each chapter concludes with a listing of terms of the trade (a new feature), discussion questions, case problems, and exercises.

When all of the materials have been carefully digested and applied to the exercises presented, students will have a better understanding of the role played by the visual merchandiser in contemporary retail settings. Those who desire to enter the field of visual merchandising will have the tools necessary to get a foot in the door.

The Visual Merchandising Concept in a Contemporary Environment

LEARNING OBJECTIVES

After completing this chapter, the student should be able to:

1. Discuss the various aspects of visual merchandising that are important to creating and installing modern visual presentations.
2. Describe the different environments in which visual merchandisers operate and the different demands of each.
3. List the different categories in the visual merchandiser's budget.
4. Explain the importance of safety in the installation of visual presentations and the precautions necessary to avoid mishaps.
5. Describe the elements that contribute to the success of window and interior displays.
6. Contrast the emphasis placed on mannequin design today with that of years past.
7. Briefly discuss the lighting changes that have taken place in the industry.
8. Tell about the various types of careers available to someone pursuing entry into the field of visual merchandising.

INTRODUCTION

The world of visual merchandising as we know it today is one in which artistic talents play a major role in creating an atmosphere that motivates shoppers to become customers. Unlike the fine artist whose creativity is a statement of feelings, or yesterday's window trimmer whose goal was to just to produce a pretty display, today's visual merchandiser must create displays with an eye on function, artistic expression, and the ultimate goal of increasing the store's profitability. The practice of concentrating a store's display budget on windows replete with costly props and backgrounds is the exception rather than the rule in today's retail environment. While some flagship stores such as Macy's Herald Square in New York City and Neiman Marcus in Dallas still feature exciting, costly displays, especially at times like Christmas, their branch stores are often in windowless structures or buildings that utilize a minimum of windows for display. In shopping malls, the major retail venues in the United States, the traditional windows have been replaced with wide-open entryways through which shoppers can view a large portion of the main selling floor. In these environments the store itself is the display, and it must be effectively enhanced to attract shoppers and stimulate sales.

With the emphasis on the whole store rather than on the windows that display personnel used to be responsible for, display people have become visual merchandisers, teams that specialize in the entire store's visual appearance. When one enters a Disney store, for example, the experience is unique. The total environment or theme concept immediately captivates shoppers, in particular children, who are quickly motivated to buy a variety of tempting items. With the animated figures encircling the sales arena, the giant screen that features Disney videos available for sale, and the mounds of stuffed animals heaped in an inviting fashion, a magical moment in shopping is achieved.

More and more retailers are using this concept, which was initiated by Banana Republic. In their original stores, merchandise emphasis was on safari-inspired clothing, and the interiors were designed to reflect that image. Until the company changed its image and merchandising philosophy, the stores were replete with netting, jeeps, palm trees, bamboo, and anything that gave the impression of a trip to the wild. Companies like Nike in their Niketowns, Warner Bros. in their retail outlets, and Hanna-Barbera subscribe to this thematic approach to visual presentation.

Another departure from traditional store design and merchandise presentation is a concept introduced by Ralph Lauren. In his retail shops, antique and reproduction fixtures transform the environment into a home-like setting. Merchandise is featured in armoires and on tables that one would find in elegantly designed residences. Enhanced by fine art and beautiful home accessories, the magic begins as the doors open into the stores. Shoppers are made to feel that they are in a comfortable home rather than in a conventional store.

Borrowing from the retailers, restaurants have successfully adopted the thematic approach. The first was the Hard Rock Cafe, followed by Motown, Jeckyl and Hyde, and Fashion Cafe, each creating an environment reminiscent of an exciting setting. The latest and perhaps most visually exciting of these eating establishments is the Rain Forest Cafe, with branches throughout the country. As customers enter, the lush vegetation immediately sets the mood to whet their appetites. In addi-

THE VISUAL MERCHANDISING CONCEPT IN A CONTEMPORARY ENVIRONMENT

Figure 1-1. The Rain Forest Cafe, in an exciting visual setting, is a new breed of business that combines dining out and retail space. (*Courtesy of Rain Forest Cafe.*)

tion to the food they serve, most of these dining emporiums feature boutiques offering a host of products bearing their logos, a marketing technique that adds to the bottom line.

Stores like The Gap with its functional fixtures holding carefully folded merchandise according to color, Williams-Sonoma with its enticing cooking utensils displayed creatively, and Crate & Barrel with its brilliant settings that make shopping an adventure, each add their own touches to make them distinguishable from other stores.

At the department store level, the lavish windows of the downtown flagships still generate a great deal of excitement. Particularly at Christmastime, stores like Lord & Taylor and Saks Fifth Avenue in New York City and Neiman Marcus in Dallas still impress critics and customers with their imaginative window displays. Lines of would-be customers congregate to view the extravaganzas set forth by the visual merchandisers. Each year the presentations seem more elaborate than those of the previous year.

While these approaches are exciting parts of today's visual environments, they do not encompass all of the design directions taken by the retail community. The challenge to visual merchandisers is to continue to develop ideas that will present the entire store in its best possible light every day, to make certain that their companies get a fair share of the consumer market.

Students about to enter the field of visual merchandising must develop the knowledge necessary to create and install presentations of merit. Throughout the text, concepts and theories as well as a host of step-by-step display techniques and innovative projects are carefully presented to assist the reader in learning how to develop ideas and tackle the everyday problems associated with visual presentation.

THE VISUAL MERCHANDISER'S WORLD

Visual merchandising, briefly defined, is the presentation of a store and its merchandise in ways that will attract the attention of potential customers and motivate them to make purchases. The role of the visual merchandiser in this effort is to carry out the merchandising concepts that have been formulated by management. These merchandising plans include what items are to be featured and in which locations they should be housed. The visual merchandiser, guided by these decisions and using all of his or her creative talents, sets out to present the best possible visual effects.

A position as visual merchandiser involves a combination of skills. Of course, it requires creativity, but it also necessitates a sense of order, dedication to design principles, and the discipline to follow directions, stay within budgets, and complete paperwork. It involves artistic talent and training and also knowledge of tools, lighting, construction of backgrounds and props, and a complete understanding of store design. Other important areas include the ability to create signs, both hand-lettered and computerized, write copy, and create and choose appropriate graphics. On any day, the demands of the job could involve many other abilities.

The specific duties depend on the arena in which the visual merchandiser works and at what level he or she is involved. Some positions require expertise in only one aspect of visual merchandising such as sign preparation or window installations, while others require a broader base so that all of the functions can be satisfactorily accomplished by one person. In major stores, visual merchandising roles tend to be specialized because there is often a large staff that carries out each project. When Macy's Herald Square, for example, plans and installs its famous annual Flower Show, scores of individuals with different talents undertake the task. On the other hand, a freelancer who creates backgrounds and props, installs the displays, and prepares copy must be a jack-of-all trades individual. Somewhere in between is the person who works for a small chain and, along with an assistant, is responsible for more than one aspect of visual merchandising.

Whatever the level of participation, each individual should understand the job to be performed and what his or her relationship is to the execution of the entire visual merchandising picture. Basically, there are three worlds in which people in the field are employed: department stores, specialty chains, and freelancing.

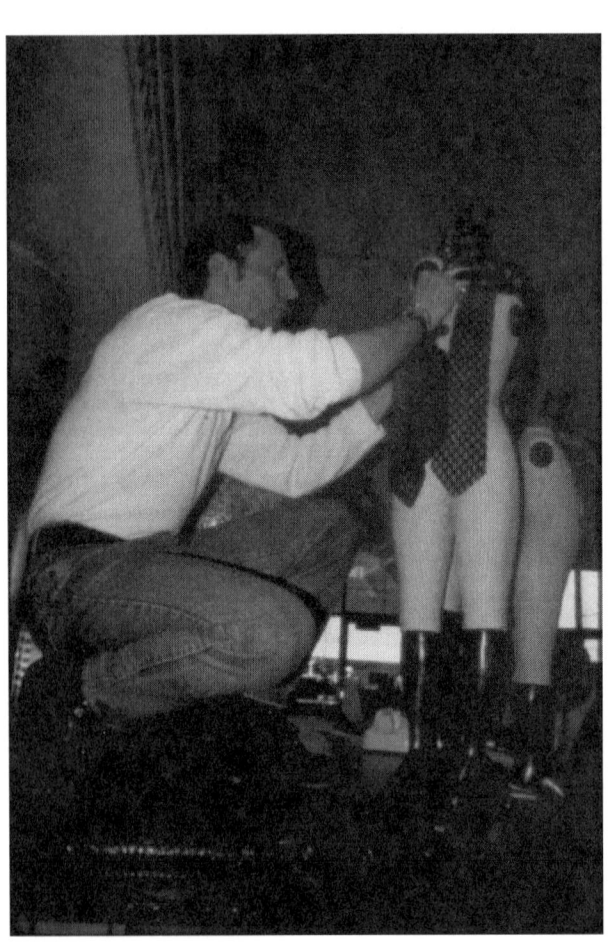

Figure 1-2. In department store flagships, in-house staffs design and install visual presentations. (*Courtesy of Ellen Diamond.*)

Department Stores

The major full-line department stores such as Macy's and the specialized types such as Saks Fifth Avenue employ in-house staffs to visually merchandise their premises. While key individuals operate from the company's flagship stores or corporate offices and are responsible for the direction of the visual merchandising philosophy and the creation of the concepts for the entire company, there are branch managers and regional supervisors who carry out the company's plans. Since the role of visual merchandise director has become so complex, the position has been elevated in most stores to vice president and in some cases, senior vice president. In addition to being the central figure in planning window and interior presentations, the visual merchandise manager has assumed numerous other responsibilities such as store design, layout, fixture design and selection, signage direction, and lighting usage.

Other members of the visual merchandising team may specialize in one or more areas. They include signmaking, graphics, prop and background construction, and trimming. Generally, each member of the team has a narrow responsibility and contributes some particular expertise to the overall challenges conceived by the head of visual merchandising. A typical department store organization chart in which visual merchandising is a subdivision of the Promotional Division shows the various job titles involved. While this is a typical arrangement for large department stores, it should be understood that each company uses a structure that best suits its needs.

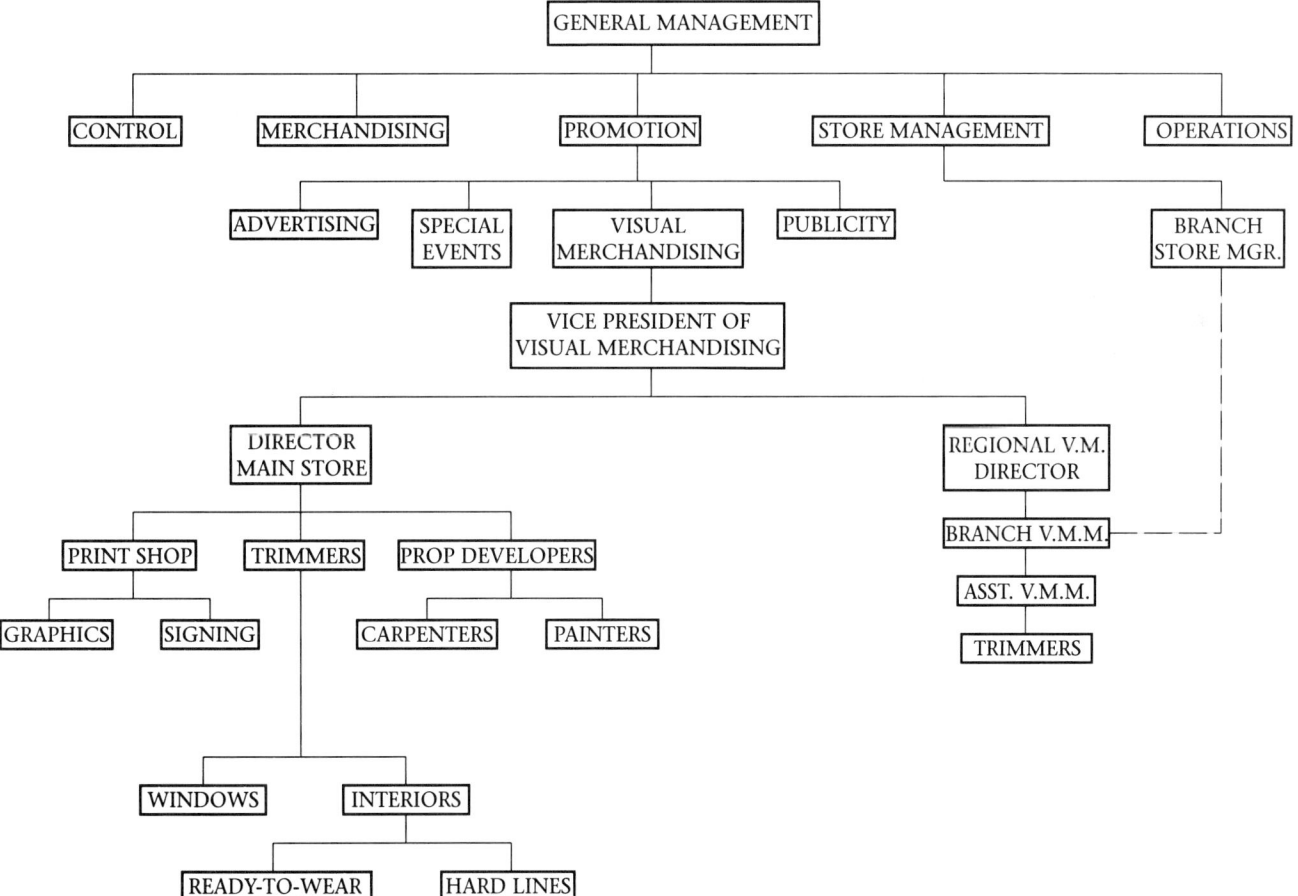

Figure 1-3. A typical department store organizational structure shows the visual merchandising department and its job titles.

Specialty Chains

Unlike the department store base of operations that generally locates management in the company's flagship store, the visual merchandising manager in chain organizations usually operates from central headquarters where all other top managers are based. The responsibility at this level is to conceive a visual concept with what is generally a small staff of designers who disseminate the ideas to those responsible for the individual stores' installations. The plans are carried out either by trimmers who travel within a particular region of the stores or by the individual store managers. In more and more companies, specific plans are set out in mock windows and interior settings in the company's headquarters and are photographed for copying by the stores. A more detailed presentation of this centralized approach appears in Chapter 2.

Freelancers

Individuals who operate their own visual merchandising businesses and provide their services to clients for a fee are called freelancers. Generally they concentrate on window presentations for independent retailers, and sometimes involve themselves in interior presentation if the store requests it.

CREATING EFFECTIVE VISUAL PRESENTATIONS

The visual merchandiser is largely concerned with the creative aspects of effective visual merchandising and the presentation of the store's merchandise in settings that will maximize sales.

The job involves the coordination of all the components of the windows and interiors, and the production of displays that will enhance the store's image and set it apart from the competition. To achieve this goal of creating an inviting environment for shoppers, a number of tasks must be performed, such as selecting the appropriate props and mannequins to enhance the merchandise. Once these ingredients have been determined, consideration must be given to sound principles of design, color conceptualization, lighting that both illuminates and creates dramatic effects, and signage that is pertinent to complete the story. The finished product should be one that attracts shoppers' attention and transforms them into customers.

TRENDS

As merchandise offerings change, so does the environment in which the goods are offered for sale. Walking through a store or past its windows, one can get a feeling about the company's image and direction. A quick look also immediately reveals whether or not the company's approach is fresh. In today's competitive marketplace, tired, shopworn mannequins, lighting that merely illuminates with no dramatic effects, fixtures that signal a time gone by, and a generally outdated appearance simply won't do. These are telltale signs that the store's efforts are stale.

There are many approaches used by visual merchandisers today to transform the selling floor and windows from ordinary to exciting. A visit to the vendors in the trade or to trade expositions will give a retailer sufficient ideas to make minor and major miracles. Through careful examination of trade periodicals such as *Visual Merchandising & Store Design*, the visual merchandiser can keep abreast of industry directions in store interiors, mannequin usage, lighting, and other areas. The latest trends, complete with pictures, are highlighted in these publications.

Some of the trends in several areas of visual merchandising are presented briefly here. More detailed explorations of these trends are presented throughout the remainder of the text.

Store Design

There is no longer a typical store design. Merchants employ the services of architects and designers who, along with visual merchandisers, create environments that are both unique and functional. The space that was once allocated to store windows has been minimized and replaced with more selling floor space. In place of the traditional windows, large panes of glass are used to allow shoppers to see a large portion of the store. The interiors range from natural settings using stone and hand-hewn woods to elegant environments with atriums, majestic staircases, marble flooring, and other touches of grandeur. Many of the major department stores are reducing the appearance of vast selling floors with the construction of individual shops or boutiques to house their special designer collections. This approach gives the customer the feeling of shopping in smaller stores rather than the cold feeling of the large department store.

Food stores are abandoning the sterile looks long associated with them in favor of surroundings that feature espresso and juice bars, preparation areas that allow shoppers to see how the products are prepared, and a host of kiosk fixtures scattered throughout the store.

Figure 1-4. This mini train station setting with boxcar fixtures builds on Osh Kosh B'Gosh's origin as a maker of overalls for railroad workers. (*Courtesy of FRCH Design Worldwide.*)

Figure 1-5. Stylized mannequins are being used in many fashion forward environments. (*Courtesy of Ellen Diamond.*)

Mannequins

While traditional mannequins are still featured by many retailers, other types have been chosen to replace them in many stores. Wire mannequins, soft sculptured types, stylized forms, and motorized models are just a few. With the cost of traditional mannequins increasing in price, many merchants have opted for forms that represent mannequins and are created by visual merchandisers. The creation of these representational mannequins is fully explored in Chapter 4, including step-by-step instructions on how to build them.

Props and Materials

The list of materials and props used by today's visual merchandisers seems to be endless. Although conventional store-bought props are available at various resource centers, more and more retailers are making use of things found in nature, such as tree branches, rocks, and sand; and found objects once reserved for the junk pile, such as old chairs, worn picture frames, and rusty farm tools. With fresh coats of paint and new finishes, they can be used dramatically in displays. Antiques and antique reproductions are also being used extensively, a trend started by Ralph Lauren.

Figure 1-6. Tree branches create a visually appealing setting inexpensively. (*Courtesy of Lord & Taylor.*)

THE VISUAL MERCHANDISING CONCEPT IN A CONTEMPORARY ENVIRONMENT

Of course, at Christmastime, animated displays and glittery props are still of paramount importance. Shoppers line up along the major department store windows to enjoy the creative offerings of the visual merchandisers.

Lighting

Although fluorescents are still used by retailers like supermarkets and warehouse clubs for general illumination, this form of lighting is no longer in great prominence in most retail stores. Today, halogen and quartz lighting and high-intensity discharge lamps are the products of choice. They not only serve the functional needs of illumination, but offer the user ways in which to achieve dramatic effects.

A variety of cans or holders are being used to house these lightbulbs, supplying a variety of looks to augment the numerous types of store fixtures.

Graphics and Signage

Although traditional two-dimensional signs are still used abundantly, signage and graphics have taken on new looks. Airbrushed murals celebrating local landmarks, multilevel murals featuring a variety of montages, animated cartoon characters that move throughout the signage, backlit transparencies, and huge photographic blowups are just a few of the exciting approaches now used in retail environments.

The use of electronics continues to pervade the retailers' premises. Fashion designer Norma Kamali began featuring each season's collections on numerous television screens in her New York City store windows. Today, the trend continues with major retailers all over the country, such as Carson Pirie Scott, Dayton-Hudson, Bloomingdale's, and Macy's, using television monitors throughout their stores to show vendor collections.

In addition to in-store video, other electronic formats are used by retailers to capture shoppers' attention. One is *Voila!*, a system by Advanced Interactive Video, Inc. of Columbus, Ohio, which is an interactive directory for use in shopping malls. The system highlights store sales and promotions and gives previews of upcoming events. It also automatically dispenses individual retailer coupons.

Instant Imagery by R.D. Button Associates, Inc. of Randolph, New Jersey is a computerized system that enables customers to

Figure 1-7. Television monitors in stores bring live action to the shopping environment. (*Courtesy of FRCH Design Worldwide.*)

see how they look in clothing without trying it on. The customer inputs his or her size and selects an outfit, which is then displayed on the person's image on a computerized screen.

Point of Purchase

In addition to the signage that abounds in retail establishments, a great deal of fanfare surrounds the use of point of purchase programs developed by manufacturers for retailer use. The Point of Purchase Advertising Institute (POPAI) reports that it now represents a $12 billion industry! Dick Blatt, its president, defines point of purchase merchandising as "displays, signs, structures and devices that are used to identify, advertise and/or merchandise an outlet, service or product and which serve as an aid to retail selling." Industry reports revealed that whenever these programs were in evidence for specific brands, sales increased significantly. Examples of how the industry has gone from one that merely used signage to one that develops full programs are included in Chapter 11.

Sound Usage

While sound is not a visual element, it is being used to enhance visual presentation. Professionals in the field agree that shoppers can turn away from visual elements, but sound is inescapable. The first early venture into sound for visual enhancement was made by Disney. In its Main Street environment in Disneyland, it determined that the attractions alone were not sufficiently stimulating. The incorporation of sound made them come to life.

Sound is being used abundantly by retailers today to set moods and give shoppers news. At Warner Bros. stores, for example, Bugs Bunny's voice is used for the store directory. More and more retailers are using music to put shoppers in a buying frame of mind. Walk through many junior departments, for example, and you can hear the rock beat that permeates the selling floor.

OTHER FACTORS IN VISUAL MERCHANDISING

There are other factors that visual merchandisers consider on a day-to-day basis, primarily budgets and safety.

Budgeting

Retailers of all sizes must grapple with how much of the budget to allocate for their visual merchandising. No matter how much is earmarked to accomplish the store's goals, it never seems to be enough.

Budgets are established in many ways, with the major department store organizations using the most structured formats. The small, independent merchant, on the other hand, tends to be less disciplined about budgeting, particularly where visual presentations are

THE VISUAL MERCHANDISING CONCEPT IN A CONTEMPORARY ENVIRONMENT

concerned. This may be because the staff does not include visual professionals who can lobby for reasonable allocations or because these merchants view visual merchandising as something to be achieved with whatever resources are left over after stock purchasing, human resource costs, and advertising.

Generally, there are three aspects to visual merchandise budgets, no matter how large or small the organization.

Display Fixturing. Equipment of a more permanent nature, such as stands, platforms, pedestals, merchandise forms, and mannequins, is generally used for a long time. Except for the major department stores where specialized forms and mannequins are set aside for specific purposes (such as the mechanical ones often used at Christmastime), this type of equipment is generally used for all presentations. Since the materials from which these forms are made are long-lasting, expenditures for this classification of display pieces are made infrequently, perhaps once a year or less often. Repairs to such equipment, such as mannequin restoration, often come out of a contingency budget.

More and more retailers are setting their sights on less costly mannequins, such as unisex types made of wire or other materials that can be used for many purposes. Creative visual merchandisers are even producing their own mannequin substitutes to feature merchandise. These forms are often very exciting, and can be made inexpensively. Using a variety of basic materials, the trimmer comes up with forms that serve the retailer's purposes. We discuss how to build these original forms in Chapter 4.

Figure 1-8. A borrowed ladder and paint cans create an appealing setting inexpensively. (*Courtesy of Mindy Greenberg.*)

Materials and Props. The settings that we see in store windows or inside stores that set the scene for a display are changed frequently. Sometimes these backgrounds are painted or adapted for repeated use, saving the retailer a great deal of expense. For specific seasons such as Christmas, when glittery fabrics, imaginative mechanical devices, and other materials indicate a specific setting, it is difficult to use the same fabrics that worked well the rest of the year. The transformation of a store at this holiday period is costly. However, because it is a time when most retailers generate a major portion of their annual sales, budget cuts are not usually made at this time. The majority of retailers overexpend themselves at this time of the year and, if necessary, cut back on the moneys used for visual presentations for the remainder of the year.

By borrowing props such as chairs, ladders, bicycles, musical instruments, etc. from other businesses or from their own merchandise departments, retailers can stretch budgets. It is the creative visual merchandiser who can develop effective presentations when costs have been greatly reduced.

Labor. A look at any major store's organizational chart for the visual merchandising department indicates that a significant amount is spent on the staff who create, construct, and install the store's visual presentations. In special situations such as storewide promotions, the labor cost is further increased by overtime pay for the staff and by hiring temporary employees to complete the project. In small stores where freelancers are generally used, expenses increase when higher prices are charged by the freelancers.

In order to cut labor costs, some small retailers have undertaken executing their own displays or at least making some changes in merchandise presentation themselves between freelancer visits. By using props that are seasonless and easy to change, retailers can reduce the labor cost of trimming.

Although the expense for visual presentations may be considerable, most retailers agree that the visual impression is very important in attracting shoppers and that any investment in creative display pays off in the end-of-the-year bottom line.

The Safety Factor

Visual merchandise design is based on such elements as lighting, merchandise selection, and the principles of display employed to ensure success. In executing designs, the installers must always make certain that the presentations are safely produced. Most retailers are reluctant to discuss careless display work that resulted in injuries and lawsuits. An electrical wire that extends past the interior display area, an overhead sign that falls, or an unsecured mannequin that topples when a customer touches it are typical of the safety problems associated with display.

Safety is an important consideration on the job, for the well-being of the visual merchandising staff as well as the customers. The potential exists for someone to be burned by hot lights, shocked by faulty electrical equipment, or tripped by poorly placed wires. In order to prevent these accidents, the following precautions should be taken when working on an installation:

- When signs or graphics are suspended from the ceiling, a sufficient amount of space must be left for shoppers to walk under them. The signs must also be out of the shoppers' reach.
- Ceiling grills or grids should be used to suspend items. The use of screw eyes directly in a ceiling might not guarantee good support. If there is any doubt about the holding ability of screws, toggle bolts should be used for plaster or plasterboard ceilings.
- All parts of a mannequin should be secured, with special attention to the base plate and rod that attaches to the buttock or ankle. The support rods should be tightened to prevent toppling. Even when

THE VISUAL MERCHANDISING CONCEPT IN A CONTEMPORARY ENVIRONMENT

mannequins are used in enclosed windows and out of the reach of shoppers, automobile and pedestrian traffic could cause them to tip over. If base plates are not used, the mannequin should be wired to the floor by a process called striking the mannequin.

- Heavy-duty nails or screws should be used to secure merchandise or props to walls. The use of pins should be avoided when long-term support is needed.
- Three-dimensional letters should be attached with bonding materials such as hot glue, double-face foam tape, or headless nails called brads. Vibration or heat from light fixtures could cause letters to fall if they are not well attached.
- Lighting fixtures should be placed out of the customers' reach. Unprotected floor spotlights should not be used in interior installations where someone could get burned by touching one.
- Extreme caution should be exercised when using hot glue guns, spray paint, or any other tool that could cause damage or injury.
- Electrical wiring should be examined regularly to make certain there is no damaged wire that could start a fire.
- Suspending wire that is strong enough for its task should be used. Although nylon filament and number 30 (invisible) wire are common choices, they do have limitations. The supports should be tested before the display is completed.

CAREERS IN VISUAL MERCHANDISING

Whether you will be employed by a major department store, starting as an apprentice and rising through the ranks; work for a chain to trim the windows of several units; or go into business as a freelancer, a career in visual merchandising will require particular skills and abilities. Some people have a natural color sense, while others might be sufficiently talented to construct backgrounds that generate excitement. Others may have the ability to hand-letter signage and price tags at a moment's notice. The challenge is to develop both what comes naturally and what can be learned from books and experience.

In order to prepare for a career in visual merchandising several practical courses are beneficial. Courses in color, design, lighting, lettering, photography, advertising layout, prop construction, and general display techniques can give the prospective visual merchandiser the background necessary for success. Schools and colleges across the country offer such courses either in degree programs or on a course-by-course basis.

Figure 1-9. A career in visual merchandising requires particular skills and abilities. (*Courtesy of Mindy Greenberg.*)

Once the preliminary tasks have been mastered, a resume should be prepared. It should be about one page in length and should briefly describe professional training, educational accomplishments, and related experiences. A good resume is needed to compete with all of the others that companies receive from candidates. Booklets from the U.S. Department of Labor and many computerized programs and books on resume writing are available. A professional resume writer can be employed to carry out the task. An appropriate cover letter should accompany the resume, outlining your interest in the position you are seeking.

In addition to the resume, a portfolio of your visual merchandising projects should be developed. It should include samples of any work that has been created by the applicant either in class or on the job.

When seeking employment, there are several places to look. Trade periodicals such as *Visual Merchandising & Store Design, Women's Wear Daily,* and *DNR* feature classified ads, and consumer newspapers do the same. Contacting employment agencies and attending trade shows can turn up important leads.

Once a prospective employer shows interest by granting you an interview, it is important to appear with a prepared portfolio of work and to present a professional and enthusiastic manner.

Proper attention to the details of a job search will ultimately match the job applicant with a suitable employer. Once you are hired, an exciting world filled with opportunity awaits you.

TERMS OF THE TRADE

centralized visual merchandising

flagship store

found display objects

freelancer

mock windows

point of purchase

POPAI

portfolio of work

representational mannequins

seasonless props

striking a mannequin

theme concept

total environment concept

visual merchandising

window trimmer

CHAPTER REVIEW

KEY POINTS IN THE CHAPTER

1. The world of display has been expanded from what was once a concentration on eye-catching windows to a concept of storewide visual merchandising that includes not only window and interior displays, but the means of presenting any and all merchandise for customer inspection, as well as creating total, exciting environments. This includes the choice and use of functional and unusual lighting throughout the premises, and signage and graphics that differentiate one part of the store from the others.

2. Merchandise presentation must be creative as well as functional so that customers can make purchases easily.

3. Borrowing from retailers, restaurants have successfully adopted the thematic approach and have transformed dining establishments into unusual environments.

4. By using the environmental or thematic approach to visual merchandising, merchants present the same setting throughout the year, without the need to change for seasons and holidays.

5. Visual merchandisers perform their duties for many different types of retailers, with each requiring the same basic preparation for success.

6. All retailers are confronted with the question of how to allocate dollars for their visual presentations. Included in their budgeting considerations are display fixturing, materials and props, and labor costs.

7. Safety plays an important role in visual merchandising. Carelessness in installation could result in injuries to store employees as well as shoppers.

8. The creation of effective presentations involves the appropriate mix of various components such as color, lighting, fixturing, and signage selection and usage.

9. In order to keep abreast of the times, today's visual merchandisers must be aware of trends in the field. Contemporary trends include store designs that depart from the traditional concepts such as natural environments, alternative mannequins, props and materials taken from places that do not require purchasing, dramatic lighting that is both functional and exciting, graphics and signage that direct customers and help sell merchandise, point of purchase devices, and the use of sound as an attracting tool.

10. A career in visual merchandising requires skill in a number of areas, each of which can be learned through formal instruction and on-the-job training.

DISCUSSION QUESTIONS

1. How does the trimmer's job in today's retail environment differ from what it was in years past?
2. Define the term visual merchandising.
3. Define the total environment concept as used by some of today's retailers and restaurateurs.
4. In what way does the department store visual merchandiser's task differ from that of the freelancer?
5. What are some of the categories covered by the visual merchandising departments of most large department stores?
6. In what way can a store that utilizes mannequins reduce its outlay for such forms while still capturing the shopper's attention?
7. By what means can a visual merchandiser cut costs for materials and props?
8. Why must the visual merchandiser pay strict attention to safety when creating presentations?
9. What are some of the safety points that should be considered when planning and installing a display?
10. What are some of the new types of illumination that provide both functional and dramatic effects?
11. What is meant by the term point of purchase?
12. What types of knowledge must the visual merchandiser possess in order to develop a career?

CASE PROBLEMS

Case 1

Faced with imminent human resources cuts in just about every division and reductions in budgeted expenditures for materials and supplies for the forthcoming year, the divisional managers at P. J. Marin, a Midwestern department store, are preparing their recommendations for the new budget. The company had been a dominant force in retailing but has fallen on hard times. The board of directors has instructed management to cut expenses until profits improve.

The company's visual merchandising manager believes that the way to become more profitable is through promotion, with visual merchandising playing a key role. Mr. McCarthy, who heads visuals, has tried to convince management of the dangers of curtailing his budget at this time, saying that an increase would be in order to help alleviate the problem. Though he advocated a visual plan that would require an increase in spending, or at least to remain at the current budgetary level, the powers at the top still directed a cut.

The budget for the visual area is divided into three parts: display fixturing, materials and props, and labor. It was suggested by the assistant visual manager that several trimmers be terminated and department managers be responsible for making interior changes. Another suggestion was to reuse last year's materials and props. Still another suggestion was to cancel the order for action mannequins that were earmarked for the active sportswear department.

The time has arrived when Mr. McCarthy must deliver a revised budget that not only will reflect dollar reductions but will still make P. J. Marin a force in visual presentation.

Questions

1. Do you agree with the company's plan to cut the visual budget? Defend your answer with sound reasoning.
2. Which, if any, of the suggestions are feasible?
3. What approach would you suggest to cut the budget and still make P. J. Marin a visually appealing store?

Case 2

Jane Livingston is a recent graduate of a prestigious art school. Her aspirations of becoming a fine artist have diminished with each art gallery's rejection of her paintings. She would someday like to break into the world of fine art with her creations, but, with funds at an all-time low, she is considering a career alternative.

Prodded by her friends, Jane is considering a field related to art, visual merchandising. Everyone feels she can easily make the transition from painting landscapes to creating attractive visual presentations because of her excellent background in design principles and color. Although she possesses the art background, she has never taken a professional course in display or visual merchandising and doesn't know where or how to begin.

One of her former professors suggested that a department store would be a perfect beginning for Jane. As an apprentice she would learn to apply her theoretical knowledge to on-the-job situations. Another acquaintance feels the chain store would be a wiser choice. Working for a major specialty chain with several hundred stores would offer a broad base of experience, he says. Finally, a relative is trying to convince her to take the freelance route. "Being your own boss would give you freedom that the other two approaches wouldn't offer," she says.

Jane has assembled a portfolio of her artwork to help break into the field of visual merchandising. She still hasn't decided, though, which route to take.

Questions

1. Does Jane have the qualifications necessary for a visual merchandising career?
2. Which route do you feel would be best for her to follow? Why?

NAME: _____ DATE: _____

EXERCISES

1. Visit a department store or specialty store to evaluate its window and interiors in terms of safety. Use the Evaluation Survey form as a guide in your evaluation and prepare a report on your findings.

EVALUATION SURVEY

Store Name _____ Store Classification _____

Mannequin placement _____

_____

Hanging signs _____

_____

Light fixtures _____

_____

Interior prop placement _____

_____

Accessible display merchandise _____

_____

2. Make an appointment to interview someone in visual merchandising and prepare an oral report to include the following information: career opportunities, salary potential, typical workday, academic preparation, and technical expertise needed for employment. The interviewee may be someone employed by a company or working as a freelancer.
3. Using this chapter as a guide, prepare a resume for a hypothetical job in visual merchandising for a department store, for a chain organization, or as a freelancer.
4. Put together a portfolio of work for use in securing a visual merchandising position. Make certain that all samples of your work (photos of displays, lettering, layouts, etc.) are carefully mounted on presentation board or in a binder.
5. Write a report on a trade publication such as *Visual Merchandising & Store Design*. The report should include the following: the name and date of the publication, a summary of at least one article, the overall format of the publication, and how this periodical helps the visual merchandiser.

Chapter 2
Planning and Developing Visual Presentations

LEARNING OBJECTIVES

After completing this chapter, the student should be able to:

1. Discuss the necessity for in-depth visual planning before installing a presentation.
2. Describe the three major approaches used by retailers to achieve visual presentations that will attract customer attention.
3. Differentiate between the in-house approach to visual merchandising and the one employed by centrally operated chain organizations.
4. Explain how some major department store organizations kick off their visual merchandising plans for the next season.
5. Discuss the detailed visual planning that is subscribed to by such department stores as Lord & Taylor, and how the branches learn about these plans.
6. Compare the windows of major department stores with those of chain operations and discuss why the former's presentations are generally of higher quality.
7. Relate how centralized chains help their units with visual installations.
8. Describe the various techniques employed by freelancers to sell their services to retailers.

INTRODUCTION

Consumers examine store windows and interiors to seek out the merchandise that will satisfy their needs. Few ever stop to realize the planning that went into making these presentations whet their appetites and tempt them to purchase. While the conception and mechanics of a display itself are secondary in importance to the merchandise being offered, it is often true that the shopper would not act on a desire for merchandise if its presentation were not so striking.

Only students of retailing, or more specifically visual merchandising, can really appreciate the trials and tribulations associated with creative visual presentations. The shopper may admire a display, but is seldom inquisitive about how it was put together. For students of retailing, an understanding of the various approaches to the planning, development, and execution of visual installations is essential. How are the visual concepts born? Who creates the formats? Who installs the displays? These are just some of the questions that must be answered to fully comprehend the work that goes into visual presentations.

Generally, there are three approaches used to achieve satisfactory displays and visual merchandising formats, depending on the size and organizational structure of the retailing operations. Traditionally, the department store organization with its visual team expends the major effort in terms of dollars and involvement in visual merchandising. One need only observe the window and interior presentations to immediately understand the complexity of the department store's visual program. A careful study of Christmas windows by such retailing giants as Lord & Taylor and Saks Fifth Avenue with all of their drama will impress upon viewers that these are major undertakings. Chains usually take a different route; many have centralized visual facilities at corporate headquarters where the ideas for visual presentations are born and then disseminated to individual units for installation by a manager, or sometimes a trimmer who works in one of the company's regions. Finally, the smaller merchant who recognizes the value of professional visual installations but doesn't have the staff to deal with the creative complexities of visual merchandising takes yet a different approach, employing the services of a freelancer.

This chapter focuses on the approaches used by department stores, chain organizations, and independent retailers to achieve visual presentations that will turn shoppers into customers.

DEPARTMENT STORE IN-HOUSE VISUAL DEPARTMENTS

Every major department store organization, whether it be of the full-line variety such as Macy's, Bloomingdale's, and Marshall Field who carry an assortment of hard goods and soft goods, or the specialized types such as Saks Fifth Avenue and Bergdorf Goodman, has its own in-house visual merchandising department. So important are these departments to the giant retailers that their directors often carry the title of vice president. Whereas formerly a store had a display department with major emphasis on windows, today it has a full-blown visual merchandising department or division with responsibility not only for windows and interior displays, but for everything that has a visual orientation, such as store design and fixture procurement.

With the enormous growth and expansion into branch stores, the visual presentations that are planned for the flagship store must be applicable to these units as well. There must be a unity of presentation in both the fixturing and the themes.

The overall effectiveness of each season's merchandise promotion is dependent on the visual staff's total familiarity with and comprehension of what has been planned, how it will be accomplished, the dates for executing the various elements, and the coordination of all the promotional departments. Too often store plans go astray because the specialized work areas work independently, as if their responsibilities and roles do not require cooperation from the other areas.

For example, an advertising campaign will only prove successful if the visual merchandise presentations complement what is highlighted in the advertisements. If the store makes a splash in the media that emphasizes bright colors and a lively theme, but the store displays are not at all bright and stimulating, the shopper who was motivated by advertising to enter the store may lose interest, once inside. If the shopper does not see any tie-in to the advertised theme, or sees a different theme promoted in-store, he or she may just leave the store, confused.

Without question, extensive planning is a key element in the success of any retailer's visual presentation. Generally, major stores begin this planning process at least six months before the installation so that prop and supplies purchases can be made, alterations of existing props and selling areas can be accomplished if necessary, and the efforts can be coordinated with the other sales promotion departments, such as advertising. Figure 2-1 features an excerpt from Lord & Taylor's Window Schedule, which carefully spells out the events that will take place in the store on a particular date. Note that each window bears a number for easy identification and a brief description of which merchandise will be featured. In order to accomplish the difficult task of guaranteeing a unified approach for the store's promotion emphasis, some major stores have a kick-off seminar for every member of the company who has some relationship to merchandising and its promotion, including advertising, special events, publicity, and visual merchandising. In addition to those involved in promotion, the audience generally includes buyers, merchandise managers, store managers, group managers, and department managers, all of whom are involved in merchandise selection and placement and whose input might help direct the store's merchandise promotions.

		UPDATED	WINDOW SCHEDULE		
WINDOWS 15 & 14 **38TH ST CORNER**	**WINDOWS 13, 12, 8, 7** **5TH AVENUE**	**WINDOWS 7D, 6D, 5D, 4D** **Dreicer Bldg** **5TH AVENUE**	**WINDOWS 11 & 9** **FRONT ENTRANCE** **5TH AVENUE**	**SMALL WINDOWS &** **SHADOW BOXES**	**SUNDAY ADS IN** **CONJUNCTION** **WITH WINDOWS**
INSTALL TUESDAY	**INSTALL TUESDAY**	**INSTALL WEDNESDAY**	**INSTALL THURSDAY**		
JULY 30 Continued	**JULY 30** Continued	**JULY 31** incl Windows 7, 8 DKNY Color TBC	**AUGUST 1** Continued		**AUGUST 4**
AUGUST 6 A-Line	**AUGUST 6** A-Line Lime/Purple with mailer	**AUGUST 7** Continued	**AUGUST 8** Yeohlee Purple Velvet 2 figures		**AUGUST 11** Nautica NYT 5 x 21
AUGUST 13 Continued	**AUGUST 13** Continued	**AUGUST 14** Nautica Women's	**AUGUST 15** Continued		**AUGUST 18** Polo Jeans NYT 5 x 21
AUGUST 20 Lauren Ralph Lauren	**AUGUST 20** Lauren Ralph Lauren	**AUGUST 21** Continued	**AUGUST 22** Polo Jeans Men's/Women's		**AUGUST 25** Lauren by Ralph Lauren NYT 12 x 21

Figure 2-1. An excerpt from a Lord & Taylor window schedule spells out displays to be installed and corresponding ads. (*Courtesy of Lord & Taylor.*)

Most companies publish a visual merchandising directions book with merchandise presentation guidelines. These books are carefully detailed so that nothing is left to chance. Figures 2-2 and 2-3 feature a Table of Contents for Lord & Taylor's Presentation Guideline for its Valentine's Day visual presentations, and a detailed Presentation Guideline Overview that covers everything from key dates to signage, special needs, presentation techniques, and fixturing. While this illustration is for Lord & Taylor, it should be understood that most other stores use the same methodology for getting their points across to all the units in the organization.

To show how detailed these planning books are, the following has been excerpted from a typical Lord & Taylor Merchandise Preparation

```
           VALENTINE'S DAY 1996
           PRESENTATION GUIDELINES
              TABLE OF CONTENTS
OVERVIEW                                           1

PART I:
MERCHANDISE PRESENTATION GUIDELINES
         WOMEN'S AND MEN'S FRAGRANCES SELLING    2
         WOMEN'S FRAGRANCES                      3-7
         MEN'S FRAGRANCES                        8-12
         COSMETIC ACCESSORIES                    13-15
         JEWELRY                                 17-20
         ACCESSORIES                             21-24
         INTIMATE APPAREL                        25-28
         MEN'S FURNISHINGS                       29-32
         GIFTS                                   33-38
         FINE JEWELRY                            39

PART II
VISUAL MERCHANDISING GUIDELINES                  1-28
```

Figure 2-2. A Presentation Guidelines Table of Contents. (*Courtesy of Lord & Taylor.*)

Guideline. While the books deal with a wealth of charts and graphs directed toward merchandise managers and buyers in addition to visual merchandisers, our examples deal specifically with the visual staff and its role in Valentine's Day presentations. It should be understood that the same format is used for every event in the store.

Figure 2-4 spells out to the trimmers exactly which props will be used for the upcoming holiday event, and specific details for each item. Additional instructions are listed under Special Notes to make certain that every detail is properly attended to.

Breaking down the instructions even further, the instructions include a summary called Steps to a Successful Seasonal Presentation as shown in Figure 2-5. This guarantees that if faithfully followed, the end result will be perfect.

In order to make certain that the actual displays are executed according to the prescribed plans, drawings for specific presentations accompany the written instructions. Figure 2-6 shows how a plexi promotional bag riser should be trimmed for the Valentine's Day promotion.

An important part of the fragrance displays for the Valentine's Day promotion requires the use of in-house produced hat boxes. Figures 2-7 and 2-8 illustrate detailed steps in the construction of the boxes, and how they should be stacked for the finished display. The step-by-step construction of the hat boxes eliminates the need to produce and ship the props from the flagship's visual merchandising department, saving the company the costs associated with packing and shipping.

Rounding out the Merchandise Presentation Guidelines package are a wealth of other ideas and instructions for the trimmers in the

VALENTINE'S DAY 1996
PRESENTATION GUIDELINES OVERVIEW

KEY DATES
TUESDAY, JANUARY 15	VISUAL SET-UP COMPLETE
TUESDAY, JANUARY 23	SIGNS IN-STORE
WEDNESDAY, FEBRUARY 14	VALENTINE'S DAY
THURSDAY, FEBRUARY 15	VISUAL TAKE-DOWN

SIGNING
  11x17 GENERIC: TO BE USED IN CONJUNCTION WITH THE VISUAL PRESENTATION
  22x28 GENERIC: USE THROUGHOUT THE STORE, ESPECIALLY AT KEY ENTRANCES
  "WHAT A PERFECT PRESENT": COSMETICS, JEWELRY, INTIMATE APPAREL, MEN'S FURNISHINGS

ITEM PRESENTATIONS
- ALL VALENTINE'S MOTIF MERCHANDISE SHOULD BE PROJECTED FORWARD AS A SINGULAR PRESENTATION WITHIN ITS PARENT DEPARTMENT.

SPECIAL NEEDS
  FRAGRANCES:
- MERCHANDISE ONE FRAGRANCE PER TABLE WHERE POSSIBLE.
- STORES CAN FEATURE FRAGRANCE GIFT SETS WITH KEY ITEMS SKUS ON ROUND TABLES WHERE POSSIBLE.
- ALL OPEN SELL SKUS MUST BE TICKETED.
- HATBOXES: L&T SIGNATURE HATBOXES CONTINUE TO BE IMPORTANT NOT ONLY FOR VALENTINE'S DAY BUT THROUGHOUT THE YEAR.
- STORES MUST REFER TO EITHER THE ENCLOSED GUIDELINES OR THE HATBOX VIDEO WHEN CREATING FRAGRANCE HATBOX GIFTS USING EXISTING STOCK OF HATBOXES.
  SMALL BOXED MERCHANDISE:
- USE ROUND TABLES WITH PLEXI LIPS AND BUILD-UP ON RISERS.

PRESENTATION
- CONCENTRATE ALL KEY ITEMS IN ONE AREA WITHIN THE PARENT DEPARTMENT TO CREATE A GIFT-GIVING ENVIRONMENT.
- BY FEBRUARY 1ST, ALL RED AND PINK MERCHANDISE SHOULD BE PROJECTED FORWARD WITHIN ITS PARENT DEPARTMENT TO ENHANCE THE VISUAL PRESENCE THROUGHOUT THE STORE.

FIXTURING
- STORES SHOULD UTILIZE ALPHA TOWER AND ROUND TABLE CONFIGURATIONS TO CREATE A VALENTINE'S DAY ENVIRONMENT WHEREVER POSSIBLE (CONCENTRATE FIXTURE CONFIGURATIONS IN COSMETICS, GOURMET/GODIVA, ACCESSORIES, MEN'S FURNISHINGS).

MEN'S FURNISHINGS
- UTILIZE ROUND TABLE WITH PLEXI LIP BUILD-UPS. MERCHANDISE ALL VALENTINE'S MOTIF IN ONE LOCATION (HOSIERY, BANDED BOXERS, NECKWEAR). THIS CONFIGURATION SHOULD BE MERCHANDISED ADJACENT TO DOUBLE/TRIPLE HUNG VALENTINE'S DAY MOTIF BOXERS.

VISUAL MERCHANDISING PRESENTATION
  TABLECLOTHS:
- USE RED BENGALINE TABLESKIRTS WITH VALENTINE'S DAY OVERLAYS (RED LOGO ON WHITE). BE SENSITIVE TO PLACEMENT, 30" - 36" AISLE (REFER TO GUIDELINE).
- STORES MAY UTILIZE ROUND ITEM TABLES OR RECTANGULAR ITEM TABLES (FOR MERCHANDISE REQUIRING CAPACITY FIXTURING).
  THE FOLLOWING PAGES DETAIL TABLE CONFIGURATIONS AND HIGHLIGHT THE APPROVED SCENARIOS WITHIN EACH VALENTINE'S DAY ZONE, 30" -36" AISLE.
  PADDED WALLS:
- ALL RED WALL PROJECTIONS FROM CHRISTMAS ARE TO BE REMOVED AND CHANGED TO THEIR EVERYDAY COLOR.
  WRAPPING PAPER:
- ALL STORES WILL BE RECEIVING THE VALENTINE'S DAY COSMETIC WRAPPING PAPER.
- THE PRE-WRAP BOX STACKS ARE TO HAVE THE TOP AND BOTTOM BOXES WRAPPED IN THE RED PAPER AND THE MIDDLE BOX WRAPPED IN THE WHITE PAPER.
  FRAGRANCES:
- TOP OF COUNTER, OPEN SELL FRAGRANCE UNITS ARE TO BE PRE-WRAPPED WITH RIBBON AND STICKER, EVERY OTHER FACING.
- CUSTOMER COURTESY WRAPPING WILL ALSO BE OFFERED FOR VALENTINE'S DAY.
- VISUAL MANAGERS SHOULD AFFIX A PRE-WRAPPED #25 SIZE BOX TOP ONTO THE 14x22 SIGN.
- REFER TO VISUAL MERCHANDISING SECTION INCLUDED IN THIS GUIDELINE FOR DIRECTION ON VISUAL SET-UPS IN STORES.
- PROPER AND ORDERLY HANDLING OF SEASONAL TRIM AND STORAGE. SEASONAL ASSETS MUST BE SAVED.

Figure 2-3. A Presentation Guidelines Overview for Valentine's Day. (*Courtesy of Lord & Taylor.*)

branches to use, from how to use streamers to the stacking of gift boxes in a display. If the trimmers carefully follow all of the outlined procedures, the stores will have uniform visual merchandising presentations for the Valentine's Day holiday.

Ongoing Visual Tasks

The visual team is not only concerned with the installation of new windows and interior displays. Their role involves much more than that. One important function is performed each and every day

VALENTINES
VISUAL MERCHANDISING SEASONAL DIRECTIVE
EVENT: VALENTINE'S DAY 1996

	YES	NO	DETAILS
ROUND ITEM TABLES	X		Specifics and Sketches Attached
RECTANGULAR ITEMS TABLE	X		As Needed - Red Bengaline
TABLESKIRT	X		Red Bengaline
OVERLAY	X		Red Logo on White - Quantities Owned Attached
GIFT WRAP	X		Red w/White Logo & White on Silver Logo
RIBBON	X		Red Background w/Hearts
BOX STACKS	X		Round & Heart Combinations 1995 - Use From Last Year See Attached
PAPER STREAMERS - WIRED	X		See Attached - As Per Guideline
RED, SILVER FORM COVERS	X		Use as per Sketch - See Attached
GILT FRAMES	X		Silver as per Sketch
FABRIC	X		Use as per Sketch - See Attached

SPECIAL NOTES:
- KEEP BOX STACKS TALL AND GRAPHIC ON LEDGES. NO DITZ
- GODIVA/SCENT SHOPS - ALPHA TABLES, BOX STACKS. SIGNING
- BENGALINE RED CHRISTMAS WALLS MUST BE REMOVED.
- USE ALL STREAMERS.

Figure 2-4. A prop list to be used by trimmers for Valentine's Day. (*Courtesy of Lord & Taylor.*)

throughout the stores. It is called the daily walk-through.

At the end of the day, just about every display inside the store has been handled by shoppers. Shirts on counter displays have been picked up and replaced, but not always in a careful manner. The outfits on mannequins have been pulled and distorted, leaving a less than perfectly dressed form. To return the merchandise displays to their original state, trimmers conduct these daily walk-throughs and freshen what the shoppers have mishandled. In this way, the display's appearance begins each day with a clean look. If this is not attended to, the store will take on a shabby appearance and the visual presentations will not attract as many shoppers' attention as was planned for.

CENTRALIZED VISUAL MERCHANDISING

As you have just learned, most department stores have in-house staffs that visually merchandise the flagship stores as well as the branches. In the chain organizations, with some numbering more than 1,000 units, this arrangement would be impractical. Stores like The Gap, Victoria's Secret, The Limited, Eddie Bauer, and Williams-Sonoma do not use professional trimmers to install the displays in their stores, but instead utilize a centralized visual program that satisfactorily serves their needs. Still others, like Crate & Barrel with approximately 60 units, use a combination of a centralized visual program and an in-store trimmer.

The centralized visual plans are extensions of the chain organization's philosophy in all of its decision making. Just as the merchandise is centrally purchased by buyers at corporate headquarters and the policies are centrally developed by top management, so too is the concept of visual merchandising centrally planned.

The Total Centralized Visual Plan

To put it simply, chains that subscribe to centralized visual planning use model windows and interiors to design their presentations; photograph the models; and send the pictures to the various stores for reproduction. In addition to the photographs, specific written directions and drawings are sent to help the visual installer complete the

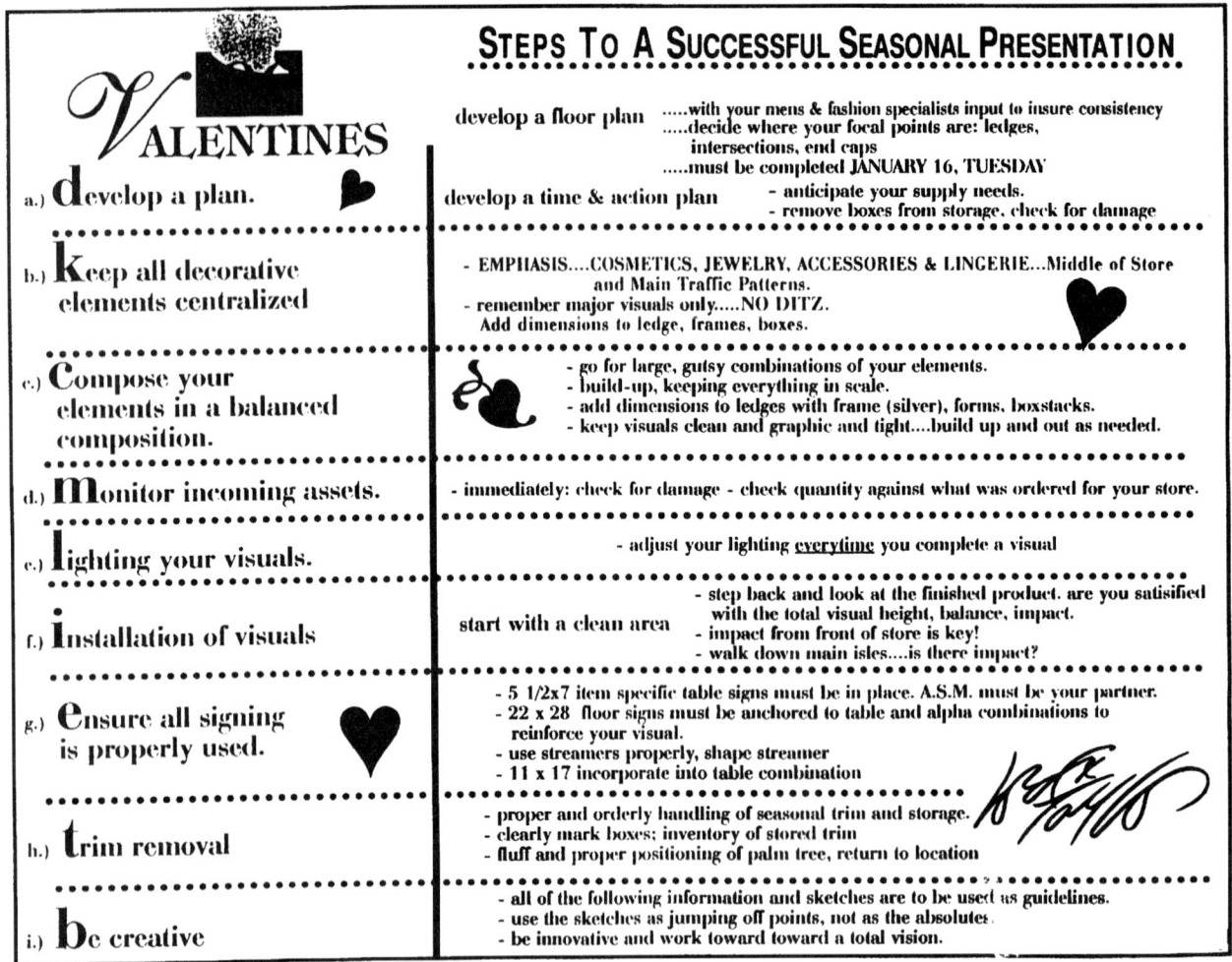

Figure 2-9. A summary of trimmer instructions for creating a successful presentation. (*Courtesy of Lord & Taylor.*)

job. The reason for the specificity of the various displays is that in the vast majority of the chain organizations, the displays are installed by a store manager or assistant and not a trained, professional visual merchandiser. Among the many companies that subscribe to this type of centralized visual merchandising is Williams-Sonoma. They send kits to the various units that contain some of the following items:

- An actual photograph like the one featured in Figure 2-9. Along with the photograph is a signage checklist.
- A graphic presentation, as in Figure 2-10, that depicts each item in the display along with numbers on the drawing that correspond to the provided list of items. In this way, if the photograph isn't totally clear to the installer, the graphic plan will take any of the guesswork out of the presentation.
- The actual signage that is featured in the display.

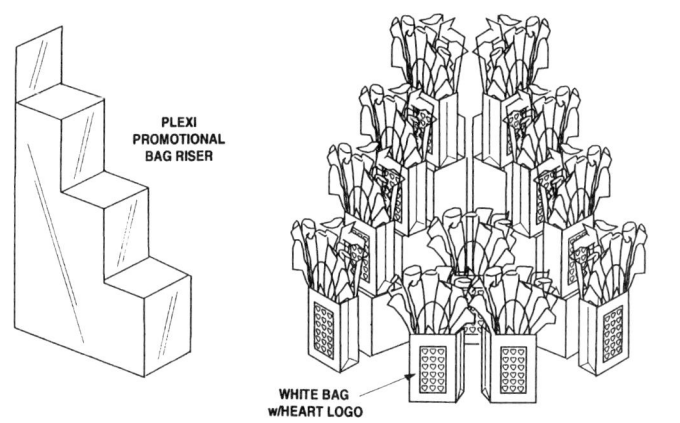

Figure 2-6. Suggested use to trimmers of plexi promotional bag riser. (*Courtesy of Lord & Taylor.*)

- Any materials that are not sold in the store but are used for display purposes. In Figure 2-11 the short bamboo spears and leaves, featured to enhance the pitcher, will be provided by central merchandising in the packet.
- Price tags, if used, are also sent to the store.

The Williams-Sonoma product line easily lends itself to duplication. In stores that feature soft goods, however, where pinning and draping of goods is often required, the results are often less satisfying. They do nonetheless satisfy the store's needs and save the company the funds that would be needed to have professional installers in each store.

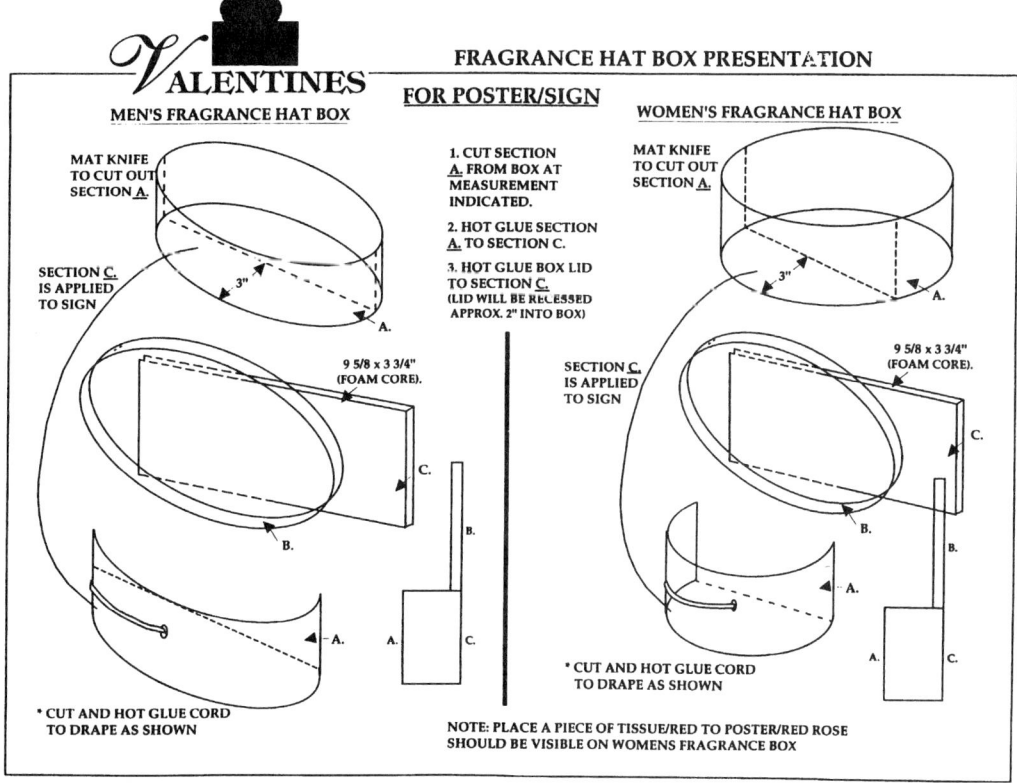

Figures 2-7 & 2-8. Detailed steps in the construction of hat boxes and how to use them in a display. (*Courtesy of Lord & Taylor.*)

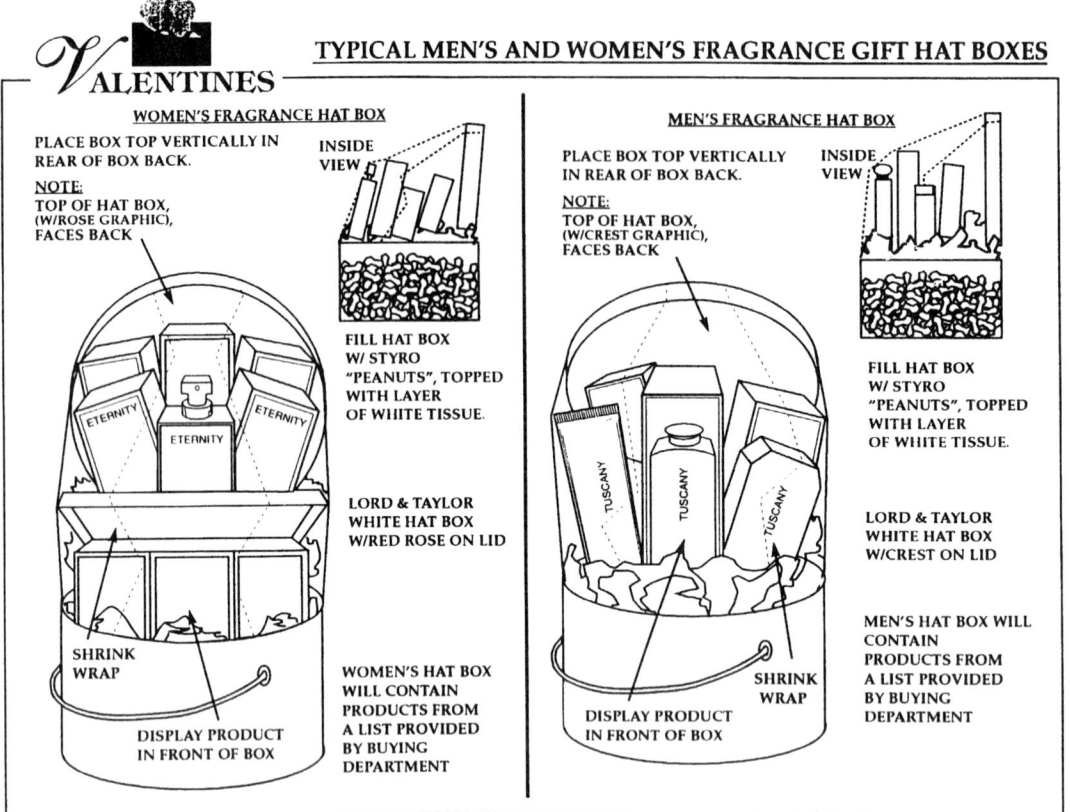

Figures 2-7 & 2-8. Detailed steps in the construction of hat boxes and how to use them in a display. (*Courtesy of Lord & Taylor.*)

It should be noted that with the trend away from traditional window structures in favor of wide-open fronts and plain glass walls that separate the outside from the inside of the store, especially in shopping malls, visual merchandising has become a little easier. In Figure 2-12 the entire store is a visual presentation, with little attention to separate, formal window displays.

Alternate Central Visual Merchandising Plans

Some companies like the concept of centralized visual merchandising in order to guarantee a uniformity of display in all of their units. However, they believe that their stores and clientele are better served if an on-staff trimmer is available to prepare the presentations. At Crate & Barrel, a home products company with more than 60 stores, the concept works as follows:

- The vice president of corporate design is involved in store design, working with buyers, checking what goods are coming into the store, and reporting all of this to the design and display people. The buyers are regularly consulted as to how they see the merchandise featured on the selling floor. This gives the centralized

PLANNING AND DEVELOPING VISUAL PRESENTATIONS

Figure 2-9. In centralized visual plans, actual photographs and signage checklists are sent to individual stores for reproducing displays. (*Courtesy of Williams-Sonoma.*)

design team the information needed to prepare guidelines for the store's visual program.
- Each store has at least one full-time design and display individual, with larger stores such as the Chicago flagship and the New York City Fifth Avenue branch having as many as six.
- The company has four regional designers who are responsible for bringing the desired display guidelines to the stores' trimmers.
- In addition to the chain of command that verbally brings the visual ideas from top management to the store level, photographs such as those in Figures 2-13 and 2-14 are used to get the concepts across.

In some chains, where the organization is divided into regions, the companies often use one or two trimmers to service all of the stores in the region. While there is no single individual present at all times in a particular store, this method does afford the chain professional visual installations approximately every two weeks.

Ice Cream

DQ	Item Description	Sku	Display Comments
3	Krups Ice Cream Maker	771402	
16	*Gelato* Book	1060623	
18	Banana Green Compote	1180728	Late; add to feature upon arrival
18	WS Crystallized Ginger	47266	
24	Bourbon Vanilla Beans	1073659	
18	Bar Mop Towel s/6	752576	
12	Oxo Scoop	1053099	

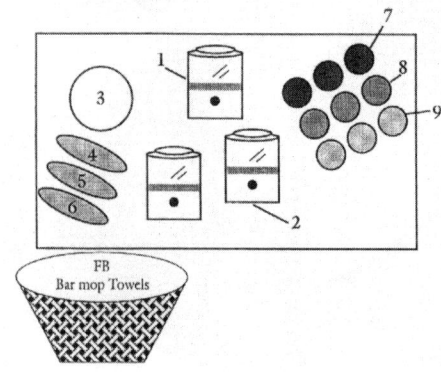

Furniture

Structure

1) Ice cream machine is on an 8" riser.
2) Ice cream machine is on 3 Australian Ginger cans.
3) Small biscotti jar is filled with vanilla beans, place on a 6" riser.
4) Banana dishes are stacked 6 high.
5) Banana dishes are stacked 5 high.
6) Banana dishes are stacked 4 high.
7) Australian Ginger is 3 high, 3 across.
8) Australian Ginger is 2 high, 3 across.
9) Australian Ginger is 1 high, 3 across.

If you do not own this furniture, place books in small floor basket.

Figure 2-10. A graphic presentation of the completed display in Figure 2-9. (*Courtesy of Williams-Sonoma.*)

FREELANCE ARRANGEMENTS

A mall or a downtown shopping area gives shoppers the impression that retailing is dominated by the major department stores and specialty chains. This is actually the case, but there are numerous stores throughout the United States that are one-unit operations or are parts of small chain organizations with just a few units. Like their larger store counterparts, they are interested in maximizing profits and realize that effective visual merchandising is essential to their goal. Short on the expertise necessary to install their own visual presentations and equally short on the funds to employ a full-time display professional, many small companies use the services of a freelancer who, for a fee, performs the visual merchandising tasks.

Freelancers work in a number of ways. Some charge an hourly fee for their time and charge for the props and materials they install in the client's interiors and windows. Others charge a flat fee per trim, while others contract for a certain number of changes throughout the year.

PLANNING AND DEVELOPING VISUAL PRESENTATIONS

Figure 2-11. A display photograph with special notes to stores. (*Courtesy of Williams-Sonoma.*)

Just as there are artists with different styles and designers known for achieving a special look, most visual merchandisers and trimmers have distinctive styles and approaches. Figures 2-15 and 2-16 feature some freelancer installations.

Bearing in mind that store windows are the silent sellers of retailing and the impression they make is vital to the store's success, the retailer should select the freelancer who is to accomplish the visual merchandising task carefully. Such factors as cost, prop utilization, and scheduling should be discussed before entering into an agreement. If an actual contract is drawn, these details are usually spelled out. In less formal arrangements, the retailer would be wise to discuss each point to make certain that both sides understand the deal.

Unlike the previous classifications where large teams of professionals carry out a prescribed plan of visual merchandising, the freelancers and retailers who employ them develop the concepts and plans together from a mutual understanding of the format, style, and direction that the presentations will have. The freelancer has several ways of showing a prospective employer his or her methods and style of work.

NOTE:
- *Posters are farthest away from doors and the cubes are closest to the door.*

Figure 2-12. When large glass fronts are used, the entire store is seen as a complete visual presentation. (*Courtesy of Williams-Sonoma.*)

Figures 2-13 & 2-14. Photographs are sent to stores to get the concepts across. (*Courtesy of Crate & Barrel.*)

PLANNING AND DEVELOPING VISUAL PRESENTATIONS

Figure 2-15. A display featuring freelancer self-made mannequins. (*Courtesy of Mindy Greenberg.*)

Figure 2-16. A window display featuring props that use a nautical theme. (*Courtesy of Mindy Greenberg.*)

First, most freelancers prepare slide or photographic portfolios that show examples of displays that they have completed. Some even develop video presentations that can be distributed to prospective clients. By examining any of these visual presentations, the retailer can immediately discern whether or not the freelancer uses an approach appropriate for his or her store.

A second route is to provide a list of stores for the retailer to visit so that the displays can be observed in person. This also enables the potential client to discuss the trimmer's work with other retailers.

Finally, a route taken by many freelancers who are just beginning their careers and do not yet have track records is to offer to do a display without cost to the retailer. This is an investment in time, but it could result in a regular professional relationship.

It should be noted that emphasis in this discussion of freelancers and small stores has been on window installations. Most independent retailers trim their interiors themselves or call upon freelancers for advice concerning merchandise arrangements and fixtures. The dollars they expend are generally for the store's face or entrance, and they do the balance of the store's visual merchandising themselves.

Needless to say, all of the planning and developing of the visual presentations include such areas as proper use of the store's window structures and fixtures; appropriate usage of mannequins, props, and materials; proper design; color and lighting choices; and the use of appropriate copy and signs, all of which must be presented in eye-catching themes and settings. All of these aspects are fully explored in subsequent chapters. In Chapter 12, we focus on how all of these aspects are coordinated in the step-by step installation of a display.

TERMS OF THE TRADE

centralized visual merchandising

daily walk-through

display presentation kits

freelancer

freelancer contract

in-house visual department

kick-off seminar

model windows

photographic portfolio

total centralized visual plan

CHAPTER REVIEW

KEY POINTS IN THE CHAPTER

1. In order to make the best use of visual merchandisers, many large department stores prepare planning books that emphasize each department's role in visual presentations.
2. The three major visual merchandising categories of retailers are those who have in-store visual departments, those who use centralized display staffs that set the tone for all units to follow, and those who employ freelancers to trim the windows.
3. The centralized plans are generally either totally centralized operations whereby model windows are installed, photographed, and sent to stores for reproduction; or an alternate plan whereby the creative aspects are accomplished centrally, and the individual units have in-store trimmers to follow the plans.
4. To emphasize the next season's visual approach, many large retailers hold planning seminars for key personnel in both the flagship and branch stores.

PLANNING AND DEVELOPING VISUAL PRESENTATIONS

5. Visual presentations should coordinate with advertising and other sales promotional devices for maximum sales effectiveness.
6. The visual merchandiser's efforts are based on the merchandise and directions initiated by the merchandise managers and buyers.
7. Most chains, especially those of significant size, use store personnel, rather than trained visual merchandisers, to dress their windows and interiors using company-provided guidelines. Some chains use traveling trimmers to visually merchandise the stores.
8. Freelancers are employed by small chains and independent retailers to execute displays. These trimmers are paid either on a per-window basis or by annual contract.
9. Freelancers promote their services to retailers through the use of portfolios that feature their work or videos that show them in action.

DISCUSSION QUESTIONS

1. Which classification of retail organization expends the most dollars for visual merchandising?
2. What are the three most common approaches used to achieve satisfactory visual presentations?
3. How do branch stores emulate the flagship store's visual format if different personnel perform the installation function at each store?
4. Through what means does Lord & Taylor make its visual presentation known to the entire company?
5. Discuss the various elements used by Lord & Taylor in its Valentine's Day Merchandise Presentation Guidelines.
6. Who provides the visual team with the information necessary to carry out appropriate visual presentation?
7. Is it necessary for the store's advertising campaigns to match its visual presentations? Why?
8. How far in advance of a season should the visual team begin its preparations for the following major presentation?
9. What are the major elements indicated in a store's planning booklet?
10. In addition to detailed, written procedures, what other devices are used to make certain that new visual displays are constructed as desired?
11. How have chain organizations with numerous units instructed their store personnel to visually merchandise their premises?
12. Why do many chains use nonprofessional personnel to trim windows?
13. Which retailer classification makes the most use of freelancers?
14. How can a freelancer tempt a retailer to use his or her services?

CASE PROBLEMS

Case 1

Since the opening of its first unit, which is still the company's flagship, Avidon's has expanded into one of the largest department store organizations in the Midwest. Over the last 20 years, the store's emphasis has been away from the downtown or main street shopping center in favor of opening units in major malls. Unlike the traditional format of the parallel-to-sidewalk window configuration used in the flagship, the newer stores have employed the windowless window concept, so the store itself is the visual presentation. The cost of mall space has mandated that traditional windows are a luxury and that the space is better used as selling areas.

In order to modernize the older units in the organization, Avidon's has decided to adopt the windowless window concept in all of the units except the flagship store. This will give the stores a fresh appearance and additional selling space.

While Avidon's has always prided itself on its visual presentations, management recognizes that it is impractical to continue to use such a large staff when windows are no longer available for trimming except at its main location. Cutting expenses will be a benefit of the new concept, but the company believes it must still visually present merchandise in a manner that will motivate shoppers to purchase.

The visual staff firmly believes that it will still play a vital role in dressing the store even though physical changes have taken place. The visual director would like to see her people assigned to the various units to arrange the inventory attractively and set up interior displays. However, the general merchandise manager believes less emphasis on formal display and more on merchandise arranging on the floor would better serve the store's needs and could be accomplished by department employees.

Questions

1. Do you agree with the store's movement away from the conventional approach to visual merchandising?
2. Should it sacrifice the windows for more selling space in all of the stores?
3. How could regular department personnel learn to visually merchandise their areas satisfactorily?

Case 2

Perry Wilson's window installations have attracted attention for the ten years since he graduated from college and started his own freelance company. By chance, his first assignment was for a men's clothing store, and he has remained a specialist in visual presentation for menswear. He has received a great deal of recognition for his work but hasn't been totally satisfied with the limitations of planning and developing visual presentations only for menswear. His unhappiness is based on two factors.

First, menswear stores traditionally make fewer changes than do women's stores. Menswear is a two-season business while womenswear is a five-season operation. In order to make a living, Perry must sell his services to many men's outlets because they require little attention over the year.

Second, and even more frustrating for Perry, is the fact that men's shops are less given to the artistic and sometimes flamboyant approaches used for the windows in women's shops. Although menswear has come a long way from the conservative image of yesteryear, the window concepts generally remain quite conventional.

Perry would like to break into women's visual presentations. Although he believes he has the talent and ability required for such display work, he hasn't been able to convince any womens' retailers to use his services. Without photographs of women's windows or recommendations from satisfied clients of womenswear, he hasn't been able to show off his expertise. He even offered to do some displays at no cost, but still he hasn't any takers.

Question

How might Perry arm himself with ammunition to overcome retailers' doubts?

NAME: _____ DATE: _____

EXERCISES

1. Prepare a Special Events calendar for a full-line department store for the month of February indicating the dates, names of the events, and visual merchandising participation for each promotion. Put your data on the form provided.
2. Visit a unit of a major chain organization (the malls are filled with them) and learn from the manager about how they accomplish their visual presentations. Prepare a written or oral report to include the following questions:
   a. Does the home office give any visual direction?
   b. Is there a formal plan or presentation provided by the home office?
   c. Who installs the actual presentation?
   d. Is merchandise selection for displays left to the store manager's discretion or does central management make the decision?
   e. How often are the visual presentations changed?
   f. Who provides the signs and other copy for visual merchandising?

Exercise 1 SPECIAL EVENTS CALENDAR

Date	Promotional Event	Visual Merchandising Participation

Chapter 3
FACILITIES DESIGN: EXTERIORS, WINDOW STRUCTURES, INTERIORS, AND FIXTURING

LEARNING OBJECTIVES

After completing this chapter, the student should be able to:

1. Understand the importance of a facility's design to the success of its operation.
2. Describe some of the exteriors that the restaurant segment of retailing is using today to attract attention.
3. Describe five types of window structures that are found in retailing.
4. Differentiate between open-back windows and windowless windows.
5. Explain the uses of shadow box windows.
6. Discuss the circumstances for using vitrines instead of open-type pedestals.
7. Describe the environmental concept for interiors.
8. List six types of fixtures that are commonly used in store interiors to display merchandise.
9. Describe an architect's plans for a company and tell why they are important.
10. Discuss the purpose of the artist's rendering of a facility's design.

INTRODUCTION

Essential to the success of every operation that deals with consumers is the ability to motivate potential customers to come inside. Advertisers spend their professional lives whetting the public's

Figure 3-1. Restaurant exteriors are designed to catch the attention of passersby quickly. (*Courtesy of Rain Forest Cafe.*)

appetite with artwork and copy that will hopefully result in a trip to the store or restaurant. While it is true that many consumers visit their favorite companies after reading a specific advertisement or set out for a specific store or restaurant for a specific item or special meal, there is a vast market of people who enjoy a visit to a mall or downtown area without a destination in mind. These consumers could be tempted by an operation that has the right appeal.

Who could encounter the entrance to the Rain Forest Cafe without wanting to go inside to see the merchandise offered for sale, and stay to have a meal? Figure 3-1 illustrates how appealing the facility is to the passersby. It is refreshing to see how many businesses in malls and other busy shopping locations are beginning to embrace extraordinary facility designs over the mundane variety.

In years past, the basic design of a new store or restaurant was generally left to a team of individuals that included store planners, interior designers, and architects. The visual merchandiser was not typically involved in such early decision making. His or her role was to set up merchandise in the windows, counters, shelves, and other interior locations as designed by other people. In the restaurant industry, the visual merchandiser was completely absent. Today, a look at many retail operations and restaurants shows that visual merchandisers are present in the initial planning. No one is better qualified to make judgments about the design of the environment. Raymond Anderson, for example, of Crate & Barrel spent four years in visual display work for the company before being named vice president of corporate design. He not only designs the company's complete facilities, but regularly involves the visual merchandisers in their creation. His visual merchandising background has given him an understanding of how a facility would best serve the merchandise offered for sale.

Other important players in facilities design are the merchandise vendors themselves. In the very showrooms to which retailers come to shop the lines, the vendors are designing their facilities to give ideas to the retailers that can be used in their shops. Bass Shoes, for example, designed its showroom as an environment that immediately raised its product line to a new level. Not only were the shoes there for purchasing, but so was an exciting facility that could easily be translated into retail environments. Many other vendors producing merchandise that ranges from computers to fashion are leaving behind their mundane showrooms and creating newer, fresher environments that epitomize

FACILITIES DESIGN: EXTERIORS, WINDOW STRUCTURES, INTERIORS, AND FIXTURING

their product lines and help the retailers borrow from these concepts. This is especially helpful to the smaller retail operation who hasn't the available in-house professional staff or the funds necessary to employ outside help. When specific plans are laid out for them, even the smallest shopkeepers can bring excitement to their stores.

This chapter focuses on the overall design of store and restaurant facilities including exteriors, window structures, interiors, and fixturing.

EXTERIORS

When Banana Republic initiated its environmental concept, it made certain that the theme would be carried right to the front of its stores. Jeeps crashing through windows into the stores' entranceways motivated shoppers to come inside to see what was happening. The excitement generated by Banana Republic in its storefronts led the way for many other businesses to put their best foot forward right at the entranceway.

Of course, not every company uses the approach initiated by Banana Republic, but all pay strict attention to their exteriors to make certain that they sufficiently motivate would-be customers to come inside for a closer look.

On a trip to a mall, a downtown shopping area, or any place where retailers and restaurants are located, you will see that each business has a different design. Some are contemporary with giant walls and lots of steel, while others feature polished brass and rich woods. Still others decorate their facades with a wealth of materials such as brick and mortar. Each company uses the exterior to develop an image and convey a message to the public. The Rain Forest Cafe, a business that combines both retail space and a restaurant facility, does an outstanding job in attracting attention. Located in shopping centers along with scores of stores and other restaurants, the Rain Forest Cafe features a jungle-like atmosphere at its entrance. With lush foliage filling the exterior, replete with replicas of animals found in the wild, a live animal trainer with a live parrot in hand hawks the crowd. His or her appearance generally draws large crowds to see the performance. Ultimately, a large percentage of the spectators come inside the facility either to purchase the goods offered for sale, to eat a meal, or both. It is a visual presentation that, at this time, has little competition.

The flagship store of Crate & Barrel in Chicago, Illinois also set out to attract shoppers with an outstanding physical facility. A huge glass silo-like structure surrounded by several levels of glass windows makes a striking contrast to other retail operations in the area. Every floor in the building is immediately seen from the outside. Because merchandise displays are presented in an exciting way, the shopper is drawn inside for closer inspection. This glass cathedral certainly gives the store an image of its own.

While the use of specific materials is important to the aesthetic quality of the design and the general impression that it leaves in the consumer's mind, function must play a vital role in the form used. Eye appeal is certainly a factor, but the design must be functional in order to properly feature what the company is trying to sell.

STOREFRONTS AND WINDOW STRUCTURES

In retailing, there are several specific categories of window structures and storefronts used at the entrances to stores. They are conceived and developed by designers and visual merchandisers. Each is designed with a specific purpose in mind, and they run the gamut from the typical downtown retailer's flagship and its parallel-to-sidewalk configuration to the popular no-window fronts found in many shopping malls. It should be understood that these are basic designs that allow for many variations.

Parallel-to-Sidewalk Windows

Retailers who have the advantage of a very large store on a main street often choose to build storefront windows that run parallel to the sidewalk and are generally back-closed to separate them from the rest of the store. These windows are preferred by many visual merchandisers because they only need to concern themselves with the merchandise being displayed in the window. There is no interference of interiors as occurs in open-back designs. In stores that employ this format, such as Macy's, Herald Square, Carson Pirie Scott, Chicago, and Filene's in downtown Boston, there are usually multiple windows in the storefront, with the entrance to the selling floor in the center of the building. It should be noted that these windows are the ones on which retailers expend the most dollars for displays. The stage-like settings they offer are perfect for extravagant displays at Christmas and other times when the store is looking to promote something special. Figure 3-2 features a typical parallel-to-sidewalk design.

Corner Windows

When a retailer has the good fortune to occupy a corner location, the design should take advantage of the fact that passersby will be converging on the store from two directions. Stores in large shopping malls vie for such locations and generally pay a premium rental for them. Given practically identical circumstances, architects, store designers, and visual merchandisers use corner locations very differently. The differences are often based upon the type of merchandise that the store will feature in the windows, and the number of entrances needed to maximize shopper traffic.

Figure 3-2. Windows parallel to the sidewalk are often found in older structures such as this Eddie Bauer store. (*Courtesy of FRCH Design Worldwide.*)

FACILITIES DESIGN: EXTERIORS, WINDOW STRUCTURES, INTERIORS, AND FIXTURING

Figure 3-3. Stores on street corners often have windows that can be seen from each of the two converging streets. (*Courtesy of Ellen Diamond.*)

In some corner designs, there is a corner window with entrances on either side of it. In others, the entrance is in the center, with two windows flanking it. In still others, the traditional windows are deemphasized for display, with just glass separating the interior from the exterior. Using this format, the entire store is presented as a visual merchandising package.

When traditional windows are the choice, a variety of styles is used. Some may be the traditional types which usually run from 8 to 10 feet high; others are the 3- to 4-foot raised showcase variety that display small items that can be closely inspected by shoppers. Figure 3-3 features a corner window.

Open-Back Windows

Retailers who believe that the entire store should be visible to the consumer from the outside, yet feel the need to feature conventional window displays, often choose the open-back window structure. While this format does give the retailer these two features, there is a drawback. Open backs sometimes invite shoppers to handle the merchandise on display, so the display can become unkempt. On occasion merchants have found children romping through such windows, knocking over merchandise and causing damage. Figure 3-4 features an open-back window structure.

Figure 3-4. The open back window provides a full view of the store. (*Courtesy of Ellen Diamond.*)

Angled Windows

In order to give more exposure to the viewer, some visual merchandisers and architects design windows that are similar to the parallel-to-sidewalk type but can feature more displays in less space. By angling the windows, they can be elongated to form a vestibule that leads the shopper to the store's entrance.

Arcades

When a store has minimum frontage on the street or in a mall, but has ample depth, the arcade front is often constructed. The arcade configuration requires setting the store's entrance back from the building line and extending the size of the display windows. Stores with limited frontage whose merchandising philosophy requires more window display space benefit from such a design.

Islands

Deep vestibules and wide frontage result in an excessive amount of space at the store's entrance. In this ample exterior space the typical arcade configuration is often used. Some stores wishing to better use the lobby area and gain additional display space build islands in the center of the vestibule. The island design enables the shopper to view merchandise from all angles. In today's economy, however, with high rent and space limitations, this structure has generally disappeared from the retail scene. Some retailers, however, make use of the island window inside the store. These islands extend the sales effort by enabling the shopper to walk around the store and view the merchandise from all angles while waiting for an available salesperson. Stores that have display islands often find that shoppers are more likely to know exactly what they would like to purchase, thus cutting down on the time it takes for the sales associate to suggest merchandise.

Windowless Windows

Retailers in mall locations often choose to construct their stores without one of the conventional window designs. The consensus among these retailers is that with ample open frontage the shopper can get an impression of the store's merchandise and will enter the premises without being enticed by a window. Windowless windows or the no-window concept requires a great deal of attention to proper visual merchandising of the store's interior, with merchandise clearly visible from outside the store. The only apparent drawback to this arrangement is the security of the merchandise. Stores that use this open design must make considerable efforts to secure their goods. Some use security guards at these entrances as a cautionary measure. When stores of this nature are closed, a security gate blocks off the entire entranceway but still permits consumers to see inside. Figure 3-5 features a windowless window.

Figure 3-5. In this windowless window the store's complete tie inventory is seen from the outside. (*Courtesy of Juno Lighting.*)

FACILITIES DESIGN: EXTERIORS, WINDOW STRUCTURES, INTERIORS, AND FIXTURING

Figure 3-6. This circular glass block front distinguishes the store's entrance from the other stores. (*Courtesy of FRCH Design Worldwide.*)

Circular Windows

In order to individualize their images, some companies develop window structures that are quite different from the traditional ones. While they do not give the retailers additional space in which to display goods, they do take the store's image out of the ordinary. The Crate & Barrel flagship on Chicago's North Michigan Avenue is an example of a giant circular window that immediately separates that structure from all of its neighbors. Figure 3-6 features a circular window that is atypical of most store designs.

Shadow Box Windows

Stores that feature small items such as jewelry require window structures that enable close inspection of the merchandise without requiring the shopper to crouch on the floor. Windows of this nature are elevated so that comfortable, clear viewing is possible. Some retailers, such as jewelers who deal in expensive, one-of-a-kind precious gems, sell directly from these shadow box cases. They have easy access from the back for the items' removal. In this way, the jeweler can display wares and make them easily accessible for closer inspection and an ultimate sale. At the end of each business day the merchandise is removed and placed in secured storage for safekeeping.

Other shadow box usage is for displays that change every week or so. These items include sunglasses, fashion jewelry, and other small items. Since there is no substantial value to these items, they remain in the shadow boxes, as is the case with other display windows. Figure 3-7 features a shadow box window.

Figure 3-7. Shadow boxes help bring small items up to or just below eye level for close inspection. (*Courtesy of Ellen Diamond.*)

INTERIORS

Although the actual interior design of any store is generally the work of an architect and a designer, the visual merchandiser is often involved to make suggestions about how the store's merchandise can best be featured. This team sets out to create an environment that is both pleasing for the shopper to experience and, at the same time, functional. They must carefully assess where fixtures will be stationed, the design and color scheme of the arrangement, the flow of traffic, the assignment of space to the particular selling departments and how they best interface with their neighboring departments, the lighting that will best illuminate the store, and other issues such as flooring, signage, and graphics.

By walking through any store that has been built in the last ten years, one will notice that greater attention than ever before has been given to individuality of design. The typical, traditional layouts and fixturing of the past no longer meet the challenges of competition. Retailers select their designs as carefully as they choose the merchandise that will fill the selling floors. A distinct image is the goal, so that shoppers will immediately recognize the differences.

The remainder of this chapter focuses on the fixturing used in today's retail environments. Color is explored fully in Chapter 7, lighting in Chapter 8, and signage and graphics in Chapter 10.

FIXTURING

Fixtures come in a vast array of materials and designs. They are chosen with the store image in mind, and their suitability for the merchandise that they will house. By examining the many fixture offerings in periodicals like *Visual Merchandising & Store Design* and making trips to the vendors who specialize in store fixtures, one can evaluate the various styles. The designs run the gamut from high-tech to wooden antique types. Within the many different styles there is a wide range of floor cases, wall cases, island display cases, shadow boxes, vitrines (closed display pedestals), open pedestals, slatwall, and show-and-sell fixtures.

Figure 3-8. Floor cases that combine storage and display. (Courtesy of FRCH Design Worldwide.)

Floor Cases

One type of fixture that combines the functions of storage and display is the floor case. Located away from the walls of the store, a floor case enables individuals to view the merchandise at close range and provides the sales associate with a counter on which to show merchandise. This type of fixture is a must for jewelry, glasses, expensive handbags, and other items that should not be handled by the shopper. Once arranged in a specific pattern, they not only present an aesthetic picture, but they can also direct the shopper through the store. Figure 3-8 features some showcases used in retail premises.

FACILITIES DESIGN: EXTERIORS, WINDOW STRUCTURES, INTERIORS, AND FIXTURING

Wall Cases

The basic element in almost any retail establishment's layout is the wall case. Whether it is a case filled with shelves for stackables such as sweaters, shirts, bottles, towels, dinnerware, glassware, shoe boxes, or table linens or is fitted with rods for hanging merchandise, it is the mainstay of the department's fixtures. It is the visual merchandiser's task to make certain that a wall case is not boring. Merely hanging merchandise on the rods or placing the folded items haphazardly will not entice shoppers to purchase. If arranged tastefully and artistically, these cases will help turn shoppers into customers. Like window displays, wall cases are often referred to as silent sellers. Figure 3-9 features a wall case that houses merchandise as well as inviting close inspection, handling, and selection for purchase, all possible without the services of a salesperson.

Figure 3-9. The wall cases shown here are the basic units that feature most stores' stackable merchandise. (*Courtesy of FRCH Design Worldwide.*)

Multipurpose Merchandise Systems

In addition to the wall cases that are permanently installed, many retailers are availing themselves of multipurpose merchandise systems that offer a great deal of flexibility. These systems can be configured easily to adapt to most retailer's needs. Some utilize pegboard with a variety of brackets that can house either shelves or hanging rods. Others use slatwall, a system that uses grooved panels into which fittings may be inserted for shelving or hanging items. Still others employ slot walls that enable the user to create a combination of shelves that can be changed quickly to meet most merchandise needs. Figure 3-10 features a multipurpose system.

Figure 3-10. Multipurpose systems provide flexibility in merchandise display. (*Courtesy of Ellen Diamond.*)

Island Display Cases and Tables

These fixtures encourage self-service. They come in a variety of designs, some with storage areas below and others merely serving as places to dis-

Figure 3-11. These tables, used in a Sears store in Mexico, allow for self-selection. (*Courtesy of FRCH Design Worldwide.*)

play items. Customers are visually encouraged to choose a piece of merchandise from a counter and purchase it without salesperson assistance. Figure 3-11 features display tables.

Shadow Boxes

When a store wishes to catch the attention of the shopper who is waiting for assistance, it might feature merchandise in a shadow box. These display environments are generally fitted with lights and are placed in strategic locations with the merchandise directly at eye level. They are often grouped in clusters of two or three to have a greater impact. To make certain that the trimmer's artistic arrangements are not tampered with, these boxes are usually fitted with glass windows. If the shadow boxes are without glass protection, they are placed out of customer reach, but within customer view.

Vitrines

Still another display fixture option is the vitrine. It is a glass-enclosed display pedestal that enables the shopper to see the merchandise from all sides. It is built high enough to permit comfortable viewing. Small items such as jewelry, belts, sunglasses, and evening bags are displayed in these fixtures.

Show-and-Sell Fixtures

Many retailers have difficulty attracting a sufficient number of sales associates to their companies. Without people who are capable of selling, the store often finds that shoppers who are motivated to shop leave disgruntled because their needs were not satisfied by a capable salesperson. In order to overcome this very serious problem, many retailers are using fixtures that are neither cases nor pedestals but further promote customer self-service and add variety to the merchant's display options. Generally known as show-and-sell fixturing, these racks and stands are a better choice for some merchandise that may get lost inside counters or on shelves. These fixtures often feature the latest merchandise arrivals and are generally placed at the entrance to a department. If the featured collection has several components, each is given space on the fixture. Often a mannequin dressed in an ensemble of the merchandise is featured next to the fixture. In this way the shopper can see the merchandise and how it looks on a figure, and then can proceed to select the pieces that are appropriate for his or her needs. Figure 3-12 features a show-and-sell fixture.

Figure 3-12. This show-and-sell fixture in Osh Kosh Children's Wear features shoes and seats for fitting. (*Courtesy of FRCH Design Worldwide.*)

In some companies, visual merchandisers send directives to the selling departments about the placement of these fixtures and how they might be best utilized to attract attention. For multipurpose use, some retailers are using systems that can be quickly assembled and reassembled to fit specific needs. Instead of using fixed show-and-sell fixtures, they use adjustable ones such as grid systems that can serve many purposes.

The abundance of fixturing on the market today is overwhelming. Almost daily, newer and more exciting fixtures become available to meet every retailer's need. The visual merchandiser keeps up with trends through catalogs, showroom visits, trade expositions, and trade periodicals such as *Visual Merchandising & Store Design* and *Identity* magazine.

The Complete Layout

The storefronts, window structures, interiors, and fixturing discussed thus far are chosen by the team employed to design each store. Each visual element is conceived and executed to have aesthetic quality as well as perform a particular function. In the past, small retailers and restaurateurs visited storefront companies and fixture showrooms for their overall design ideas. Very often, these consultants didn't consider the whole project, but only their end of the layout. Today, even the smallest organization understands the need for a total, unified retail premises package. Coordinating the complete layout is a must if the desired company image is to be achieved.

Architects who specialize in retail establishments and restaurants are called on to design entrances, window structures, and interiors for even the smallest of spaces. In fact, the smaller the square footage, the more important it is to ensure the best use of the space. More and more vendors are addressing the retailer's needs for store design by designing their showroom facilities in ways that can easily be translated into retail space. Not only does this take the guesswork out of store design, but it saves the retailer the expense of having plans drawn for his or her premises.

If individualization is called for, the use of an architect is the best approach. After meeting with the architect, the retailer is usually shown a rendering of the anticipated design with a list of materials suggested for use in construction. Figure 3-13 features an artist's rendering.

The rendering is a realistic picture of the project. It shows the exact colors that will be used; simulated merchandise on racks and in shelves, in showcases, and in windows; and detailed wall and floor

Figure 3-13. Artist's renderings give the client a visual idea of the project's concept. (*Courtesy of FRCH Design Worldwide.*)

coverings. Samples of flooring, wall coverings, fixture materials, lighting, etc., accompany the rendering; nothing is left to chance. This enables the merchant to study the next best thing to a photograph of the proposed store or restaurant. Since the project is still in the planning stages, this is as close to reality as possible.

Large companies generally involve their visual merchandisers at this point and throughout the construction phase to make certain that the plan will be suitable for maximum merchandise exposure.

Once the plan has satisfied the company's decision makers, minutely detailed architectural drawings are prepared for use during construction. Drawn to exact scale, these plans give specific sizes and elevations and show the location of every fixture, illuminated areas, and other details on which the construction will be based.

It is only through careful planning that the end result will satisfy the needs of the company. Figure 3-14 features a cross section of an architect's finished products that have captured the needs of retail clients. Each has been honored with numerous design awards, such as Store of the Year from the National Association of Store Fixture Manufacturers.

FACILITIES DESIGN: EXTERIORS, WINDOW STRUCTURES, INTERIORS, AND FIXTURING

Monterey Bay Aquarium

Figure 3-14. Award-winning designs that represent a cross section of retailing. (*Courtesy of J.T. Nakaoka Associates Architects.*)

Sharper Image Spa

Rampage

Ansel Adams Gallery

TERMS OF THE TRADE

angled windows
arcades
back-closed window structures
circular windows
corner windows
environmental visual concept
facilities rendering
floor cases
island display cases and tables
island windows
multipurpose merchandise systems
no-window concept
open-back windows
parallel-to-sidewalk windows
shadow box windows
shadow boxes
show-and-sell fixtures
slatwall
slat walls
vitrines
wall cases
windowless windows

CHAPTER REVIEW

KEY POINTS IN THE CHAPTER

1. Visual merchandisers play an important role in the facilities design of a company.
2. The visual merchandising director is involved in the planning of exteriors, window structures, interiors, and fixturing.
3. In addition to playing an important role in visual merchandising for stores, many professionals in the industry are now involved in designing environmental settings for restaurants and creating displays for vendor showrooms.
4. More and more attention is being focused on interiors so that they will project different images than the competition.
5. Unusual window structures and exterior designs, such as the silo-like exterior used in Crate & Barrel's Chicago flagship, help make

a retailer appear immediately different from neighboring businesses.
6. Parallel-to-sidewalk windows are generally the choices of stores with wide street frontage.
7. In an effort to maximize shopper awareness, stores that are located on a corner often plan windows and entrances on both streets.
8. Open-back windows provide display space as well as a view of the store interior from the outside.
9. Arcade fronts form vestibules, some of which are sufficiently large to house island windows and increase display space.
10. Many retailers use the windowless window that increases selling space by eliminating conventional windows and giving the shopper a view of the interior.
11. Store and restaurant facilities are taking on new, individualized designs to help make a lasting impression on the shopping experience.
12. Floor cases and wall cases not only house the merchandise but, if properly placed, can become traffic-stopping displays.
13. Vitrines enable the shopper to examine merchandise from all sides.
14. Show-and-sell fixturing enables the customer to examine the merchandise closely and often to select it without salesperson assistance.
15. Multipurpose merchandise systems offer a great deal of flexibility on the selling floor.
16. Slatwall is a system that uses grooved panels into which fittings can be inserted for shelving or hanging items.
17. An artist's rendering of a proposed facilities design permits the retailer to visualize the finished product.
18. Architects' plans are drawn to scale, indicating every aspect of the design.

DISCUSSION QUESTIONS

1. What role does a visual merchandiser of a large company play in designing a store?
2. Why do retailers desire a different look for their stores?
3. How are many restaurants now distinguishing themselves from others in their facilities design?
4. Why are some merchandise vendors redesigning their showrooms?
5. How does the Rain Forest Cafe attract passersby to stop and take a closer look?
6. Describe the typical window structure of a department store's downtown flagship store. Why is this design used?

7. What advantage does the corner window configuration give to the retailer?
8. While the open-back storefront affords some advantages, describe some shortcomings of this design.
9. How can narrow frontage be transformed into more window space?
10. Why do merchants, particularly in malls, often subscribe to the windowless window concept?
11. What purpose does a circular window serve?
12. Why are store interior designs being given more attention by retailers than ever before?
13. What are the two major types of merchandise fixtures that retailers use?
14. Discuss the advantages of multipurpose merchandise systems.
15. Describe show-and-sell fixturing.
16. What is a vitrine?
17. How does the artist's rendering help the retailer?

CASE PROBLEMS

Case 1

Jolie Couture is a high-fashion retailer specializing in clothing for the sophisticated female. Typical of its clientele is the customer who spends freely on original designs and appreciates pampering and special service. The company was established 35 years ago with its first shop in Palm Beach, Florida, and has grown to an organization of 10 salons in places such as Dallas, Texas and Beverly Hills, California.

The company is about to embark on a new venture. It plans to open a series of stores under the name Jolie Couture II that will be a separate division of the company. These stores will be upscale, high-fashion shops but will be different from the original store's concept. While Jolie Couture specializes in original designs from all over the world as well as custom-made, in-house styles, the new stores will concentrate on designer labels, with little emphasis on custom design. They expect to attract a larger market since the merchandise assortment will be more readily accessible to more women.

While the concept has been enthusiastically received by the various levels of management, there is still one problem that hasn't been resolved. Peter Gordon, director of visual merchandising for the company, has presented his concept of the physical structure of the new stores. His ideas are in contrast to those in evidence at the original Jolie Couture shops. In the original locations, the storefronts have windows that do not allow observation of the interior. Each unit in the chain features a pair of parallel-to-sidewalk windows framed in marble. The style suggests elegance and has proven to be a successful showcase for the store's custom merchandise.

Peter's recommendation for the new shops is quite different. He wants to use the entire store, elegantly furbished, as a window. He suggests a floor-to-ceiling glass front that would enable passersby to see into the store. The glass front would be dramatically illuminated from the outside.

Martha Peabody, vice president for merchandising, is not in total agreement and feels strongly that the concept will take away from the exclusivity now enjoyed by the company. The management team is divided in its feelings, half agreeing with Peter and half with Martha.

Questions

1. With whom do you agree? Defend your answer.
2. How could both parties be accommodated? Suggest a design that could satisfy each group.

Case 2

In each of the first five years in business, Caryn-Sheri Unlimited has enjoyed a significant increase in sales. So successful is the shop that the partners are embarking on an expansion program. They plan to open two new units within the next five years and additional shops if they continue to be profitable.

Caryn-Sheri Unlimited specializes in active sportswear for women at a price point that appeals to those in the $35,000 to $60,000 income bracket. The stores were designed to resemble a workout or exercise facility. The decor uses various types of equipment found in a gymnasium to display the merchandise.

While both partners are enthusiastic about expansion, they are in complete disagreement over the focus of the store design for their new venture. Caryn, the more practical partner, believes the new stores should duplicate the first in all aspects. The interior and the window design have proved to be beneficial. Why mess with success? Sheri, the more creative partner, believes that while they are successful, they are limiting their market to those interested in the merchandise only for use in physical exercise. She favors a design that would minimize the gymnasium atmosphere and develop an environment showing the merchandise in other uses. Her rationale is that much more could be sold if the message were that active sportswear is equally suitable for streetwear. Caryn counters that a chain organization should have all of its units similar to each other. She believes that a different design might take away from the appeal that has contributed to their success.

Questions

1. Is it necessary for all stores in a company to have a uniform appearance?
2. With which partner do you agree? Why?
3. Can a plan be developed to satisfy the beliefs of both partners? Describe such a plan.

NAME: _____ DATE: _____

EXERCISES

1. Visit a shopping center and evaluate six stores in terms of their window structures and interiors. Make sure you select six different types of windows, as outlined in this chapter, and complete the information requested on the form provided.

2. Select a merchandise classification such as home furnishings or men's clothing and develop a plan for a store that would visually merchandise the offerings to their best advantage. The store will be located in a mall and occupy a 15-foot front and a depth of 100 feet. The structure is just open space now. Use the form provided to complete a design plan for the store. Make sure you complete all of the categories in developing your design.

Exercise 1 WINDOW AND INTERIOR EVALUATION

Store Name	Window Type	Interior Decor	Effectiveness of Visuals

NAME: _____ DATE: _____

Exercise 2 DEVELOPING A STORE PLAN

MERCHANDISE CLASSIFICATION: _____

Category **Justification**

Store Front/Windows

General Decor

Interior Display Fixtures

Chapter 4
Mannequins and Other Human Forms

LEARNING OBJECTIVES

After completing this chapter, the student should be able to:

1. Describe four classifications of mannequins found in stores.
2. Differentiate between the traditional human forms and those that are stylized.
3. Discuss a major innovation in the use of representational mannequin forms.
4. List and describe four reasons for the manufacture of human form mannequins as component parts.
5. Identify the component parts of a mannequin.
6. Explain the reasons for the different types of base-to-leg attachments found on mannequins.
7. Describe the stages of dressing a mannequin.
8. Discuss the advantages of fibers such as Kanekalon and Luraflex in wig construction.
9. Compare the advantages and disadvantages of permanent mannequin makeup to the makeupless variety.
10. Explain why human forms other than full mannequins are used in display.
11. Compile a checklist for use in purchasing mannequins and other human forms.
12. Create his or her own mannequins to be used in place of those produced by the mannequin industry.

INTRODUCTION

Of all the component parts of a display, the one that is often the focal point of an area of emphasis is the mannequin. Mannequins have always been the mainstay of the visual merchandiser's bag of tricks, but they have taken on new excitement. In the past, the forms were lackluster replicas of people, and not much attention was given to carefully adorning and posing them to convey a fashion image or to enhance a theme. A quickly dressed mannequin was itself the goal, rather than being one element in a total display design, as is the case today.

In order to generate excitement, some visual merchandisers cluster several mannequins together. Not only does this eliminate the need for other props, but it presents a striking appearance. If the mannequins used are particularly unusual, it adds even more to the presentation.

Visual merchandisers have come to recognize the mannequin's value in terms of sales and now choose them as carefully as the buyer does the store's merchandise. The selection of a mannequin is a precise and time-demanding process. Visual merchandisers, especially those with sophisticated retail operations, will travel far and spend huge sums to bring back the best available mannequin. Production and purchasing were once accomplished exclusively in the United States, and usually close to the store's base of operation, but today's quest for the perfect mannequin is often an international adventure. New John Nissen Mannequins, Belgium; Adel Rootstein, London; and Poil Kyoya, Tokyo, are just some of the companies that do business with American visual merchandisers. Figure 4-1 features a mannequin designer refining a new product.

In addition to the mannequins available from manufacturers, many trimmers are using creations that they construct themselves. These creations and the various types of professionally produced mannequins are discussed later in this chapter.

Along with full form mannequins, there are models such as 3/4 torsos, hosiery legs, and shoulder and head forms. As the full form figures have changed in design and materials, so have these display devices.

This chapter focuses on the types of mannequins and forms, component parts and their workings, how to dress a mannequin, proper care and maintenance, wig selection, makeup, a checklist for use in the selection of mannequins and other human forms produced in the display industry,

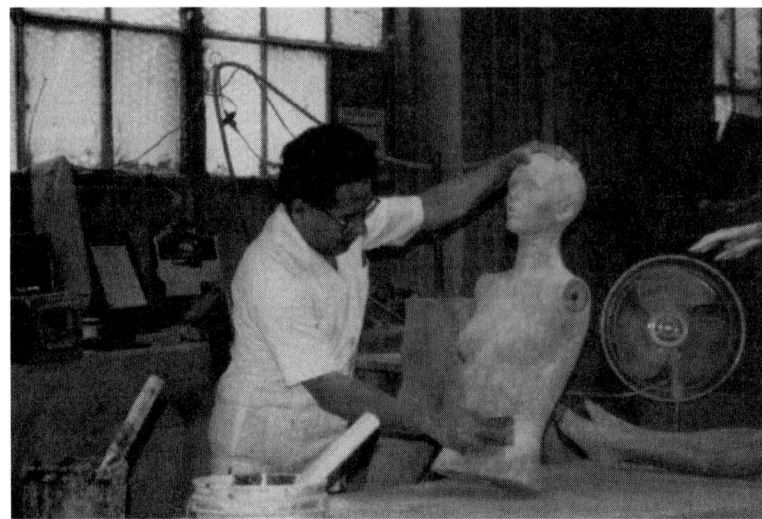

Figure 4-1. The creation of a mannequin requires a great deal of attention and finishing. (*Courtesy of Ellen Diamond.*)

MANNEQUINS AND OTHER HUMAN FORMS

Figure 4-2. Traditional mannequins are the mainstays of visual departments. (*Courtesy of Ellen Diamond.*)

Figure 4-3. Stylized forms give the trimmer an alternative to the traditional mannequin design. (*Courtesy of Ellen Diamond.*)

and step-by-step instructions for the creation of one's own mannequin.

TYPES OF MANNEQUINS

A visit to any visual merchandising trade show, such as NADI's (National Association of Display Industry) ShopEast and ShopWest, underscores the variety of mannequins available to the retailer, from realistic to avant garde. Following are some of the types of mannequins available today and their potential uses.

Traditional Human Forms

While abstract or stylized mannequins provide excitement in windows and interiors, their use is somewhat limited. Stores with restricted budgets and conventional merchandise offerings must rely upon models that typify their images. This is not to imply that image must be limited to dowdy because only ordinary mannequins are available. Today's traditional mannequin can be sophisticated yet serviceable for different types of attire. It is equally appropriate wearing a business suit or sportswear. It affords the retailer the advantages of adaptability and versatility. Through the use of different wigs, makeup, and arm and leg positions, it can be transformed to create many different impressions.

Although stores such as Marshall Field, Macy's, J.L. Hudson, and Bloomingdale's use the fashion forward mannequin, their visual merchandising departments are also heavily stocked with traditional mannequins. Figure 4-2 features traditional mannequins.

Stylized Human Forms

For the store seeking an image that will separate it from the rest of the pack, but still wishing to remain sophisticated, there are many mannequins that follow traditional lines but offer a change of pace. Their figures might feature a skintone finish other than human flesh color, a brush stroke body surface akin to a fine artist's brush stroke, or hair that is sculpted to give a clay-like feeling and sleek appearance. What remains the same in this group of mannequins as in the traditional variety is the reality of the pose, the retention of the human features, and the versatility to effectively display a wide variety of merchandise. The major retailers in this country and abroad rarely use this type of mannequin as their display mainstay but use them for specific departments in the store. Figure 4-3 features children's stylized forms.

Futuristic Human Forms

A retailer may seek to depart totally from the realistic look of a traditional mannequin, or even the slightly exaggerated look of a stylized form, but still wish to rely on some version of the human form. The emphasis may be on unique coloration or accents, such as the hair, that depict unconventional shapes such as cones. Other futuristic mannequins may be unusually tall or finished with shiny surfaces, each designed to attract attention. Figure 4-4 features futuristic forms.

Figure 4-4. Futuristic forms serve some retailers as attention-getters. (*Courtesy of Ellen Diamond.*)

Representational Forms

Many retailers are resorting to the use of forms that fill the same purpose as traditional or stylized mannequins. The major reason for the use of these forms is economy. While a fine traditional mannequin may cost as much as $1,000, these representational forms are quite inexpensive. With shrinking visual merchandising budgets in many retail operations, these forms seem to fit the bill. Made of a variety of materials such as steel tubing, wooden dowels, brass, and PVC piping, the forms are actually display hangers on which merchandise may be satisfactorily displayed.

These simple devices are easy to trim, may be used for both men's and women's clothing, and serve many purposes. They are particularly useful in the branches of many chains where professional visual merchandisers are not available to make mannequin changes. The simplicity of these structures makes it easy for a salesperson to make the needed adjustments. Figure 4-5 features a unique representational form.

Trimmer Constructed Mannequins

When money for mannequins is severely limited, more and more trimmers are creating their own. They are similar to the manufacturer-made representational forms, but are made of inexpensive materials at a fraction of the cost of any other mannequin. Figure 4-6 features trimmer constructed mannequins.

Later in this chapter, a step-by-step illustration is provided to show how these invaluable display pieces can be constructed quickly and inexpensively.

COMPONENT PARTS OF MANNEQUINS

Mannequins come in a wealth of styles, shapes, and materials. Some are made as self-contained units, as is the case with many of the representational forms. There are no separate parts to maneuver or adjust.

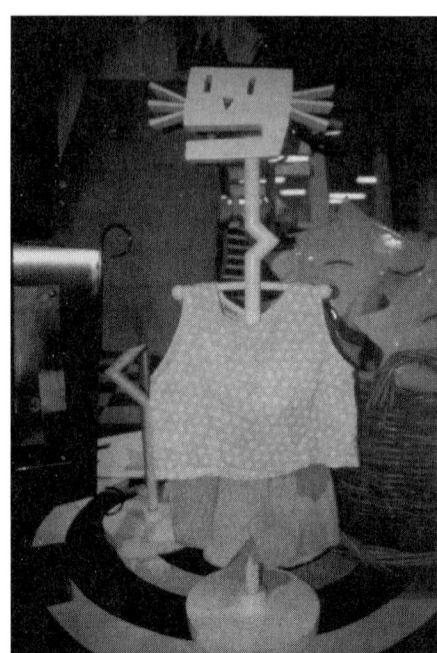

Figure 4-5. This unique representational form is inexpensive as well as eye-appealing. (*Courtesy of Ellen Diamond.*)

MANNEQUINS AND OTHER HUMAN FORMS

Figure 4-6. Trimmer constructed mannequins save the retailer from high costs yet provide display interest. (*Courtesy of Ellen Diamond.*)

Figure 4-7. Leg structure.

Figure 4-8. Torso.

Most other mannequins are constructed as a package of pieces which, when assembled, constitutes the full human form. The reasons for the components are:

1. *Ease in changing garments*

Since mannequins, unlike humans, cannot bend or change position to accommodate trying on a garment, parts such as the arms and legs must be removable for dressing.

2. *Flexibility*

If mannequins were capable of only one position, visual merchandisers would need many more for variety in their presentations. With the interchangeable legs, arms, torsos, and wigs, a mannequin can be adjusted to serve many purposes. Just a change of the leg portion can transform a stander to a sitter.

3. *Storage*

It is often easier to store the mannequin in parts. Arms and wigs, for example, require very little space and could be stored easily on shelves.

4. *Care*

No matter how careful the handlers are, mannequins are bound to suffer chips, scratches, and breaks. If the figure were a one-piece assemblage, refinishing to repair the damaged parts would require that the full figure be shipped to the mannequin repair company. It is certainly easier and less expensive to transport only the damaged part rather than the full form.

The component parts of the mannequin and the devices that enable them to be attached to form the full figure are depicted in Figures 4-7 to 4-13. The model illustrated is a female figure, but the male and children's counterparts are produced in the same manner.

The leg structure is usually a one-piece construction. In some cases, for maneuverability when displaying pants, one leg is detachable. At the top of the leg portion there is a wide, dowel-like fitting that attaches to the torso and secures the two principal parts of the body (Figure 4-7).

At the base of the torso is a hole to receive the dowel-like fitting described in Figure 4-7. While the leg portion might be adjusted slightly in a particular direction, the torso is stationary (Figure 4-8).

Most mannequins are secured by a removable steel rod that extends from a weighted glass or metal base to the uppermost back portion of the leg. When secured at both the bottom (base) and top

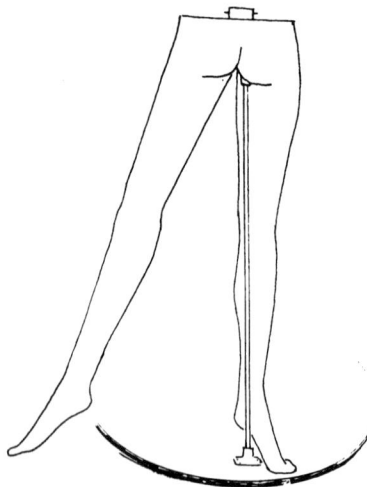

Figure 4-9. Base attachment.

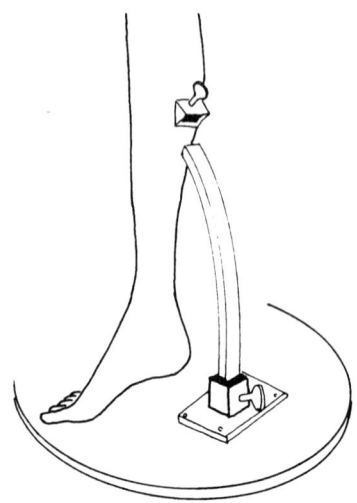

Figure 4-10. Base attachment.

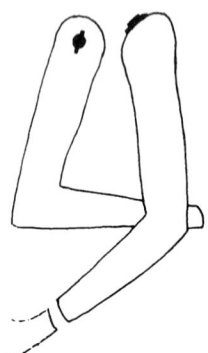

Figure 4-11. Arms.

Figure 4-12. Hands.

Figure 4-13. The completed mannequin is the sum of its component parts.

(leg of mannequin), the figure is in a steady position (Figure 4-9). An alternative method of securing mannequins is to wire them to the floor. Using this method, neither the steel rod nor the base is necessary for securing purposes.

Often mannequins are used to display pants. For that purpose, some forms are equipped with short steel rods that extend from below the leg calf. This short rod can easily be concealed under the pant leg. In Figure 4-9, the long steel rod attachment can be a problem in pant dressing, so the shorter version is used (Figure 4-10). If either of the rods get in the way of the pant leg, as might be the case when the pant is very tapered at the bottom, a seam in the garment may have to be opened to complete the mannequin's dressing.

The arms of the mannequin have metal devices that fit into receiving holes on the upper sides of the torso. The fitting is designed to permit the arms to rotate and stop at different intervals for varied positioning (Figure 4-11).

Hands are fitted with devices that lock into receiving holes in the mannequin's arms. When both parts lock, the arm and the hand make a perfect fit (Figure 4-12).

When fully assembled, the components yield a full mannequin on which any type of clothing can be displayed, as in Figure 4-13. As already mentioned, the beauty of modern mannequin construction is that the upright figure may be changed to a sitter with a simple change of the leg structure.

DRESSING THE MANNEQUIN

If the proper attention is paid to assembling and disassembling a mannequin as it is being dressed and undressed, the figure will retain its freshness and usefulness for a long time. The illustrations in Figures 4-14 to 4-17 show the technique and steps used in dressing a mannequin. The order is simply reversed for undressing.

To dress the assembled mannequin, first remove the legs from the steel rod and base. Then turn the legs upside down to receive the skirt or pants. If the mannequin is to wear hosiery, it should be added before placement of the outer garment. With the legs upright in the proper position, it is time to add the shoes. Then reattach the legs to the rod and base. The trimmer must select the leg component carefully, making certain that it is appropriate for the garment to be displayed. For example, in the case of pants, the best choice is a leg base that attaches to the steel rod as shown in Figure 4-10. If this is not used, it could be difficult to reinsert the steel rod. The longer steel rods, as featured in Figure 4-9, would bind the pant leg and prevent insertion back into the base. Some companies manufacture a mannequin that eliminates the traditional attachment rods that have been illustrated, and uses a device that connects the base under the mannequin's foot. A disadvantage of this design is that if hosiery and shoes are to be used, both items must have holes cut in them. While some stores do damage the shoes and hosiery, it should be noted that they cannot then be sold. Figure 4-14 shows a skirt on the form; Figure 4-15, pants on the proper base.

If a dress is being featured, it is possible, after the hosiery and shoes have been placed, to then attach the torso to the leg portion and slip the dress over the head of the mannequin onto the body. Hands-on experience provides the trimmer with a sense of how each garment is best handled and placed on the mannequin. The novice will require a good deal of trial and error experimentation before mastering the task.

In the case of separates, next place the torso onto the leg component just described and then put on the shirt, sweater, or blouse. If the design buttons down the front or back, it is easy to insert the arms later. Such designs are dressed in much the same way as humans put them on their bodies. Sweaters other than cardigans must be pulled over the head. At this stage, the blouse should be left unbuttoned with pullover sweaters hanging loosely. This is important because sometimes it is difficult to attach the arms to the torso. Leaving the clothing loose enables the individual to more easily slip the arms in place (Figure 4-16).

At this point, attach the hands to the arms by lining up the two related devices, one found at the base of the arm, the other at the wrist portion of the hand. Once rotated properly, they will lock into place. Then slip the arms into the garment's sleeves and attach them to the torso, again rotating until locked into place (Figure 4-17). If the sleeve opening is too small to receive the hands in this manner, it might be

Figure 4-14.
Dressing a mannequin in a skirt.

Figure 4-15.
Dressing a mannequin in pants.

Figure 4-16. Dressing a mannequin in a sweater, blouse, or shirt.

Figure 4-17. Adding the arms and hands.

necessary to detach the hands from the arms, insert the arms through the blouse or under the sweater, lock the arms in place, and then attach the hands. Again, experience is the best teacher.

The wig can be added after the garments are in place and adjusted with pins, if necessary. If pins are needed, they must be applied to the back of the garment, out of the shopper's sight.

MANNEQUINS AND OTHER HUMAN FORMS

WIGS AND MAKEUP

Too often a display features the latest fashion, yet the mannequin does not have a totally fresh look. The hairstyle might be out of sync with the clothing or the hair might be damaged or discolored, like human hair that has been neglected. Another basic problem could be the mannequin's makeup. The wrong color emphasis, discoloration of pigment, lackluster application, and nicks and scratches all detract from the featured merchandise. Whether for humans or mannequins, to give the impression of perfection, the whole presentation must be carefully developed.

Wigs

Figure 4-18. Wigs help create a specific look for the mannequin. (*Courtesy of Greneker.*)

In order for the visual merchandiser to present the latest fashions successfully, there should be a number of wig styles from which to choose. A mannequin can be immediately transformed from a casual, sporty look to one of sophistication and elegance with a different wig. Fashion has so many influences and changes so rapidly and radically that different hairstyles are essential to capture the mood of each trend. One season the hair is long and ironed straight, the next, short and curly. A blonde might be more suitable for a particular outfit, but a redhead might better complement an emerald green ball gown. Figure 4-18 features a traditional mannequin's wig.

The keys to appropriate wig use are variety, flexibility, and adaptability. When a style is in vogue, the display person should be able to respond immediately without making a trip to the supplier. If the visual merchandising department has a variety of wig types, hair lengths, and fibers, the task will be simpler to accomplish.

The horsehair, lacquered wigs that were once dominant in the display world are outdated. While the material enabled creation of the most elaborate coiffures, once they were lacquered into place, the styles were permanent. Very few stores still use these wigs. They are easily detected. Shiny and stiff when new, they quickly fall into disarray and soon have separate clumps of hair that no longer form to the head's contour.

Just as hair has taken on a more natural, relaxed look, so have the wigs used on mannequins. The demise of horsehair has given way to newer fibers such as Kanekalon, Elura, and Luraflex. Each is soft and closely resembles human hair. Kanekalon has the advantage of being inexpensive, but cannot be restyled from one shape to another without being washed each time. Elura can be reset, but its shortcoming is a slightly artificial look. Luraflex is extremely versatile for wig use. It is natural in appearance and can be restyled as often as necessary to complement the changes dictated by fashion.

Novelty fibers are much in evidence in today's windows and interiors. For that special promotion, the store that is fortunate enough to have a large visual merchandising budget often invests in unusual wigs. Raffia, lamé, and wool have been used to project specific fashion looks. They are not the mainstay of a store's wig collection, but they can be seen in fashion forward stores throughout the world.

Care is vital if a wig is to remain attractive and useful. Storage in individual containers, washing regularly to get rid of hairspray, and careful setting and combing can lengthen the life of a wig.

Of course, many visual merchandisers are using stylized mannequins that feature molded wigs made from the same materials as the mannequins. They cannot be changed or adapted to a specific need. However, some retailers prefer these forms because the hairstyles are always in place and need not be fussed with. With these mannequins, the problems associated with wig refurbishment are eliminated.

Makeup

Most retailers, except for the fashion forward department stores, order mannequins complete with total, permanent makeup. Chain stores and independent retailers generally choose makeup that is acceptable for just about any style that is to be fitted on the mannequins. While this is not best in terms of complete coordination with the garments to be displayed, it provides the least difficulty for the store: no smudging or smearing, no makeup on clothing, and no need for a specially trained person to design or apply makeup for each display change.

Figure 4-19. Makeup applied permanently prevents smudging. (*Courtesy of Greneker.*)

Figure 4-19 features a mannequin with makeup applied at the factory.

In an organization that considers specialized makeup imperative to each individual visual presentation, artistic creativity is needed. These stores simply order mannequins that are devoid of makeup or have very light makeup that can be strengthened as necessary. The selection of makeup at such a store's cosmetic counters is generally sufficient to meet this need. Because care should be taken to choose makeup that is appropriate to the mannequin's skin color, it is best to consult the cosmetic department specialist about color and application procedures. Sometimes, when a couture collection is being featured in the store's windows, the designer creates specific makeup colors and styles to accompany the designs. In these cases, the designer or a company representative should be contacted for instructions.

MANNEQUINS AND OTHER HUMAN FORMS

The following are some basic rules for mannequin makeup:

1. Make sure the face is cleaned often whether the mannequin's makeup is permanent or fresh. Correct any damage to the skin as necessary.
2. Makeup is used to highlight and complement the merchandise. Unless the display is a tie-in with a cosmetics company or a high-fashion clothing designer, the makeup should be used only as an enhancer. It shouldn't stand out or compete with the purpose of the display.
3. The fashion pages of *Harper's Bazaar, Vogue, Women's Wear Daily, W,* etc., should be examined for cosmetic trends.

OTHER HUMAN FORMS

The full human form, whether realistic, stylized, or representational, is certainly central to many clothing displays in windows and interiors. Complete mannequins, however, do not meet all of the visual merchandiser's needs. Those who design and install displays make significant use of other human forms in conjunction with mannequins or alone. Some windows or interior spaces are too small to house a full form, or the merchandise might be best featured on another type of display form.

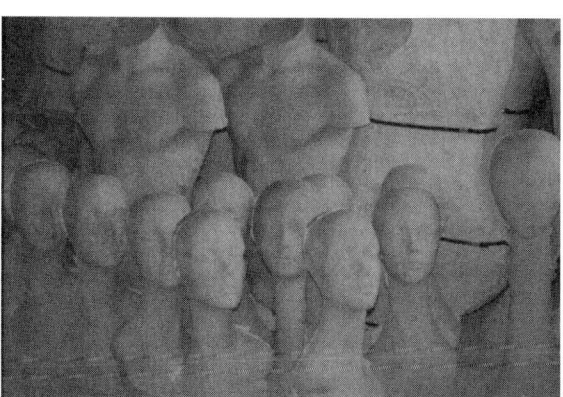

As mannequins come in a variety of materials and images, so do other forms. Some of those found in visual installations are women's torso or 3/4 forms for swimsuits, blazers, and ensembles; male suit forms that are actually more popular than the full figures for men's clothing; shoulder and head forms for scarves, millinery, and accessories; blouse forms; and hands, hosiery legs, and shoe forms. Figure 4-20 features a variety of the forms being produced that are popular in today's presentations.

Figure 4-20. A variety of forms in their unfinished states that will become part of a visual department. (*Courtesy of Ellen Diamond.*)

PURCHASING MANNEQUINS AND OTHER HUMAN FORMS

Rarely is the display budget so plentiful that the visual merchandiser can select mannequins and other human forms without considering cost. Since a top-of-the-line mannequin costs about $1,000, mannequin purchases require careful planning.

By examining such periodicals as *Visual Merchandising & Store Design,* published in the United States, and *Retail Attraction,* published in Great Britain, one can assess the variety of mannequins and forms available, their producers, and their approximate cost. Most companies have showrooms for inspection of their lines and often have representatives who travel to the stores. They may provide photographs for those who cannot take advantage of the personal contact. Of course, a trip to the showroom or a trade exposition is best. Visual merchandisers should visit vendors much the same as store buyers do in shopping the lines of merchandise. This is a purchase that lasts a long time; it should not be accomplished haphazardly.

CREATING A MANNEQUIN

Many trimmers are creating their own mannequins for the retailers they service. The benefits are versatility and extremely low cost. Often the materials used in these constructions cost only a few dollars! This is quite a saving when compared to forms that are purchased from manufacturers.

While professional trimmers are using these mannequin forms, it should be noted that the retailers themselves can, after learning some of the techniques, create their own mannequins and cut their visual merchandising costs considerably. Manufacturers and wholesalers can also make use of these forms. At trade expositions, in particular, they can be quickly and cost-efficiently assembled to display their hottest numbers. Instead of calling upon the services of a professional, they too can satisfy their own display needs.

The following paragraphs and accompanying photographs illustrate the manner in which children's, men's, and women's forms are created and dressed.

Children's Mannequin

The supplies for this construction are easily obtained from a crafts store: a Styrofoam base, a wooden dowel, a round Styrofoam ball, a wooden crosspiece, and wire (number 24 is perfect for this task).

Follow these steps for perfect results (see Figures 4-21a, b, and c).

1. Place the dowel (length to be determined by the desired height of the child) into the Styrofoam base. Make sure it is centered so that it will not topple.

MANNEQUINS AND OTHER HUMAN FORMS

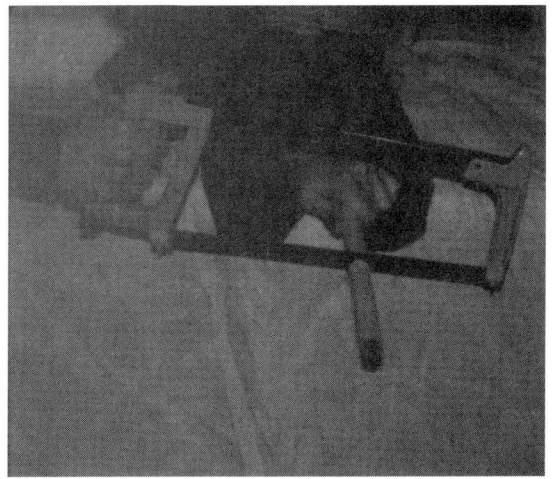

Figure 4-21. Some stages of construction of a children's mannequin that has been created by the trimmer. (*Courtesy of Mindy Greenberg.*) Figure 4-21a. Dowels are cut, wired together, inserted into a Styrofoam base, and topped with a Styrofoam ball that serves as the head.

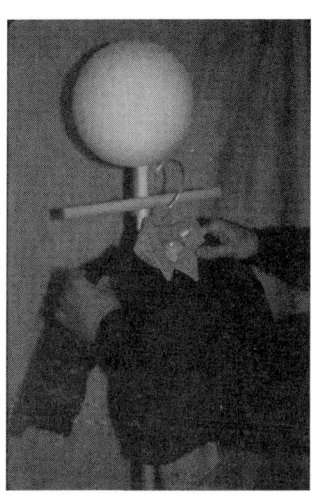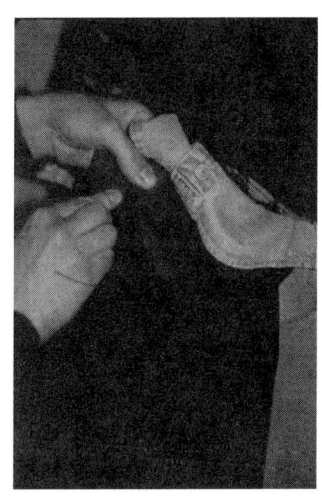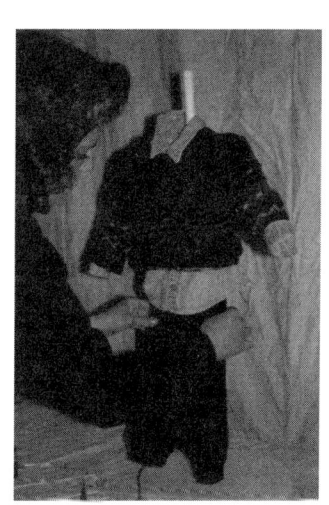

Figure 4-21b. Top pieces are fitted on hanger. Bottom piece is either fitted on hanger, wired, and suspended from crosspiece, or pinned directly to top pieces.

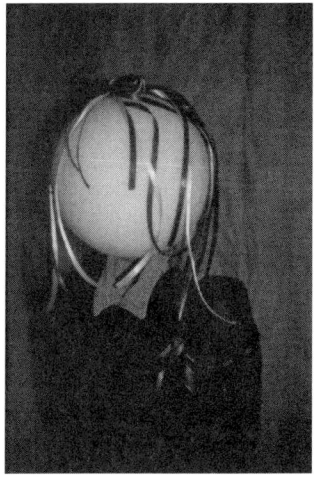

Figure 4-21c. The head is fitted with ribbons or hat, accented with child's prop, and set in place.

2. Wire the crosspiece of wood (also a dowel that may be cut from the upright piece) to the dowel implanted into the Styrofoam.
3. The mannequin is ready to be dressed. First, place the top pieces such as shirts and sweaters over the arm dowel. Next, put pants on a hanger, as shown in the illustration, and drop hanger on wire from arms crosspiece. Make certain that the wire is securely tied to crosspiece.
4. Pin the end of one sleeve to garment.
5. For fullness, stuff the arms, pant legs, etc., with tissue paper.
6. Attach the Styrofoam ball, which serves as the head, to the top of the upright dowel.
7. Pin a hat to the top of the head, or try something whimsical such as using many short lengths of ribbon for hair on the head. Another material to use for hair is jute. A bandanna might be used on top of the hair. The face might then be painted to give the mannequin a fun look. The creativity of the trimmer can add many elements to make this a unique mannequin.
8. The mannequin should then be placed in a setting to depict a theme, or simply placed against a wall.

Men's Mannequin

For a full-form male mannequin the following supplies will be needed: one 6-foot piece of 2×4 lumber, a 1×12 square for the base, a 1×2 to anchor the 2×4 to the base, and 2 hangers, one a suit type and the other with clips. A drill and screws for assembly will also be needed. (See Figures 4-22a, b, and c.)

The following steps complete the project:

1. Assemble all of the pieces of wood as shown in the appropriate photograph.
2. Place a screw at about 8 inches from the top of the 2×4 from which the clothing will be hung on the hanger.
3. Put the clothing on the suit hanger. A shirt with a sweater over it looks very attractive.
4. Add a length of wire to the bottom hanger on which the pants will be clipped. Hang this wired hanger from the screw in the 2×4 and let the pants drop to the desired length.
5. Pin the arms of the shirt to suggest motion and place one sleeve in a pant pocket.
6. Arrange a bulky sweater over the shirt.
7. Cover the neck that shows at the top of the hanger with a pair of gloves.
8. Add a hat.

MANNEQUINS AND OTHER HUMAN FORMS

 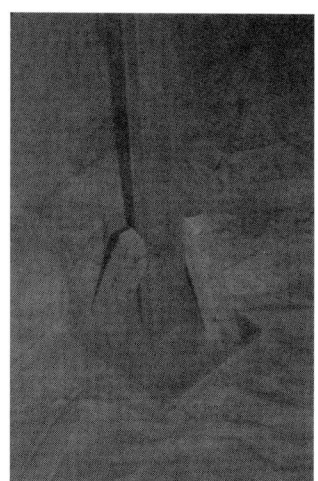 

Figure 4-22. A men's mannequin being created on the job by the trimmer. (*Courtesy of Mindy Greenberg.*) The wooden components are assembled, top pieces are placed on suit hanger and suspended from screw on upright 2×4.

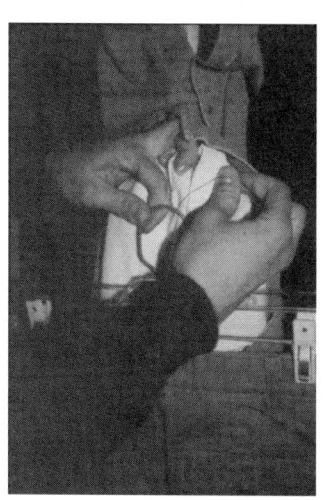  

Figure 4-22 (cont.). The bottom hanger is wired, to be dropped from screw. Pants are clipped to hanger and adjusted to receive top pieces, with top sweater then layered.

Figure 4-22 (cont.). The hat is stuffed to resemble a head, with gloves inserted for additional interest.

9. Place shoes at the base of the form, one over the other.
10. Place the completed form against a solid wall or within a theme setting.

Women's Mannequin

The materials needed for this presentation are 1 or 2 hangers, depending upon the design, wire, and branches. (See Figures 4-23a and b.)
The following steps will produce the finished display:

1. Use a clothing rack to assemble merchandise.
2. Hang the clothing on the hanger. For pants, an additional hanger may be used.

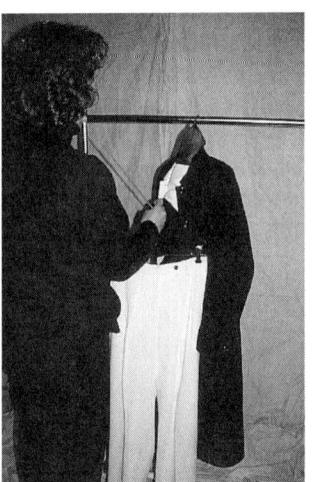

Figure 4-23. The women's form is being created for eventual suspension from a prop. (*Courtesy of Mindy Greenberg.*)
Using a clothing rack to create form, layer the merchandise on one or two hangers, as needed. In the illustration, a pant hanger has been wired to hang from the upper hanger.

Figure 4-23 (cont.). Merchandise is adjusted, suspended from a decorative branch, and accented with props.

3. Place upper pieces on hanger. Cut a piece of wire from which pants on bottom hanger can be suspended from neck of top hanger.
4. Layer clothing to achieve interest.
5. Sleeves should be placed in pockets or pinned in an interesting manner.
6. Attach branches to ceiling grid of window, or directly to ceiling.
7. Hang the finished garment display from the branches.
8. Place a coordinating scarf at neckline to conceal exposed hanger.

These illustrations are merely some examples of how trimmer-made mannequins can be created. These guidelines can easily be altered. The professional, creative trimmer will come up with dozens of alternate techniques. The novice who is willing to spend some time mastering the techniques will also be able to create the mannequins. Experience will lead to new ideas.

TERMS OF THE TRADE

blouse forms
display hanger
Elura
fashion forward mannequin
futuristic human forms
head forms
horsehair wigs
hosiery legs
Kanekalon
Luraflex
mannequin
receiving holes
representational forms
shoe forms
shoulder forms
stylized human forms
suit forms
traditional human forms
trimmer constructed mannequins
women's torso

CHAPTER REVIEW

KEY POINTS IN THE CHAPTER

1. Today's mannequins bear little resemblance to the lackluster variety that was once popular.
2. The availability of mannequins has significantly increased, with resources around the world.
3. Mannequins are available in many forms, from the traditional variety to the avant garde.
4. A stylized mannequin is used by the retailer whose clientele is sophisticated and desires fashion forward concepts.
5. Representational forms are so versatile that they can be used to feature either male or female clothing.
6. Many trimmers are creating their own mannequins today, that are both inexpensive and serviceable.
7. Component construction of mannequins affords ease in dressing, flexibility, more convenient storage, and easier care.
8. Using component parts, the mannequin can be transformed from one look to another.
9. In dressing a mannequin it is essential to follow a prescribed plan so that the garments are more easily handled.
10. To ensure a total look, it is important for the wig to be compatible with the merchandise.
11. Wigs are available in many fibers, each having specific advantages when compared with the horsehair variety.
12. Many of today's mannequins feature hair that is made of the same material as the mannequin and is permanent.
13. Makeup should complement the garment featured, not overpower it.
14. Where there are space limitations, other human forms are used in place of full mannequins.
15. These other human forms, such as the torso, head and shoulder unit, hands, legs, etc., also give variety to visual installations.
16. When purchasing mannequins and other human forms, it is important to consider durability, style, versatility, store image, wigs, makeup, and variety of poses.

DISCUSSION QUESTIONS

1. Contrast the mannequins of the past with those used in visual merchandising today.
2. What does the term *silent seller* mean in terms of mannequin usage?

3. Describe the differences between traditional and stylized mannequin forms.
4. How does the futuristic human form differ from other mannequins used by retailers?
5. Representational mannequins are said to be more versatile than the other types. What accounts for their versatility?
6. Discuss the four major advantages of constructing mannequins in component parts.
7. What are two major types of base attachments used to secure mannequins? Why must both types be available?
8. Describe the first step in dressing a mannequin.
9. How does the trimmer overcome the difficulty associated with inserting the arm component into the torso while putting on the garment?
10. Is the horsehair wig used significantly today by the visual merchandiser? Why?
11. What are the disadvantages of Kanekalon and Elura?
12. Name the fiber that has the best properties for wigs and discuss the advantages to the hair stylist.
13. Most mannequins in use have permanent makeup. What are the advantages and disadvantages of permanency?
14. Discuss two rules of makeup usage for mannequins.
15. For what reasons are some retailers resorting to creating their own mannequins for displays?
16. What are some of the resources for the materials used in making one's own mannequins?
17. Why do visual merchandisers use other human forms in their presentations besides mannequins?
18. List five human forms other than mannequins and describe their functions.
19. With so many different mannequin types available, how does the retailer know which variety to purchase?
20. What factors should be considered in the purchase of mannequins and other human forms?

CASE PROBLEMS

Case 1

Litt Clothiers, Inc. has been in business for ten years. It began as a small specialty shop that catered to middle-income women.

Specializing in apparel and accessories, the store built a solid reputation and has maintained a profitable position with its conventional image. The store's interior was designed to complement the merchandise assortment that featured fashion as well as basic or staple clothing, with an occasional and usually successful attempt at some fashion forward items. In keeping with the decor, the mannequins in the window and interior installations were traditionally oriented. They were of high quality, yet their use showed little pizzazz or innovation.

About five years ago, the company expanded into the adjacent building, nearly doubling the store's total square footage. The menswear division, a new part of the business, did well in this new addition. Now the company has discovered a new market, the teenage children of its customers. After considerable research, the company decided to convert its lower level into a sales floor aimed at the younger set.

Among the problems to be dealt with is how to visually merchandise the new department in order to differentiate it from Litt's traditional, upstairs selling floors. Since the concept is new, past practice cannot guide the decisions.

Of considerable importance is the selection of mannequins. Since the new department will feature youthful male and female clothing, there seems to be a need for many mannequins, but only a modest budget is available. Some planners feel that seven female and three male mannequins, stylized to give a contemporary look, would be a workable number. The menswear buyer feels that the new youthful menswear would be shortchanged, that not enough of the new clothing could be shown to make an impact. With the opening set for 90 days from today, the dilemma still exists.

Question

How could the mannequin problem be solved to the satisfaction of all concerned? Bear in mind the store's budgetary restraints. Your answer should be backed by specific examples.

Case 2

Five years ago, Amanda's opened its doors for business and began a most profitable venture in junior clothing retailing. The merchandise assortment featured just about everything the customer would need to complete her wardrobe. Clothing appropriate for the junior executive at work, active sportswear, and evening wear were the classifications that dominated the selling floor.

The company's success has enabled it to refurbish the store. New flooring, lighting, fixtures, and wall coverings have been selected and work is about to begin in the store. While management would like to expand its existing selling floor, the acquisition of new space is impossible. With the boom that has taken place in the area, there is virtually nothing for the company to acquire.

In an attempt to capitalize on the space they have, Amanda's has decided to minimize sales support space and expand sales areas. Among the areas affected by the reallocation of space is visual merchandising. Although a significant sum has been earmarked for new mannequins, the visual merchandising department's manager has been informed to limit plans for the refurbished store to 10 mannequins instead of the 15 they presently use. While it is true that some of the mannequins rested in storage while others were on display, the new edict raises doubts about the ability to visually merchandise active sportswear, for example, on the same mannequins used for displaying evening wear. Still, the storage space, now limited in size, couldn't handle storing any mannequins until they were needed. The new mannequins must be able to accommodate all types of merchandise effectively. Already cut to the bone in storage space, the new mannequin purchase has yet to be resolved.

Question

Given the space limitations and the limit of 10 mannequins, how could the visual merchandiser solve the problem? Remember that the same merchandise assortment will fill the newly refurbished store.

EXERCISES

1. Contact a large department store's visual merchandising manager or assistant manager and conduct an interview on the store's policy, endeavors, and considerations in the purchase of mannequins and other human forms. A list of questions should be prepared in advance, such as:
   a. From whom are the store's mannequins purchased?
   b. What is the price range of the mannequins used by the company?
   c. Is permanent makeup preferred or does a cosmetics expert apply what is needed?

   Be prepared to ask other questions and outline the information received for presentation to the class.

2. Visit two major stores in your area and closely observe the mannequins in the windows and interiors. Evaluate each store's forms in terms of the items listed. Get permission to photograph several of each company's mannequins and affix the pictures, labeled with the store's name, to the form provided. Include complete information for each category. If the windows are on the street, it is best to photograph them at night using 400-speed film without a flash.

This also works best for interior photographs. (Keep this in mind for all of the photographic exercises in this text.)

3. Write to several of the manufacturers featured in such periodicals as *Visual Merchandising & Store Design,* requesting photographs, drawings, and information on the latest mannequins.

NAME: _____ DATE: _____

Exercise 2 MANNEQUIN EVALUATION

NAME OF STORE: _____ **NAME OF STORE:** _____

Mannequin classification		
Skin tone		
Wig types		
Makeup types		
Uniqueness of design, if any		
Overall evaluation Sample photographs (Affix to additional sheets of paper as necessary; label photographs clearly)		

Chapter 5
Materials, Props, and Tools of the Trade

LEARNING OBJECTIVES

After completing this chapter, the student should be able to:

1. Discuss the trend in visual merchandising toward installing eye-catching windows without vendor-produced props.
2. Compare the characteristics of masonite, Homasote, and plywood.
3. Describe the many uses of foam boards.
4. Contrast the use of fabric for backgrounds with the use of display paper.
5. List the various commercial sources for props and discuss the advantage of each source.
6. Define the term *found objects* and relate their value to visual merchandisers.
7. Identify five items sold in many stores that double as display props.
8. Explain the various methods by which retailers can acquire display props.
9. Compile a list of essential tools needed by trimmers to accomplish most display installations.
10. Discuss the difference between tools of the trade and accessories of the trade.

INTRODUCTION

The dramatic nature of a display and the impact that it makes on a shopper very often are attributed to the elements in the display rather than to the merchandise. While the most important feature of a visual presentation is the merchandise, the background is necessary to enhance what the store is trying to sell. Visual merchandisers are the first to admit that the major ingredient is the merchandise, no matter how exciting the presentation might be.

Materials and props might be compared to cosmetics. The right makeup choice and application will improve one's appearance but the facial structure stays the same. A black velvet backdrop, enhanced by dramatic lighting, will present a ball gown in a sensational setting and perhaps lend elegance to the gown's design, but it is the gown itself that will appeal to the shopper and encourage her to try on the item.

Often a display overwhelms the observer with too many devices. Windows and interior presentations of this nature may confuse the shopper. So overwhelming is the visual effect that the purpose of the display, selling the product, is not realized.

Today's professional visual presenters are more aware than ever that functional display is the proper way to motivate purchasing. Except for some elaborate settings during the Christmas season and major store events for which institutional (image-building) emphasis is placed on windows and interiors, display people are concentrating more on the development of themes that require fewer background props and materials.

Although display settings and props are still being produced and sold, an inspection of many windows and interior presentations shows the widespread use of props that are not from visual merchandising environments. The use of window shutters through which items such as belts may be woven or ladders displaying different items on their steps are just two examples of such props.

By resorting to these practical props, you can present effective displays within a limited visual merchandising budget. With the trend toward cutting costs for visual presentation, these objects are perfect props.

This chapter focuses on the various props and materials featured in displays and the tools that trimmers use to install displays.

MATERIALS

When consumers want to redecorate their homes, they have many alternatives available to them. A fresh coat of paint might be enough to create a new appearance. Paint can be used to create different effects such as marbleizing, brushed suede, mottling, striating, and raised surfaces, making paint a wonderful, inexpensive element. Decorative wallpaper or fabrics might be used to create a special look. Visual merchandisers have the same tasks to perform, but the redecorating is frequent. When home decoration is called for, the end result lasts for many years. In visual merchandising, display installers are called upon as often as once a week to transform display areas from one theme or setting to something that is totally new and different. The homeowner is often willing to spend a large sum on materials because of the long-lasting nature of the installation, but wallpaper at $50 per roll is simply out of the question when a display window may be timely for only one week.

Having considered the cost, versatility, and function of the material, the visual merchandiser is ready to make selections. While the choice of materials is often expanded by the display person's own creative instincts, there is a wide assortment readily available at costs to serve even the most limited budgets.

Construction Boards

Many types of boards are found in displays. Their uses are numerous, with each having certain characteristics that enable the visual merchandiser to achieve special effects.

Foamboards. This lightweight, paper-covered Styrofoam board is the mainstay of most display departments. It is produced by many companies. Fome-Core by Monsanto is a common one. Another of the more widely used foamboards is Sintra, which is a thick variety that is long-lasting. It can be quickly cut into any shape, scored to create columns or rectangular forms, covered with fabric by using glue or staples, and even painted with excellent results. Available in several thicknesses, it is easy to cut with a utility or X-acto knife. Many trimmers prefer to use foamboard for irregularly shaped pads to fit into oddly shaped places. Unlike other boards, its flexibility enables it to be bent slightly for curved effects. A disadvantage of the product is its tendency to fray or bend at the edges. If carefully handled, however, it can be used again and again to create the most unusual forms. Figure 5-1 features a foam board creation.

Figure 5-1. Foamboard is very versatile and can be cut and painted as in this illustration. (*Courtesy of Ellen Diamond.*)

Oaktag. This is a sturdy, paper composition material with a shiny surface. It is very inexpensive, is available in many colors, and can be cut quickly into any desired shape. It can also be painted. Visual merchandisers often use this material to cut such shapes as hearts for Valentine's Day displays, artists' palettes to feature paint installations, and stylized faces for cosmetic presentations.

Masonite. A composition board that comes in thicknesses of 1/8 inch to 1/2 inch and sizes up to 4 × 8 feet, masonite is used extensively in the display area. It has a longer life than foamboard but is much heavier to handle. It can take more bending than foamboard and is therefore often the choice when curved walls are to be faced. It is an excellent surface for painting background scenery. A disadvantage, however, is that it is difficult to staple and so is usually avoided for making pads.

Homasote. Made of compressed cardboard, this product is a favorite for pads. It is durable, comes in 4 × 8-foot sheets ranging in thicknesses of 5/8 inch to 3/4 inch, and is lightweight.

Plywood. When a solid, stiff construction is required, most people use plywood. In thicknesses that range from 1/8 inch to 1 inch, plywood comes in three grades: unfinished, one side finished, or both sides finished. When used as panels covered in fabric, the unfinished, least expensive variety is acceptable. If painting is required and only one side is to be viewed, then the better grade should be used. If both sides must be finished, then the top grade is the choice.

Miscellaneous Types. Other types of boards used include chipboard, a wood-chip composition board; upson, heavyweight cardboard; and gatorboard, a thick Styrofoam panel.

A trimmer will not depend on a type of construction board to perform a certain way until he or she has sampled the abilities and limitations of the board. Once the trimmer has sufficient hands-on experience, the choice of materials becomes second nature.

Fabric

Available in a variety of colors and patterns, fabric adds richness and quality to a display. While color is easily achieved through paint, fabric applications are quicker (no need to allow time for drying) and richer in texture. Versatility and durability are fabric's assets. Although the initial cost is considerably greater than paper, fabric can be used over and over again if properly handled. Many trimmers rely heavily on felt, especially if a wide surface needs covering. Its unusual width of 72 inches generally eliminates seaming, and its elasticity enables it to be stretched to remove wrinkles and creases. The color selection is such that it offers a color range as wide as an artist's palette. Figure 5-2 features a fabric storeroom from which selections are made.

Bengaline and moiré are two fabrics that are being used extensively by trimmers. The durability of these two fabrics and their richness make them ideal for extensive use. Very often, pads are covered in one of these two materials. Figure 5-3 features fabric-covered pads ready to use.

Burlap, also available in a wide color range as well as in the neutral burlap color, is another favorite. Its coarse

Figure 5-2. Fabrics are available in many types to suit the needs of display installations. (*Courtesy of Ellen Diamond.*)

MATERIALS, PROPS, AND TOOLS OF THE TRADE

Figure 5-3. Fabric pads, ready for installation by the trimmer. (*Courtesy of Ellen Diamond.*)

fiber and open-weave construction provide a textured surface, popular in many rustic displays. It, too, is used to wrap pads, but can also be featured as a draped material

Satin is a standard for draping. In displays that require drapery walls, satin is the most popular. Its lustrous sheen projects a feeling of elegance. Most satins used for display purposes are rayon-based, because of their inexpensive cost, but crease easily. Wrinkle removal is most easily accomplished with a commercial steamer after the fabric has been applied to the walls.

Velvets, lamés, mylars, brocades, and jacquards are other fabrics used when opulence is desired by the trimmer. Unlike their counterparts used in clothing construction, these fabrics are made of inexpensive fibers, which considerably lowers their cost. Like satin, they also drape well and give the trimmer the ability to create a rich environment.

Paper

The most widely used display paper is seamless paper. Available in widths up to 14 feet, with 8 feet being the most popular width, seamless paper is available in a wide color range at a very low price. It affords the trimmer an excellent material without the trouble of hiding seams. It can be used as it comes off the role or painted to depict a theme. Often, the trimmer tears the edges of the paper to give it an artistic look. The one disadvantage of paper is its short life. Unlike fabric that is durable and can be reused, paper rarely has more than one life. While it lacks strength, it does have the advantage of low cost.

Occasionally, regular household wallpaper is used in installations. Its infinite variety, at every pricepoint, makes it perfect when a particular theme warrants its use. Many trimmers are known to scout the wall covering close-out stores for such papers at bargain prices.

Other commonly used papers include the embossed type for a dimensional feeling, patterns, wet looks, cellophane, foil, string, and grasscloth. Each gives a different effect at minimal cost.

Paint

Most visual merchandisers use latex-based paint because it dries quickly and requires just soap and water to clean spills and brushes. A visit to today's paint shop shows the extensive range of available colors and the tools available to create a wealth of surfaces and finishes. From the smoothest satin surfaces to the most textured varieties, the results are quickly achieved with an assortment of rollers that are easy to use. Paint has a long life and is used in areas where relative permanence is needed.

Carpet

Some stores desire a permanent floor covering in display areas that has rich textural and visual qualities and will complement many types of merchandise presentations. Carpet provides such a base. It is available in many colors and surfaces. Added to the large variety of velvets and plushes is the new range of sisals and berbers that give a dimensional look. They are available in many colors, are relatively inexpensive when the life of the product is considered, and can be cleaned easily.

Wood

Many stores, particularly smaller specialty shops, use finished wooden floors in their windows, with other materials reserved for interior use. Parquet and geometric designs are extensively used as permanent bases. Many woods come prefinished with polyurethane coatings for a lustrous finish. The only disadvantage of wood is that it can be scratched during set-ups. However, this can be avoided if the trimmer uses felt-based pedestals and other props whose sharp edges are protected.

Miscellaneous

Ceramic and vinyl tile, netting, grass mats, straw rugs, rope, and many other materials are used in display. Visual merchandisers are always seeking different materials to achieve specific effects. It is not unusual to see real hay, sand, pebbles, or imitation snow covering a display floor. It is left to the ingenuity of the trimmer to come up with materials that were not earmarked for display but would make interesting enhancements to visual installations.

PROPS

Try to visualize the characters in a play or a movie speaking their lines in an environment devoid of props. It would be difficult to understand the production's time frame or setting. Set decoration quickly establishes a mood or theme, whether for the theater or for anything that requires a visual orientation.

In the display world, considerable attention is given to securing props that will help present merchandise effectively. Visual merchandisers take several routes in acquiring these props. Some have the advantage of in-store shops to create many of the items required. Others rely on display houses for their needs. In addition to these

MATERIALS, PROPS, AND TOOLS OF THE TRADE

two sources of supply, people in display are using more props that do not come from either category, instead using found objects: items that were produced for other purposes, pieces of furniture, and merchandise intended for other uses.

Found Objects

Creative displays are often built with items that were truly pulled from the junk pile and refurbished, or items that were manufactured for other uses but serve as wonderful props for window and interior settings. By using these props, visual merchandising directors can often stretch limited display budgets.

The diligent display person can find some visual merchandising treasures on the trash heap, if he or she possesses sufficient creative talent. Discarded crates that were used to ship produce, empty soda bottles, garden equipment such as rakes and hoses, picture frames, barrels, and old photographs make wonderful props. With a little sandpaper, paint, and cleaning compounds, the shabbiest of these can be transformed into priceless display gems. Figures 5-4 and 5-5 illustrate found objects used in display.

Figure 5-4. Produce packing crates, found as disposable trash, are excellent display props. (*Courtesy of Ellen Diamond.*)

Furniture

Many pieces of household furniture make wonderful display props. Stores like Victoria's Secret, for example, use a variety of settees, loveseats, and boudoir chairs for displaying intimate apparel. Regular dining tables found in the home also make excellent props to feature the stacking of merchandise for interior display presentations. Chairs, lamps, pedestals, and other furniture items are being used for display. Figure 5-6 features an assortment of pedestals used by trimmers.

Large department stores have these items in stock for sale, and can borrow them for display purposes. Other retailers wishing to use furniture often arrange with stores in the area for their use. If credit is given in the display for the furniture source, the lender is generally happy with the accommodation.

Merchandise Used As Props

Screens, shutters, window shades, ladders, antiques, vases, urns, musical instruments, and garden tools all make excellent props. Figure 5-7 features urns and vases being constructed. In full-line department stores, many of these items are on the selling floor, and as in the case of furniture pieces, can be borrowed. For limited-line stores, where only one type of merchandise, such as apparel, is offered for sale, the acquisition of

Figure 5-5. With a fresh coat of paint, the picture frame becomes a standard prop in many trimmers' installations. (*Courtesy of Ellen Diamond.*)

Figure 5-6. Pedestals, often sold in furniture departments, double as exciting display props. (*Courtesy of Ellen Diamond.*)

these props is different. In the case of musical instruments, for example, a music shop could be contacted for temporary use of the items. Offering to install a sign reading, for example, "Instruments available for purchase at Acme Music Company," will usually seal the deal. Figures 5-8 and 5-9 feature merchandise used as props.

Freelancers often purchase inexpensive items and sell them or loan them to their clients. Some borrow them from other stores, promising window credit as discussed earlier. An antique dealer would be an excellent source for the acquisition of merchandise to be used as props.

If enough thought goes into merchandise prop procurement, the sources of supply are numerous.

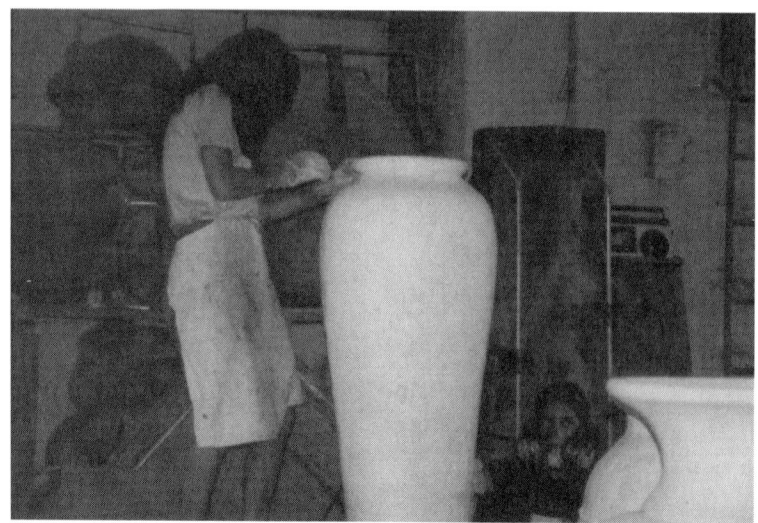

Figure 5-7. The urns and vases being created here will be valuable props. (*Courtesy of Ellen Diamond.*)

Figure 5-8. Ladders are excellent props on which merchandise can be displayed at varying heights. (*Courtesy of Ellen Diamond.*)

MATERIALS, PROPS, AND TOOLS OF THE TRADE

Display House Props

By visiting a display house, the visual merchandiser can acquire a vast assortment of professionally produced props as well as ideas for future presentations. Most vendors change their showrooms to coincide with the seasons. The seasons, however, do not coordinate with the actual calendar. For example, Christmas installations appear in the display houses during the summer so that visual merchandisers can plan their Christmas presentations early enough for an appropriate delivery date.

Visiting all of the vendors in their showrooms can be a tedious and time-consuming task, especially for stores that are far from their suppliers. To make the task easier, vendor display products may be seen at trade shows. Two major shows are held each year under the sponsorship of the National Association of Display Industries (NADI). ShopEast is located on Pier 92 in New York City in December, and ShopWest in Long Beach, California in July. Another important show, Visual New York, is presented in individual showrooms in May and December in New York City. The participants are located close to each other, making the shopping experience rather easy. In most of these trade expositions props, materials, mannequins, lighting, signage materials, and fixtures are offered for sale. Figures 5-10 and 5-11 feature props that are readily available at display houses.

Figure 5-9. Music stands holding sheet music are inexpensive, eye-catching props. (*Courtesy of Ellen Diamond.*)

Figure 5-10. This boat makes a great immediate impact. (*Courtesy of Ellen Diamond.*)

Figure 5-11. A variety of props, such as this tower, are typical of display house offerings. (*Courtesy of Ellen Diamond.*)

The props bought at the display houses are very often refreshed and used again and again. They become part of the store's prop collection. Common to the prop collections of most major stores are items such as urns constructed from Fiberglas or Styrofoam and finished to resemble more expensive materials; bamboo poles in a variety of lengths; artificial flowers and leaves, both stylized and realistic; columns of varying heights; and garlands, banners, artificial trees, rope, and PVC piping used to create different shapes. Some of the display house materials are featured in accompanying display photographs.

In addition to the display house props, a visit to major hardware stores such as Home Depot and to craft stores can provide ideas and materials that can be used for interesting displays.

In-House Construction

Many major department stores have display warehouses in which they store their props, assemble display house purchases, or refinish items that were previously used in windows and interiors. The more fortunate visual merchandising staff also has an in-store construction shop equipped to build props. Figure 5-12 features an in-house trimmer constructing a prop. This display team can have almost anything built to specification in a short time. Equipped with the various tools of the trade, discussed in the next section, the shops can produce even the most intricate designs.

While these shops are usually found at the department store level, some industrious freelancers maintain construction facilities in which they produce their own props for use at their clients' locations. Although most freelancers purchase their props, the do-it-yourself approach enables them to develop unique items and make a profit on the background as well as the time it takes to install a display. Figure 5-13 shows how common brooms have been transformed into mannequins.

Figure 5-12. A creative flower pot being constructed by a member of the in-house visual team. (*Courtesy of Ellen Diamond.*)

Figure 5-13. Inexpensive brooms come alive in the hands of a talented trimmer. (*Courtesy of Ellen Diamond.*)

MATERIALS, PROPS, AND TOOLS OF THE TRADE

TOOLS AND ACCESSORIES

The tools used to execute a display vary from one project to another. If the props are purchased from a display house, all that might be necessary to complete a display is a staple gun to apply fabric to pads or paper to a wall, a screwdriver to assemble parts if necessary and to secure mannequins, a hot glue gun for adhering purposes, a pair of scissors, wire, pins, a hammer, and nails. If the job involves construction of props as well as installations, then other tools may be needed, some of which are unfamiliar to the layperson and might be used only occasionally by the trimmer. One such item is the cutawl, a type of electric saw that can cut around any desired shape.

Large store organizations often have the largest assortment of tools, because they are involved in every aspect of visual merchandising ranging from a simple mannequin change to total refurbishing of a department. While the tool assortment found in these companies is vast, the majority of the items never leave the shop. The trimmer takes only a few tools to the job, the bulk of which will fit easily into a tool box. Figure 5-14 depicts the trimmer and tools needed to install a display.

The tools discussed in this chapter and shown in Figures 5-15 to 5-17 include the minimum tools of the trade, the extra tools for display use, and the accessories of the trade that are musts for the tool box and construction shop.

New tools and accessories that will make the visual merchandiser's task easier or pave the way to more exciting visual effects are constantly appearing in vendor's catalogs. Every trimmer develops favorite tools and display accessories, but it is important to remain open to new ways of doing the job.

Figure 5-14. The basic tools fit into a tool box for easy transportation to the installation site. (*Courtesy of Ellen Diamond.*)

Figure 5-15. Minimum tools of the trade.

Minimum Tools of the Trade	
Tools	Uses
Claw hammer	to hammer nails as well as remove nails and other fasteners
Tack hammer	small hammer for driving pins into solid structures
Flat screwdriver set	various sizes used for regular screws
Phillips-head screwdriver set	various sizes for use on phillips-head screws
Staple gun	to attach fabrics, paper, wire, and props to walls, floors, ceilings, and pads
Staple remover	to remove staples left over from previous installations
Awl	to mark and set a hole to be drilled
Pliers	to turn metal screw eyes, to open and close chain links, remove nails, etc.
Scissors	to cut fabric and paper
Mat knife	to cut paper, oaktag, construction board, foamboard
Wirecutter	to cut wire and some chain
Hacksaw	to cut metal
Wood handsaw	to cut wood, masonite, Homasote, paneling, dowels, etc.
Wrench	to turn nuts and bolts
T square	to measure perfect right angles
Steel rule—36"	to measure lines and to use as cutting edge with mat knife
Metal tape—12'	to measure widths and lengths longer than a 36" steel rule
Drill	to drill holes

Figure 5-16. Extra tools for display use.

Extra Tools for Display Use	
Tools	Uses
Cutawl	to cut intricate designs or patterns in wood (electric saw)
Sabre saw	to quickly cut straight or curved lines (handheld saw with various blades)
Table saw	to quickly make straight or mitred cuts
Electric sander	to quickly sand rough, wooden surfaces
Set of wrenches	to loosen and tighten any size nuts and bolts
Drill press	to electrically set a hole
Jeweler's saw	for fine cutting of metal objects
Hot glue gun	to melt wax pellets into a form that may be used to bond two surfaces (has heating element and trigger mechanism)

MATERIALS, PROPS, AND TOOLS OF THE TRADE

Figure 5-17. Accessories of the trade.

Accessories	Uses	Accessories	Uses
Steel pins	headless pins used primarily with garments	Glues	hot glue for bonding most surfaces, epoxy for glass, Elmer's for paper and wood, and rubber cement for short-lived use of paper
T-pins	to pin heavier objects	Nuts and bolts	to join two pieces of wood or metal
Staples	to tack paper and fabric; available in lightweight or heavy-duty	Molly screws	to use in soft surfaces where studs aren't present
Screws	used when nails are not strong enough; easier to remove than nails	Wire	to "fly" merchandise; No. 30 type is nearly invisible
Screw eyes	to attach the wire used to hang signs, props, and merchandise	Monofilament fish line	to invisibly suspend merchandise from the ceiling or to secure baseless mannequins
Masking tape	to "mask" painted edges and to tape elements of short-lived displays; available in 1/4" to 2" widths	S-clips	to hang merchandise from ceiling grills
Double stick tape	to bond two surfaces	Nails	used in prop construction, securing props, hanging signs, etc.; available in common and finishing (headless) types, sizes 4-penny to 16-penny
Cellophane tape	to affix paper signs and twine because it is invisible to the consumer		

TERMS OF THE TRADE

    awl
    cellophane tape
    chipboard
    claw hammer
    construction boards
    cutawl
    display house props
    double stick tape
    drill press
    flat screwdriver
    foamboard
    found objects
    gatorboard
    Homasote
    hot glue gun

jeweler's saw
masonite
mat knife
molly screws
monofilament fish line
NADI
oaktag
pads
phillips-head screwdriver
S-clips
sabersaw
seamless paper
staple gun
T-pins
table saw
tack hammer
upson
utility knife
wirecutter
X-acto knife

CHAPTER REVIEW

KEY POINTS IN THE CHAPTER

1. Background props and materials should enhance a display but not overpower the merchandise that is available for sale.
2. Except for elaborate holiday displays such as for Christmas, many visual merchandisers favor functional display.
3. Using found objects and merchandise originally intended for other purposes as props, the display team is able to accomplish exciting presentations without severely taxing the budget.
4. Of all the construction boards used in visual merchandising installations, foamboard heads the list in most departments.
5. Fabric affords the trimmer the advantage of reusing the material.
6. Felt is a versatile fabric used in display because of its ability to be stretched, a wide color range, and its unusual 72-inch width.
7. Props are available from display houses, but equally effective and professional-looking props can be created by the visual merchandiser.

MATERIALS, PROPS, AND TOOLS OF THE TRADE 101

8. Major department stores often have in-house construction areas that produce props and revitalize old ones.
9. A trimmer should have a basic assortment of tools that easily fit into a toolbox for use at the actual display site.
10. Trimmer accessories are items such as pins, nails, staples, wire, etc., that need constant stock replenishment.

DISCUSSION QUESTIONS

1. What is the most important element of a visual presentation?
2. Why do visual merchandisers often shy away from dazzling backgrounds?
3. How can a display's cost be minimized at the same time its effectiveness is maximized?
4. Describe foamboard and its uses in visual merchandising.
5. Discuss the advantages and disadvantages of masonite for displays.
6. Why is felt used extensively by individuals who create displays?
7. Which textured fabric is a favorite of the display world?
8. How can a trimmer achieve a colorful background without fabric or paint?
9. How can the visual merchandiser acquire display items that are both interesting and cost-efficient other than from display houses?
10. Define the term *found object.*
11. List five in-store merchandise items that can be used as display props.
12. In terms of actually building a display, what advantages does the visual merchandiser of a large department store have over a freelancer?
13. Which tools are considered necessities for the trimmer's toolbox?
14. Describe the difference between a wood saw and a hacksaw.
15. How do display accessories differ from the tools of the trade?

CASE PROBLEMS

Case 1

Unlike the giant department stores that have a wealth of display space in windows and interiors, Sheri's Boutique is a small, single-store operation that thrives in very limited quarters. In approximately 900 square feet the store manages to bring an excellent profit to its owner.

Located on the main shopping street of La Jolla, California, it faces stiff competition from four unique shops. Although each has a distinct personality and image, all of the stores appeal to the same market. Too small to advertise significantly, Sheri's Boutique believes that creative window displays will entice the most discriminating shoppers to enter the store.

For the past two years, the store has employed Caryn Joy to trim the small, closed-back window. Her displays receive favorable attention and have built up business. Caryn recently moved away and Sheri has been unable to hire anyone who could match Caryn's talent. Without creative windows, the store's business will suffer.

Sheri has watched Caryn for the past two years and has assisted her with each trim. Sheri never did a display herself, but she is being encouraged by her husband, Marc, to try it. While both believe the goal of effective display could be achieved without relying on a freelancer, they recognize the challenge of their present window structure. It requires a good deal of time for background changes. There is also the issue of props, which had always been on loan from Caryn. Now the store will have to purchase and store its own. Sheri and Marc would consider redesigning the window structure if display would be easier to accomplish and prop costs could be cut.

Questions

1. What type of window structure would you suggest?
2. How could prop and material use be minimized?

Case 2

Elements, Inc., a department store with six branches, has fallen on hard times. While it continues to show a profit, the past year was not as good as earlier years. Changes are underway.

The company hired a consultant to research the situation and make suggestions about reorganization and different operating methods. He found the overall problem to be one of rising costs without a comparable increase in sales and he made several suggestions to improve the financial position.

At the meeting to cut costs in accordance with his suggestions, top management zeroed in on the visual merchandising department. Close inspection of that area's expenses indicates a steady increase in purchases for display presentations as well as a significant cost increase in the operation of the in-house construction facility. While creative work that will motivate shoppers to purchase is still considered a necessity, management is determined to cut visual merchandising costs.

Mr. Mitchell, the company's senior vice president, is in favor of eliminating the in-house construction area. This would significantly cut the store's overall payroll. Opponents of the plan believe the move would result in less effective visual presentations. Although it seems to be a drastic step, the company must cut costs to remain a profitable enterprise.

So far, all of the store's departments have made recommendations for cost-cutting measures except for visual merchandising.

Questions

1. If the in-house construction shop is eliminated, can the store still have creative displays? How?
2. Could the shop be maintained while cutting the overall expenses of the visual merchandising department?
3. How can the store provide interesting visual presentations while cutting costs?

NAME: _____   DATE: _____

EXERCISES

1. Visit a mall or any major shopping center and examine all of the store windows. After studying each display, choose three different ones that feature the following props in their installations:
   - found objects
   - store merchandise used as props
   - commercially produced props

   Photograph your three choices and mount the pictures on the forms provided. Be sure the information about each photograph is complete.

2. Make arrangements to visit a display company that sells tools and accessories of the trade to visual merchandisers. If a visit is difficult to accomplish, write to a company requesting information on the tools and accessories it offers for sale to the professional display person. In both situations, try to obtain photographs, brochures, pamphlets, etc., that describe the items sold by the company. Companies that offer such tools are easily found in such periodicals as *Visual Merchandising & Store Design* and *Chain Store Age,* and in local Yellow Pages directories.

   Once you have obtained the information, prepare a catalog on the tools and accessories of the display trade, indicating which are necessities and which are the extras. Drawings and/or photographs of each item will make the catalog a more meaningful publication from which tools and accessories can be selected.

NAME: _____ DATE: _____

Exercise 1 **DISPLAY PROPS**

Chapter 6
Principles of Design

LEARNING OBJECTIVES

After completing this chapter, the student should be able to:

1. List the five principles of design that may be found in visual presentations.
2. Differentiate between symmetrical and asymmetrical balance and tell how each is accomplished by the trimmer.
3. Explain the numerous techniques employed to achieve emphasis in a window.
4. Describe the importance of proportion in a display.
5. Discuss rhythm and how the trimmer accomplishes it in an installation.
6. Distinguish between rhythmic repetition and continuous line.
7. Identify the use of rhythmic radiation in a display.
8. Achieve harmony in the execution of a visual presentation.
9. Justify the use of contrasting elements in a display design.
10. Relate five methods for achieving contrast in a display.

INTRODUCTION

Fortified with both exciting and functional fixtures, materials, and mannequins, the visual team is one step closer to installing merchandise displays that will capture shoppers' attention. In doing this, the visual merchandiser must always keep the principles of design in mind and carefully use them from the time the theme's concept is born until it is finally executed.

We have all heard or been involved in discussions about good or bad design as seen in a room, a building, a piece of furniture, or apparel. Good design should not be confused with taste, which involves personal choice or preference. The merit of any design is judged on a set of principles that includes balance, emphasis, proportion, rhythm, and harmony. These same principles may be applied to works of fine art, architecture, or any creative endeavor. In the case of visual presentations, when the principles are properly executed and professionally blended with other elements such as color, lighting, and signage, they result in a presentation that achieves its goals.

When these artistic principles are applied in the field of visual merchandising, they must be considered along with the store's merchandising concept, image, type of customers, geographic location, and other factors that make up the company's business philosophy. The design principles are the same; but the settings in which they are applied affect how emphasis or rhythm is carried out.

This chapter illustrates all of the design principles in actual presentations that have been photographed, coupled with analytical drawings to make them more easily understood. You will notice that a trimmer generally employs more than one principle in a given display.

BALANCE

The word balance describes an equality of weight, something distributed evenly on two sides. When we think of a scale, we understand it to be balanced if both sides are at the same level with each supporting a similar object.

In Figure 6-1, two objects, identical in size and weight, are featured. The center line of the scale is the exact middle with each side representing equal weight or importance.

When the principle is carried over to visual designs in a window or interior presentation, it is not adhered to as scientifically or mathematically. In order to give equal importance to objects in the display, they should be placed with care

Figure 6-1. A balanced scale supports equal weights on both sides.

PRINCIPLES OF DESIGN

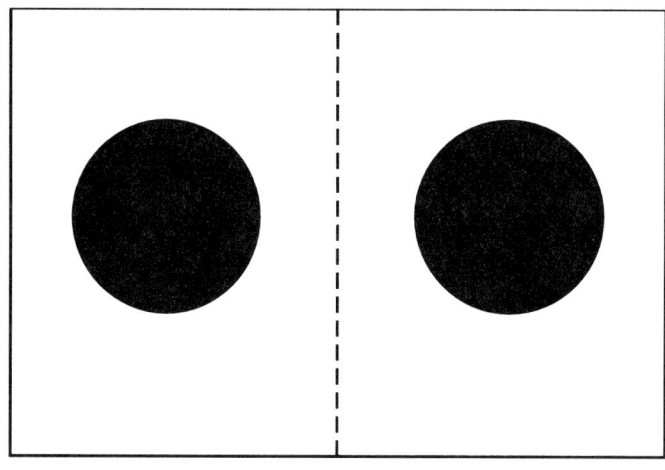

Figure 6-2. An imaginary line shows the balance between two geometric forms.

on either side of an imaginary line. Figure 6-2 shows two shapes in perfect balance. The broken line is imaginary, as the trimmer would envision it, and shows that both sides are equal or in balance.

Symmetrical Balance

Perfect balance may be fine for some displays, but the majority of presentations would be monotonous if there were not other design possibilities.

In the photograph and analytical drawing of the accompanying symmetrically balanced display in Figure 6-3, the trimmer has

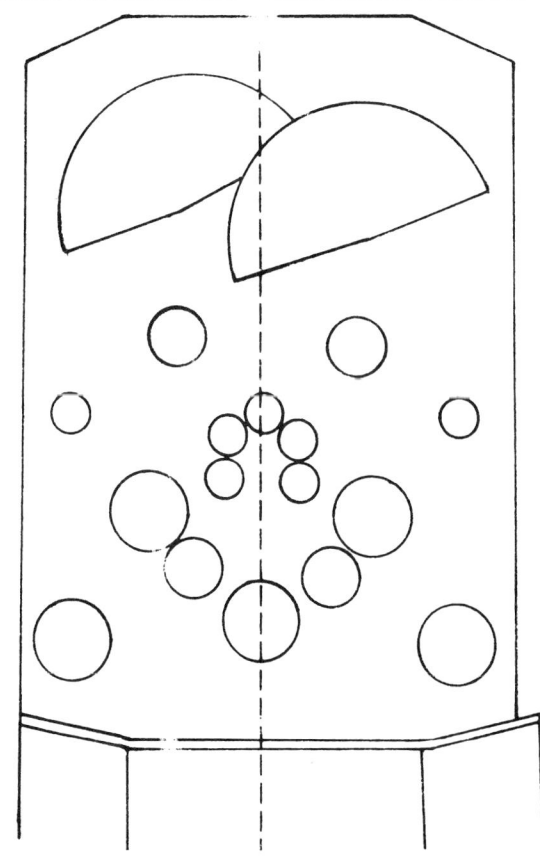

Figure 6-3. Perfect formal balance is achieved in this display. (*Courtesy of Ellen Diamond.*)

resorted to formal balance. While it guarantees the assignment of equal weight to each half of the design, its effectiveness is limited. Novice interior designers often fall into the trap of formally balancing a room. They place a sofa in the center of a wall, end tables on either side with identical lamps adorning them, and a rectangular cocktail table in front of the sofa. Each side is a mirror image of the other. While considered correct in terms of balance, this arrangement could be uninteresting if not carefully executed. Formal balance gains effectiveness if the merchandise is appealing, the colors are rich, and the two halves of the display, while formal in balance, do not feature identical items. The formality of the design is in the shapes employed rather than in duplication of designs and colors.

In Figure 6-3, we see classic formal or symmetrical balance in a window display. The illustration is presented in two parts, the first being the actual presentation and the second a drawing of just the sizes and shapes. The broken line is imaginary and is used only to demonstrate the balance of each side to the other in the display. The interest is generated directly by the merchandise and not by the creativity of the trimmer.

Asymmetrical Balance

Asymmetrical or informal balance is more relaxed and allows better use of the trimmer's creative talents. In this arrangement, while the total weight on each side of the imaginary center line is about equal, the shapes used to balance each other could be different, such as two smaller pieces balancing a larger object. In the drawing depicting asymmetrical balance, an imaginary line divides the display in half. The large circle on the right side in Figure 6-4 is balanced by the three smaller circles on the left. Each side achieves a sense of balance, though using different objects.

The visual merchandiser uses this simple concept in complex ways. While being governed by the fundamental principles as depicted in Figure 6-4, imagination, creativity, and originality come into play when actual asymmetrical balance is used. When the actual photograph of the window is analyzed in the drawing in Figure 6-5, the sense of balance can be understood.

It should be noted that the bottles and steamers on the right are carefully offset by the woks and garlic on the left. Each half of the design represents an equal mass and comes across to the observer as having good balance.

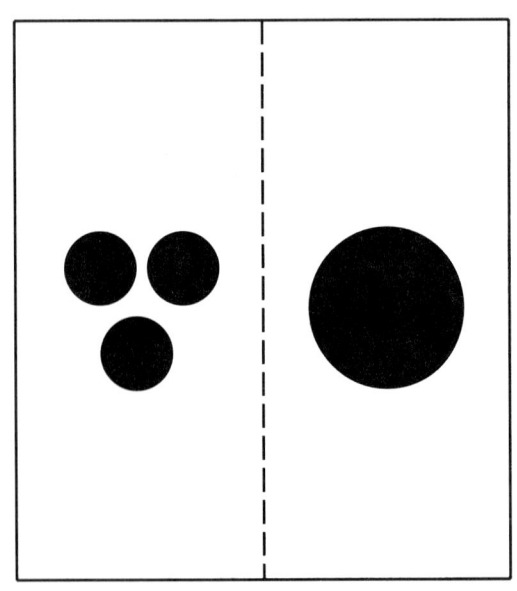

Figure 6-4. In asymmetrical balance, the halves may carry different shapes but have equal weight.

Figure 6-5. An analysis of asymmetrical balance using the display and a drawing to represent the shapes. (*Courtesy of Williams-Sonoma.*)

EMPHASIS

Every visual presentation should be built around something of particular interest, often referred to as the focal point. The focal point is the dominant or central point of a display, with everything else playing a secondary or subordinate role. It may be a piece of merchandise, a prop, a concept, or a feature. In a model room setting, for example, the designer might use a famous painting, carefully illuminated, as its focal point of emphasis. You want the viewer to notice it immediately as the central focus and then to retain the image as a motivation to purchase. If a presentation has too many focal points, the result can be confusion rather than emphasis.

Emphasis can be achieved through a variety of techniques, the most common of which are size, repetition, contrast, and unique placement.

Size

When you walk into a room crowded with unfamiliar people, the first person you notice is usually the tallest one; for example, the basketball player among people of average height. Similarly, in the design of a visual presentation, dominance is easy to achieve with something large. It might be an oversized prop, as depicted in Figure 6-6. Many visual merchandisers use very large graphics in conjunction with traditionally scaled merchandise to draw attention.

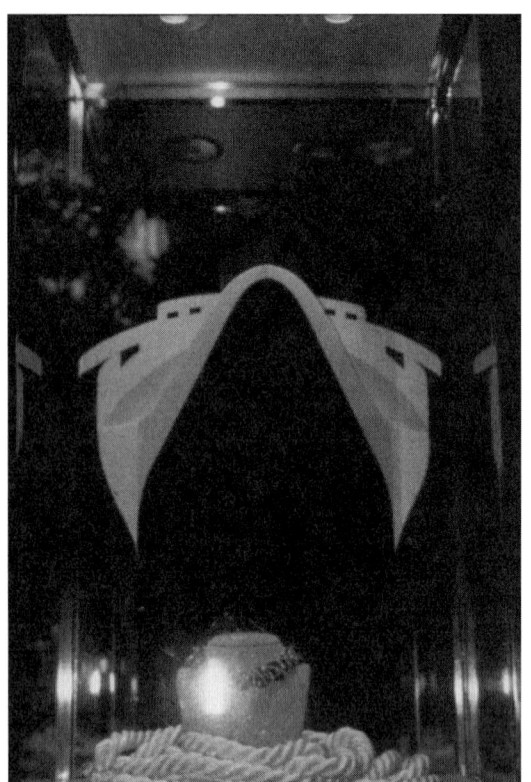

Figure 6-6. The oversized oceanliner, in contrast to the jewelry, draws attention to the display. (*Courtesy of Ellen Diamond.*)

Repetition

Repeating a color, shape, pattern, or texture allows dominance to emerge. The eye quickly focuses on the repetitive element, and the abundance of these similar elements underscores their importance to the customer. In Figure 6-7, the repetition of the merchandise attracts the eye.

Contrast

Another means of portraying dominance or emphasis is with a color, texture, or concept that is in complete contrast to the other elements of the display. For example, in an arrangement where all of the geometric prop shapes are round, as shown in Figure 6-8, the circular shapes surface as the dominant image, in contrast to the merchandise forms. You will understand this concept better after examining the analysis of shapes that accompany the photograph.

Certain concepts are frequently employed to achieve contrast in design, the most common of which use size, lights and darks, shapes, textures, and directions.

Size Contrast. Interest can be captured by placing an oversized object in the display. It is obvious that the dinosaur overpowers the other elements in the display in Figure 6-9. If you remove the dinosaur by placing your hand over it, the display becomes mundane. This element plays off the others, providing a focal point to catch shoppers' attention.

Lights and Darks. By including a single light object in a generally dark display or vice versa, an immediate visual force is created. White bridal gowns against a much darker background or men's black formalwear against a light background are good examples of this type of contrast, as is the display of a bride in a white dress with a groom in a black tuxedo. In Figure 6-10, the contrasting stripes of the merchandise draw interest.

Figure 6-7. The lining up of five identical items of merchandise exemplifies repetition. (*Courtesy of Ellen Diamond.*)

PRINCIPLES OF DESIGN

Figure 6-8. The spoked wheels perfectly contrast the merchandise forms. (*Courtesy of Ellen Diamond.*)

In a room setting, the interior designer often paints three walls in a soft tint, and then colors the remaining wall in a very dark shade of the same hue. This gives the dramatic effect of light and dark contrast.

Shape Contrast. A uniform presentation of the same shapes can be tedious. If a table display features only one shape, such as round dinnerplates, the display lacks interest. With the inclusion of various shapes, such as a rectangular or oval basket and folded napkins in rings, the display is more artistic and interesting.

Textural Contrast. Introducing an unusual or unexpected texture in a display is another way to capture interest. Wristwatches, for example, are usually shown in a luxurious setting of satin-lined gift containers or exquisite jewelry boxes. In one watch display, the trimmer decided to go after the rugged individualist with a display using rope and ragged packing cord. Fine timepieces are set against textures that are rough and common; the visual result is outstanding.

Figure 6-9. The enormity of the dinosaur prop offers contrast to the merchandise. (*Courtesy of Ellen Diamond.*)

Figure 6-10. The striped black and white merchandise draws attention to the display. (*Courtesy of Ellen Diamond.*)

Figure 6-11. The one shoe facing in the opposite direction of the others provides directional interest. (*Courtesy of Ellen*)

Directional Contrast. A display in which all of the elements face the same direction has its uses, but there are other possibilities. Including an element that seems to move in the opposite direction from all of the others provides an interesting contrast. One shoe in Figure 6-11 faces right while the other shoes and pedestals face left, creating an extraordinary presentation.

Unique Placement

Unexpected or unique positioning of an item can immediately capture the customer's attention and make a point. Suspending mannequins in midair and dressing them in activewear as seen in Figure 6-12 grabs the shopper's attention and focuses it on how active and attractive he or she can be in clothes bought in this department. Put the same outfit on a conventionally posed mannequin and the result would not be as exciting.

The concept of emphasis and how best to achieve it in each display situation comes with experience. While the techniques mentioned are tried and true, the creative visual merchandiser is always trying to develop new approaches to capture the shopper's eye.

Figure 6-12. Suspended mannequins capture the shopper's attention. (*Courtesy of Ellen Diamond.*)

PROPORTION

The principle of proportion involves the comparative relationship of the design elements to each other. When each element of the design is properly proportioned, the whole will have a pleasing effect to the eye. That is not to say that each part is carefully measured to make certain that it is in perfect proportion, but it is our visual perception that tells us whether each of the parts is proportionate to the entire layout or design composition.

Often the word scale is used in place of proportion. Interior designers speak of appropriately scaled furnishings to fit the available space.

PRINCIPLES OF DESIGN

Figure 6-13. The mannequin's size is out of proportion to the window. (*Courtesy of Ellen Diamond.*)

Figure 6-14. A smaller-scaled, representational form better serves the display in Figure 6-13. (*Courtesy of Ellen Diamond.*)

To understand the importance of scale or proportion, consider an interior design situation. Professionals who design and decorate residences find that the average square footage of living space is shrinking. Cost and overcrowding in some areas have necessitated that individuals make do with less room than was once considered necessary. Therefore, furnishings for such quarters must be scaled to fit the shrinking living space. Not only would an overstuffed sofa not fit into the living room, but even if it could, its size would make it visually disproportionate for the space. Numerous furniture manufacturers now offer home furnishings that are scaled for smaller residences to provide suitable proportions.

The visual merchandiser must also address the proportion principle in a number of situations. First, in planning a presentation, he or she considers the size of the space in the window, showcase, floor case, or interior display case. Not only must the merchandise fit well into the display space, but the mannequins, forms, and props must be properly proportioned for the presentation. Figure 6-13 features a mannequin in a window whose scale is ill-proportioned. The trimmer chose a life-size mannequin for the outfit; however, the mannequin is too close to the ceiling and this is visually disturbing.

Substituting a representational form that is properly scaled for the window makes the display more appropriately proportioned and more pleasing to the eye.

In the previous examples, the problem was space-oriented. Proportion must also be carefully considered when choosing the various elements of the display to make certain that each is proportional to the others for an overall good design. In the lamp and table drawings, one is unacceptable, while the other is more pleasing. The lamp placed on the small table is an example of poor proportion or scale. When the same lamp is situated on a larger table, the total design is more pleasing

In achieving designs of pleasing proportion, remember that it is not necessary to measure spaces and display elements. Exact mathematical ratios should be reserved for scientific endeavors, not design work. It is how the various elements interrelate to form the total image that is important.

RHYTHM

When all of the elements of a design are properly located so that the eye travels smoothly from one part to another, then flow, movement, or rhythm have been achieved. This is an extremely important principle because it makes the eye take in every part of the display before it focuses and rests on a specific focal point or area of emphasis. It is the task of the presentation's designer to make the eye move in a specific pattern. As we examine the works of famous artists, we discover that rhythm is carefully executed through repetition, continuous line, progression, radiation, and alternation. These methods are also employed by visual merchandisers in their display arrangements.

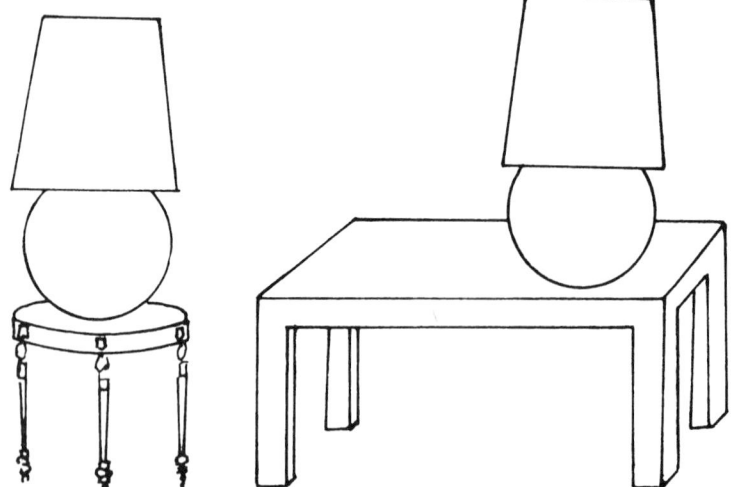

Figure 6-14a. Proportional relationships among the elements can make or break a display. (*Courtesy of Ellen Diamond.*)

Repetition

In a display using the principle of repetition of shapes, the eye is led in one direction by multiples of the same shape. The placement of three identical forms in a row moves the eye across the display in Figure 6-15.

Continuous Line

Interior designers frequently use moldings or borders to achieve this principle of rhythm. These linear devices lead the eye around an installation. In the display depicted in Figure 6-16, a simple garden hose is artfully draped to bring the observer's eye from the upper left area of the display down to the featured merchandise. In addition, repetition of shape is also employed to carry the eye back and forth across the levels of the presentation.

Figure 6-15. The three identical forms help lead the shopper's eye. (*Courtesy of Ellen Diamond.*)

PRINCIPLES OF DESIGN

Figure 6-16. A simple garden hose helps to move the eye through the display. (*Courtesy of Ellen Diamond.*)

Progression

Rhythm can be accomplished by employing gradation of line, shape, size, or color. Textile designers sometimes provide interest in fabric coloration by offering a design in a range of the same color from the lightest to the darkest. Visual merchandisers borrow from this concept when trimming a window in tints and shades of one specific color. Another technique to show progressive rhythm uses the same shape in increasing or decreasing sizes as shown in the different sized circles in Figure 6-17.

Radiation

Rhythmic movement may radiate from a central point, as in the rays of the sun or the spokes of a wheel. In fact, trimmers sometimes use circular props such as wagon wheels to move observers' eyes outward from a central point in a display. The merchandise itself may be arranged to radiate from a focal point without a special prop. In the drawing in Figure 6-18 depicting ties on a wheel, the trimmer has used rhythmic radiation.

Figure 6-17. The progression of circles attracts attention. (*Courtesy of Ellen Diamond.*)

Figure 6-18. Ties displayed in a radiating pattern establish rhythm. (*Courtesy of Ellen Diamond.*)

Figure 6-19. The ties, at alternating heights, add rhythm to the display. (*Courtesy of Ellen Diamond.*)

Alternation

When certain shapes or colors are used alternately, they give a design rhythm. The alternating red and white stripes on the American flag are a powerful example of this rhythmic technique. The alternate use of light against dark colors or warm with cool colors can also give a design rhythm. Using awning-striped materials for display settings is one way trimmers employ the alternation technique. In Figure 6-19, the ties are placed at alternating heights to produce rhythm.

HARMONY

When all of the elements in a design properly blend to form a unified picture, the principle of harmony has been achieved. It is analogous to a theatrical presentation. If the scenery, lighting, and characterizations are uniformly satisfying, the play is successful. When one of the actors demonstrates substandard ability, the play is not as effective. The unity of the various elements is necessary for a positive, overall production.

Harmony of design seems to imply that all of the elements must be exactly the same; for example, using merchandise that is all red, in shapes that are all the same, and in textures that are similar. Such a display would be harmonious but not very interesting. In design, a display can include some variety and still be considered harmonious.

In planning a visual presentation, if the central theme concentrates on a specific color, a variety of shapes and merchandise textures should be employed to provide excitement. Using too many variables could cause confusion and could be just as improper as monotony. Experience teaches a designer how to use variety to create memorable, harmonious presentations. In the beach window featured in Figure 6-20, summer is the theme. All of the key elements utilize the beach design, and ultimately underscore the purpose of the window to the observer. The variety of shapes, textures, and materials blend harmoniously.

Figure 6-20. This display epitomizes the harmonious blend of elements. (*Courtesy of Ellen Diamond.*)

PRINCIPLES OF DESIGN

Mastery of some of the design principles, such as balance, is easy to accomplish. Others take a little longer to use effectively in visual presentations because they are not scientific definitions; they are open to interpretation. We have introduced you to these basic principles, but experience is the best teacher when it comes to applying them in dynamic visual merchandising.

TERMS OF THE TRADE

alternation
asymmetrical balance
balance
continuous line
contrast
directional contrast
emphasis
focal point
harmony
progression
proportion
radiation
repetition
rhythm
scale
shape contrast
symmetrical balance
textural contrast
unique placement

CHAPTER REVIEW

KEY POINTS IN THE CHAPTER

1. In order to construct a display that is technically correct, its plan should be evaluated in terms of principles of design.
2. Balance, the equal distribution of weight in a design, can be accomplished with the symmetrical (formal) or asymmetrical (informal) plan.
3. The term *emphasis* suggests that there should be a central or focal point to a display achieved through size variation, repetition of shapes, contrast, or unique placement of a key element.

4. Contrast can be achieved easily through the use of atypical sizes, variation of lights and darks, different shapes, different textures, or changing the direction of a key element.
5. Proportion must be considered carefully so that all elements of the design will relate in terms of size.
6. To achieve rhythm and move the observer's eye through the display, the trimmer should consider the use of repetition, continuous line, progression, radiation, or alternation.
7. Contrasting elements can bring rhythm to a display in addition to establishing emphasis.
8. Harmony suggests that unity of the elements is essential to an effective display.

DISCUSSION QUESTIONS

1. What are the five principles of design that should be considered in the development of a display?
2. Is it necessary for each side of a display to be perfectly or formally balanced by the other side? Why or why not?
3. How can a display be easily balanced yet safeguarded against the monotony of a symmetrically balanced window?
4. Define the term *emphasis* and describe its importance to a visual design.
5. What elements can be used repetitively to create interest in a display?
6. Describe the concept of proportion and why it must be considered in any visual presentation.
7. The term *rhythm* usually applies to music. How does it apply to three-dimensional design?
8. In what way can a trimmer use repetition as a rhythmic principle to catch the shopper's eye?
9. Why is continuous line usage effective in a display installation?
10. Describe how progression can be used to create rhythm.
11. What display props are appropriate for rhythmic radiation?
12. Select a synonym for harmony and discuss its importance to design.
13. How can contrast be employed successfully in a design while not interfering with the concept of harmony?
14. In what way can the excitement of an all-red window be heightened through the use of the contrast principle?
15. What is the difference between textural and directional contrast?

PRINCIPLES OF DESIGN

CASE PROBLEMS

Case 1

Boring and *monotonous* are perhaps the two most appropriate terms to describe the windows at Brown & Co., a children's specialty shop in southern Florida. The operation is a typical small store that grosses $250,000 annually, employs five people whose primary responsibility is sales, and is comanaged by John and Edith Brown, the proprietors.

In addition to the responsibilities of buying and merchandising, handling customer complaints, and arranging adjustments, the Browns have tried trimming their store windows. The company formerly employed a freelancer who accomplished the task satisfactorily but didn't achieve outstanding results. When the trimmer decided to retire, the partners investigated other freelancers but could not find anyone to fit their budget. They felt the costs simply outweighed the benefits they would derive from professional window displays. The only route left was to do the windows themselves.

Edith, originally a fine arts major in college, felt that her early training would be applicable to visual merchandising. She was familiar with color selection, as well as some of the rules of balance, proportion, and harmony. Armed with this knowledge she trimmed her first window, a back-to-school installation. She purchased the display accessories usually associated with this theme from the area's display house and perfectly balanced them in the window, so perfectly that one side was a mirror image of the other. The result was a dull presentation that didn't seem to catch her customers' attention.

Not yet willing to cry "help" to a freelancer, the Browns want to try again. They just aren't sure how to make the new effort a traffic-stopper.

Questions

1. What principles were neglected that could improve the first display's appearance?
2. What props could you suggest that the Brown's use instead of traditional back-to-school banners, rulers, etc.?
3. Aside from formal instruction, how might they increase their knowledge of achieving exciting displays?

Case 2

The Sweater Emporium, as its name implies, is a retail operation that deals exclusively with sweaters, specifically for women. The company's two stores are almost identical, with interiors and windows that are virtually the same size. Thus their visual merchandising efforts are alike.

The stores have been in operation for one year and considering that they started on a shoestring, their accomplishments have been noteworthy. Save for their visual presentations, the rest of their efforts can be considered professional. As is the case with many smaller retailers, display is a sorely neglected area. The costs are often prohibitive. While their efforts in terms of window presentation are mildly satisfactory, the partners, Marc and Mitch, want to improve their efforts.

After reading a few books on the principles of design and observing other stores for ideas, they concluded that their problem is not one of inability but one of limited merchandise. Everything they read about or observed indicated that a variety of shapes and sizes is necessary to give a window a more artistic appearance. However, sweaters are sweaters. They are soft, similar in shape, and possess the same basic characteristics. Accessories retailers have an assortment of merchandise types that allow for better design. Sportswear, menswear, home furnishings, and children's wear, too, offer an assortment of merchandise. Without changing their merchandise mix, Marc and Mitch believe they are unable to achieve what they want in terms of visual presentation.

Questions

1. How would you suggest that they improve their windows with the merchandise they now feature?
2. What design principles could help them alter their lackluster displays?

EXERCISES

1. Photograph four window displays, each on a different theme. Attach photographs to the forms provided. Beside the space for the photograph on each form is a space for analysis. As you have seen with some of the photographs in the text, do a companion draw-

NAME: _____ DATE: _____

ing for each of your photos to illustrate how the principle of balance was employed in the window.

2. Prepare drawings on the form provided that demonstrate each of the subdivisions of rhythmic design. Do not use any of the illustrative drawings from the text.

Exercise 1 **PRINCIPLES OF BALANCE**

Exercise 1 (continued)

NAME: _____ DATE: _____

Exercise 2 DRAWINGS OF RHYTHMIC DESIGN

Chapter 7
Color: Fundamental Concepts and Applications

LEARNING OBJECTIVES

After completing this chapter, the student should be able to:

1. Discuss the importance of color in industries such as visual merchandising.
2. Define the terms *hue, value,* and *intensity.*
3. Choose color schemes based on the color wheel that are technically correct.
4. Prepare a color presentation that is monochromatic yet has contrasting elements to avoid monotony.
5. Design a color scheme using accepted theory that provides the greatest amount of color contrast.
6. Identify the neutrals used in color combinations and discuss their importance to color schemes.
7. Describe the effects of warm and cool colors on individuals.
8. Explain the emotional concept of advancing and receding color.
9. List the six primary and secondary colors and the emotional moods generated by each.
10. Discuss the visual merchandiser's limitations in personal color preference when planning a presentation.

INTRODUCTION

Using color is the best way to add excitement to a visual presentation without increasing the cost of the installation. Our most famous art treasures abound with color, and it is that element that captures the immediate attention of the viewer. Avant garde artists, in particular, use the vibrancy of color to make strong initial statements.

The movie industry, television, and the legitimate theater depend on color to give otherwise bland productions enormous visual appeal. Fashion and design periodicals seldom use black and white photographs; most are in color. Even some movie classics, originally black and white productions, have been colorized by computer. While some professionals dislike this trend, those who understand today's marketplace recognize that color can revive interest in old movies.

It is obvious that the use of color is essential in attracting attention to a subject. While fine artists must be skilled at mixing their own pigments to achieve a variety of colors, visual merchandisers rarely do the actual mixing of paints, with the possible exception of trying to achieve a specific color for a background or props. Their mixing of colors refers to arranging colored items tastefully. However, the display person must have the same understanding of color and its concepts and applications as a fine artist in order to capitalize on color's advantages. The visual practitioner in retailing and related fields needs to know the correct combinations of color for achieving special effects, how to best use color in a window or interior presentation, and the psychological impact of various colors. This chapter presents a foundation in color principles, terminology, and themes.

DIMENSIONS OF COLOR

The layperson's vocabulary of color usually extends as far as knowing the names of general colors. A customer will ask to see the blue shirt, red dress, or yellow scarf. If you closely examine a stack of red sweaters in a store, however, you realize that the word *red* by itself doesn't totally describe the color. Some reds look orange-red, while others seem to be purple-red or blue-red (which we often refer to as maroon). Two reds may look like the same basic color, but one may be lighter than the other. It is necessary, therefore, to explore the variations in color so you will be prepared to use them in visual merchandising.

Hue

In simple terms, hue is the name of the color. Just as people are referred to by their individual names, colors are known by their hues. Yellow, green, blue, and purple are some of the hues or names of colors. Pure colors, or hues, by themselves tend to become monotonous in a visual presentation.

Value

When describing the lightness or darkness of a hue, we are speaking of its value. By adding white to a hue, we lighten it and achieve a tint. With the addition of black, a darker variation is produced, known as

Figure 7-1. The color wheel is based on the three primary colors and the colors that result from mixing them.

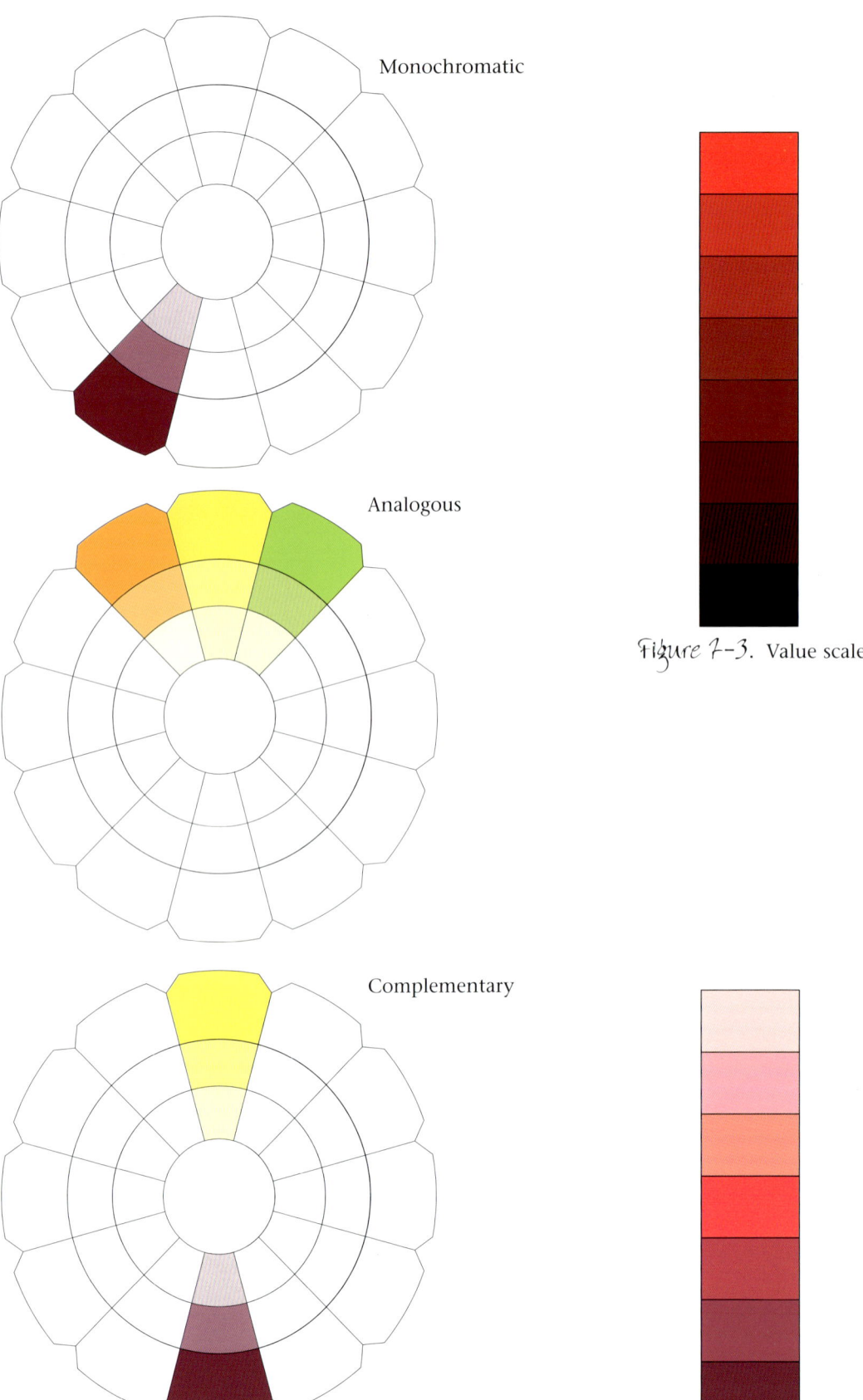

Monochromatic

Analogous

Complementary

Figure 7-2. Common color combinations based on the color wheel.

Figure 7-3. Value scale.

Figure 7-4. Intensity scale.

Figure 7-5. Monochromatic display. (*Courtesy Ellen Diamond.*)

Figure 7-6. Analogous use of colors. (*Courtesy Ellen Diamond.*)

Figure 7-7. Complementary color scheme. (*Courtesy Ellen Diamond.*)

Figure 7-8. Creating a painted backdrop. (*Courtesy Ellen Diamond.*)

Figure 7-9. Silkscreening signage. (*Courtesy Ellen Diamond.*)

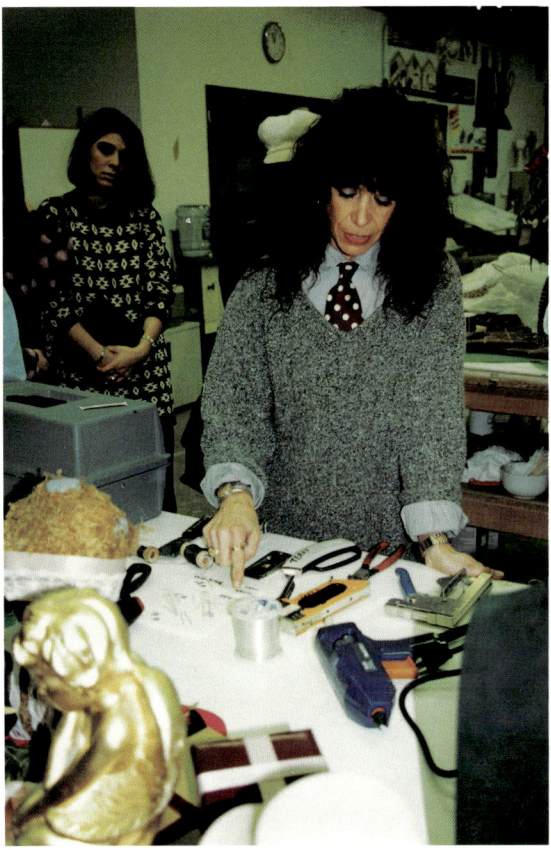

Figure 7-10. Using the tools of the trade. (*Courtesy Ellen Diamond.*)

Figure 7-11. Installing the presentation. (*Courtesy Ellen Diamond.*)

Figures 7-12 and 7-13. Unique fixturing transforms interiors into exciting environments. (*Courtesy FRCH Worldwide and Rain Forest Cafe.*)

Figures 7-14, 7-15, and 7-16. Carefully executed store windows stop traffic. (*Courtesy Ellen Diamond.*)

Figure 7-17. This imaginative display, using ties in a creative manner and dramatic lighting, epitomizes contemporary visual merchandising. (*Courtesy LSI.*)

a shade. With each addition of white or black to a color, its hue doesn't change, only its value. In creating a window in which red is dominant, the installer adds interest by including different values of red, such as pale pinks or dark reds.

Intensity

The saturation or purity of a color is referred to as its intensity. A color's intensity is actually its brightness or dullness. Artists vary intensity by adding middle gray to the pigment or adding the complement of the color, which is discussed later in the chapter, for duller intensity. The color is most alive and brilliant in its purest form. While the mixing of colors to alter their intensity is usually the work of a painter, the visual merchandiser needs to know all about them in order to plan presentations.

The visual merchandising staff of a store and their freelance counterparts must know how hues are used to achieve harmonious as well as exciting effects and how values and intensities of colors can be arranged most effectively. It is this color comprehension that enables trimmers to maximize the effectiveness of their displays just by adding color, rather than adding props, materials, and other more costly display elements.

THE COLOR WHEEL

The system of color that is most often referred to makes use of the color wheel. By understanding the relationships of the colors and applying them in terms of their location on the wheel, the visual merchandiser is more likely to come up with color schemes or themes that achieve the goal of attracting customer attention. The color wheel, pictured in Figure 7-1, is based on three primary or basic colors from which all other colors are produced. The appropriate mixing of these primaries produces secondary colors, while the blending of an adjacent primary and secondary results in a tertiary color. The wheel shows the continuous transition of color and is the foundation upon which most color schemes are based. In close proximity to the color wheel, examples are shown of the three most common color schemes based on the wheel, a value scale, and an intensity scale. In the remainder of the color section, you will find examples that underscore the importance of color to several aspects of visual presentation.

COLOR HARMONIES

A color scheme, arrangement, or harmony is easily accomplished by following specific rules that are based on the color wheel. Colors may be used together harmoniously in a design, depending on their locations on the color wheel and the value and intensity of each. In order to have a better understanding of the various color harmonies, it is advisable to refer back to the wheel and the value and intensity scales.

The arrangements used most often by visual merchandisers and others wishing to maximize the effects of color are examined here.

Monochromatic

This color arrangement uses only one hue. While initially this might not seem very stimulating, its proper employment has the potential for visual elegance. Using tints and shades of one hue, then highlighting with the neutrals of black and white, one can achieve a show stopper. Additional interest can be provided if the materials of the merchandise and background vary in texture and pattern.

Analogous

Colors that are next to each other on the color wheel may be used in combination to form the analogous color scheme. This arrangement gives the trimmer greater freedom to use differently colored merchandise, unbound by the limitations of a monochromatic scheme. Since the merchandise in most stores is varied in color, the analogous design enables a variety to be featured in one presentation. Many retailers of clothing and home furnishings create in-store color combinations that are analogous and add to the excitement by following the same scheme in the store's windows. As with the monochromatic scheme, neutrals, tints and shades, textures, and patterns can also be used for greater artistic results.

Complementary

When color selection builds on two colors that are opposite each other on the wheel, the result is a complementary color scheme. When these colors are held side by side, the intensity of each is heightened. A Christmas display is a good example because bright red packages against a green Christmas tree provide high-intensity color that demands attention. While this impact is often desirable, quieter effects can also be achieved with complementary colors. Using tints or shades of complementary colors will be more subtle but still offers the excitement of each playing against the other; for example, the soft pinks and pale greens of spring.

Split Complementary

An interesting effect can be achieved by using one basic color with two colors that are on either side of that color's complement. In doing so, the trimmer has more colors to work with and can create a design that is infinitely more exciting than the monochromatic, analogous, or complementary schemes. Split complementaries, in a variety of values and intensities and underscored by neutrals, can be the basis for a very creative visual installation.

Double Complementary

Expanding on the complementary arrangement that features two colors at directly opposite positions on the wheel, the double complementary approach uses two sets of colors, or four basic colors, for the presentation. The use of four hues can cause visual confusion unless they are applied with great care. One way of avoiding a problem is to predetermine which of the four will be highlighted and which will play subordinate roles. Using one or two of the colors as dominant forces and the others as accents can have magnetic results.

Triad

This harmony involves the use of three colors on the wheel that are equidistant from each other. If you superimpose a triangle on the wheel it will help you discern which colors fit this arrangement. As in other cases where several colors are used, it is best to vary the use of these hues by toning down their intensities and values or by using only one in a dominant role.

The six color harmonies discussed are presented in Figures 7-18 to 7-23 to graphically show their arrangements.

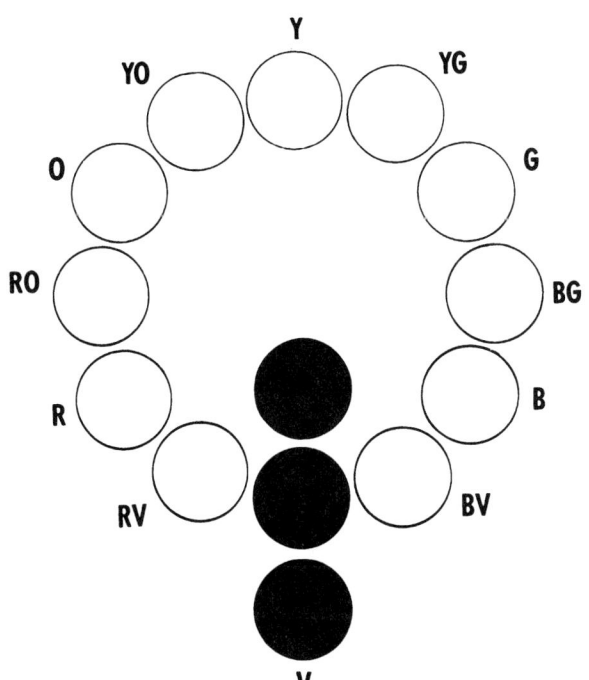

Figure 7-18. The monochromatic arrangement. The shaded area is the specific color used in the monochromatic scheme. Tints and shades of the color add depth to the display.

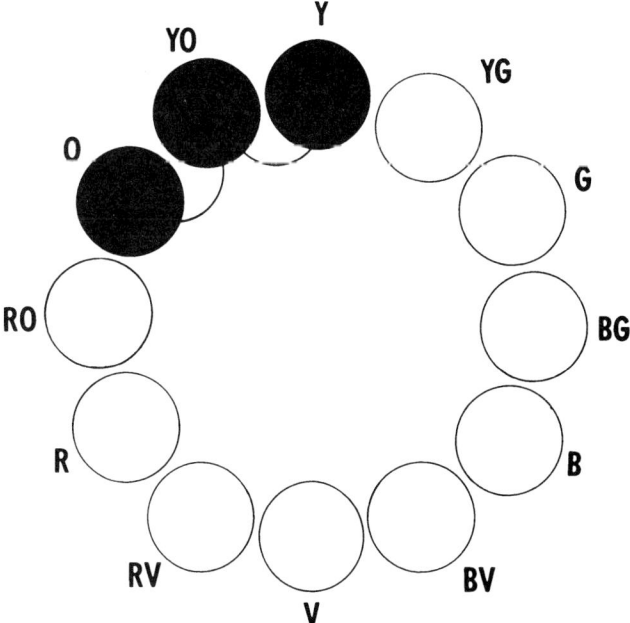

Figure 7-19. The analogous arrangement. The shaded areas of yellow, yellow-orange, and orange provide a range of tints and shades to be used with neutrals for an analogous color scheme.

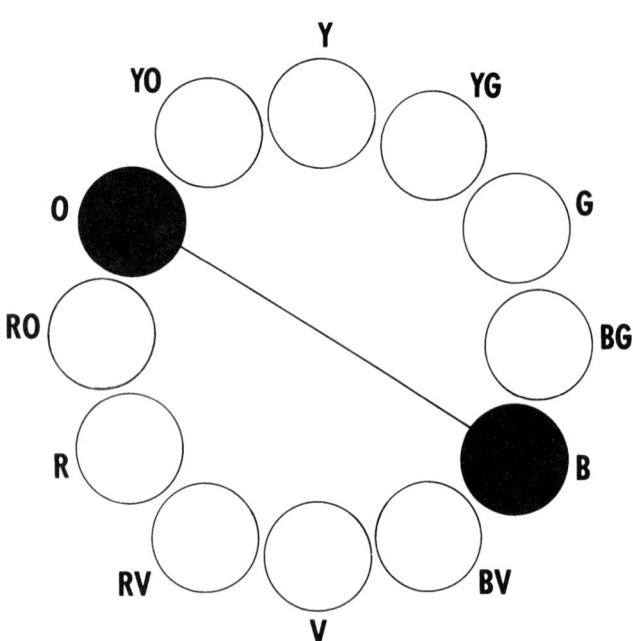

Figure 7-20. The complementary arrangement. The use of pure blues and oranges with neutral black or white provides color intensity that is unmatched by other schemes.

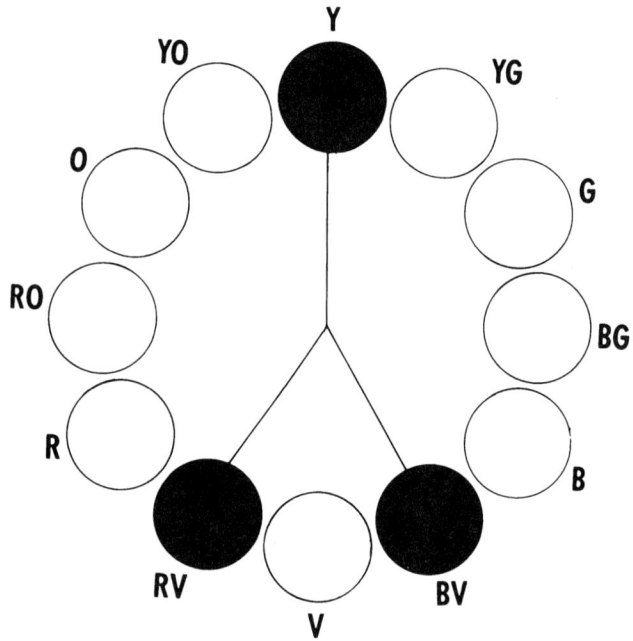

Figure 7-21. The split complementary arrangement. Yellow as the basic hue, in combination with red-violet and blue-violet, results in a harmonious split complementary scheme.

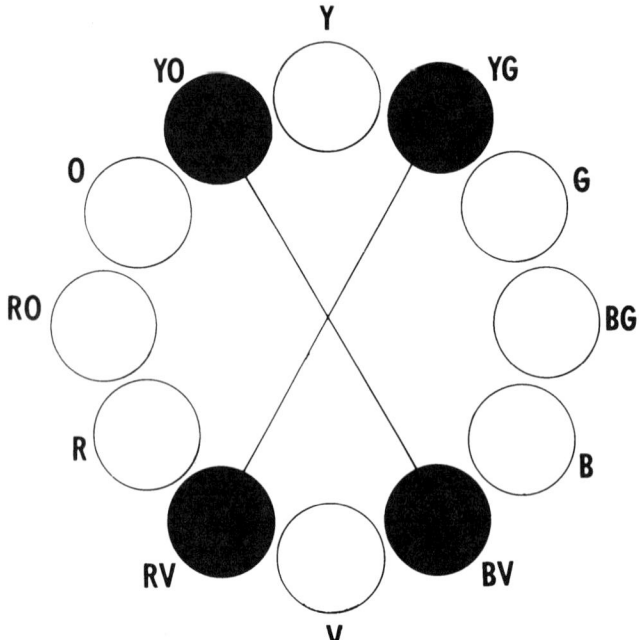

Figure 7-22. The double complementary arrangement. The shaded areas indicate that yellow-green, yellow-orange, blue-violet, and red-violet are used in this double complementary color scheme.

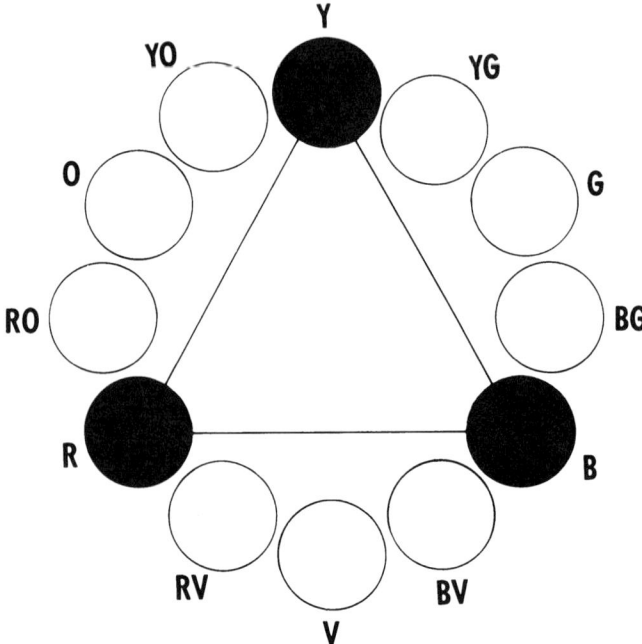

Figure 7-23. The triad arrangement. A superimposed triangle shows the equidistant location of the primary triad colors: yellow, blue, and red.

THE NEUTRAL INGREDIENTS

Through the discussion of color harmonies, we have learned that hues are primary colors or secondary colors with other colors achieved through their combinations. While black and white are often called colors, they are not technically colors. Along with gray and tan, they are neutrals that may be used in conjunction with colors or by themselves to create presentations of interest. A very elegant image is produced in a formal display featuring female mannequins dressed in white gowns escorted by male mannequins in black tie dress.

No matter how they are perceived technically, the neutrals play a vital role in window displays, interior presentations, and department colorization.

CHOOSING A COLOR SCHEME

In our personal, everyday lives we make color choices that are generally based on taste and preference, not on a season, a theme, the time of year, or anything else. While we might want to learn about restful colors or colors that provide excitement (discussed in the next section), the bottom line in making a color selection is strictly personal.

In visual merchandising, however, choices are somewhat dictated by the merchandise to be displayed or the statement to be made. You might personally favor red, but if the designers concentrate on blue this season, you must decide how best to enhance blue. By employing the color wheel and the schemes that have just been explored, you will be able to fulfill the requirements of the project and capture shoppers' interest. This is not to say that arrangements of color must be adhered to as strictly as the schemes imply. Professional designers, whether their forte is clothing, home furnishings, interiors, or general display, often use their creative abilities to go against the conventional rules for visual impact. The rules of color are intended to be guidelines, not limits, to creativity.

In developing color combinations, many visual merchandisers use a fabric of interest as a starting point. A print or stripe that has considerable eye appeal might lead the trimmer to pull out a particular tone and use it for the background or prop color. Vendor-produced graphics (discussed in Chapters 10 and 11) might feature a color scheme upon which a presentation could be based.

Paintings are often inspirational sources of interesting color harmonies. The Mondrian works with their bold geometrics and strong color combinations, for example, have served many visual merchandisers with color schemes. Just as clothing designers explore costume institutes like the famous one at New York City's Metropolitan Museum of Art for inspiration, so might visual merchandisers make the rounds of art museums. Nowhere is it written that any set of rules must always be followed in selecting color schemes and, given the wealth of resources available, visual merchandisers who operate within a rules framework are shortchanging the companies for which they work. By making it a regular practice to stay on the lookout for interesting color combinations, whether in the way(s) mentioned, or by scanning fashion and home furnishings magazines, examining color presentations at color forecasting services such as Color Association of the United States (CAUS), or by using the color libraries at such forecasting services as Promostyl and Cotton Incorporated, visual merchandisers enhance their ability to bring life to presentations.

PSYCHOLOGY OF COLOR

The role that color plays in a window or interior store setting is much more than that of providing something pleasant for the shopper to see. While everyone has a favorite color, few understand the rationale behind their choices. Color has a significant effect on our emotions, and the skillful use of color in displays can motivate us to buy. In order to capitalize on the psychological effects of color, it is important to understand some of the ways that color can be applied to create the best emotional environment to encourage purchasing.

Warm and Cool Colors

Scientifically speaking, colors don't actually provide warmth or coolness. They do not have physical properties that dispense heat or cold. Instead, the temperatures that we associate with specific hues are a result of physical sensations we experience from certain colors.

Blue and green are considered cool colors, with purple sitting on the fence. If the purple is predominantly blue, it is considered cool. Red, orange, and yellow are warm hues. In designing a color scheme for a fur salon, the dominant color might be blue. With its cool and icy characteristics, it is almost certain to create an environment in which the shopper might experience an emotional chill and want to bundle up in the warmth of fur. Conversely, the use of yellows and oranges in a resort shop could quickly evoke the warmth of the sun and tempt the shopper to try on a swimsuit. If an experiment were done in which the colors were reversed in the preceding examples, it is likely that the shoppers' reactions to the merchandise would be quite different.

Advancing and Receding Colors

Although colors do not actually move, there is a feeling that some colors advance while others recede. When observed from a distance, the warm colors such as red and orange seem to appear nearer to us than do their cool counterparts, greens and blues. Bearing this in mind, the visual merchandiser who wishes to employ color to enlarge or shorten a display area should be aware of the tricks that colors play on our minds. If a display area or a department is small and the desire is to make it seem more open and spacious, a pale, less intense blue would be in order. If, on the other hand, a warm, cozy feeling is the desired result, a bright red would be an appropriate choice to bring the walls in.

The Emotional Effects of Color

The right color choice can immediately create a mood. Most of us have either felt mood changes due to specific color use or have heard others speak about mood swings they have experienced as a result of a particular color. Although blue is generally the color preferred by most people, with red second, there is no safe color that will have the same effect on all people. The interior designer's task of color selection for a home is easy; he or she discusses it with the client. However, the selection of a color for retail departments, interior presentations, or window displays is a shot in the dark. In trying to predict the effects of certain colors on customers, the visual merchandiser counts on the following typical responses to color.

When trying to achieve excitement and a scene that will arouse the senses, red is an excellent choice. When used monochromatically in its pure form and contrasted with tints of pink and shades of maroon, it has an impact unattainable by most other combinations.

Orange is a warm color that when darkened to rust gives an earthy feeling. If the customer is to be reminded of the upcoming autumn season, there is no better color to use. Fall leaves, resplendent with oranges and yellows, immediately give us the emotional feeling of warmth.

Blue, the favorite color of most people, suggests coolness and serenity. The peacefulness of the color might be the reason it is a favorite. What better color than that of the sky to evoke a calming emotional experience?

Green is an excellent choice for a restful setting. For spring presentations, the greens of the grass and budding plants give the viewer a feeling of emotional comfort. By itself in a visual presentation, however, green doesn't have the properties sufficient to create a positive picture. It is best combined with yellows and oranges to create a springlike feeling or contrasted with red, its complement, for pure excitement, as in the case of Christmas decorations.

Purple, the symbol of royalty, is a color to be used for dramatic purposes. In its pure or shaded forms it emits a feeling of drama or mystery. As a tint, its effect is generally cooling.

Yellow is a warm color that produces a cheerful effect. When it is used alone, however, it may be monotonous. It is best used in combinations with other colors or perhaps, if a monochromatic scheme is the goal, with white.

The neutrals, black, white, tan, and gray, while not technically considered colors, are still transmitters of emotion. Black might imply depression, but when featured in an elegant setting of eveningwear it imparts a message of richness and sophistication. White can generate a cold feeling but can add a striking balance to any color scheme. The elegance of the white bridal gown, when contrasted with any color or black, immediately heightens the emotions. Tans and grays add other dimensions to colors. Tans contribute to the earthiness of a visual presentation, while gray embellishes a display with an air of sophistication.

Although each color has a different emotional impact, visual merchandisers soon learn that the choice of color to feature in an installation is not theirs alone. The designers of clothing, accessories, and home furnishings dictate what colors are in vogue, and you must be sufficiently knowledgeable to enhance their offerings. Unlike the fine artist whose paintings reflect a personal preference and whose color palette is his or her own creation, visual merchandisers create with much less freedom of choice.

TERMS OF THE TRADE

advancing colors
analogous colors
color harmony
color wheel
complementary colors
cool colors
double complementary colors
emotional effects of color
hue
intensity
monochromatic
neutrals
primary colors
receding colors
restful colors
secondary colors
shade
split complementary colors
tint
triadic colors
value
warm colors

CHAPTER REVIEW

KEY POINTS IN THE CHAPTER

1. Color plays a vital role in visual merchandising; its appropriate use is of utmost importance in the success of the store's interior and windows.
2. Without creative use of color in installations, it is unlikely that shoppers will stop to examine the merchandise offered for sale.
3. Color is discussed in three terms: hue, the name of the color; value, the color's lightness or darkness; and intensity, the saturation or purity of the color.
4. A color wheel is a system of color location and the relationships of one to another.
5. There are three primary colors: red, yellow, and blue; and three secondary colors: orange, green, and purple; along with neutrals of black, white, gray, and tan.
6. Monochromatic schemes use one central color, while analogous and complementary schemes use two main colors.
7. By adding white to a color, a tint is achieved; with the addition of black, the result is a shade of the color.
8. A complementary scheme enhances the two colors' strengths.
9. Neutrals are used to add interest to color schemes or may be used by themselves in specific situations.
10. Visual merchandisers must set personal color preference aside and enhance, through appropriate means, the colors of the merchandise to be displayed.
11. In addition to the color wheel, visual merchandisers could be inspired by unusual coloration in a painting or by the prints and patterns of materials.
12. Color plays an interesting part in our moods. There are warm and cool colors that create specific feelings in us and colors that appear to advance and recede.
13. Different colors cause different emotional reactions in individuals. Blue, the favorite of most, is peaceful; red provides excitement; and purple gives a feeling of royalty or drama.

DISCUSSION QUESTIONS

1. What fields, other than visual merchandising, make color one of their most vital ingredients in capturing attention?
2. Since the visual merchandiser doesn't mix paints to achieve different colors, what color mix must he or she use?

3. Define the term *hue*.
4. How does one change a hue?
5. Differentiate between value and intensity.
6. Why is it important to understand the concept of the color wheel?
7. Distinguish primary colors from secondary colors, and list the names given to the colors that fall between the two on the color wheel.
8. In what way can monotony be avoided in a monochromatic color scheme?
9. Select an analogous color scheme and one that is complementary. Which scheme results in greater color intensity?
10. How does the split complementary scheme differ from the regular complementary configuration?
11. Which color scheme employs three colors that are equidistant from each other on the wheel?
12. Name four neutrals and describe the roles they play in color presentations.
13. Besides the color wheel, what other sources of color inspiration are available to the visual merchandiser?
14. Define the terms *advancing* and *receding* in color selection.
15. What are the cool colors and the warm colors?
16. Of what significance are cool and warm colors to visual merchandising?
17. Which is the favorite color of most people? Why?
18. What emotional effect is generated by red?

CASE PROBLEMS

Case 1

The Landing is a department store organization based in the Northeast. It has a downtown flagship operation and six full-size branches in the surrounding suburbs. In business for 35 years, the store's sales have continued to increase each year. As with most other department stores, The Landing carries a wide assortment of hard goods and soft goods with emphasis on clothing and accessories for its female clientele.

After a successful five-year attempt to trade up, the company is now ready to experiment with the addition of a fur salon to cater to the upscale female customer. But where? The stores are already bursting at the seams, and there is no possibility of acquiring additional selling space at either the flagship or its branches. The solution seems to be reallocation of floor space to accommodate the new furs.

The general merchandise manager believes that restructuring the space assigned to hard goods is the answer. Since this merchandise brings less than the markup achieved by fashion items, it is natural, she says, to use some of the space for the new fur department. The hard goods buyers believe that a decrease in their selling space would severely hamper sales and would give the impression that The Landing is no longer a full-scale department store. The latter conclusion has been voiced by others in top management.

Last week, the divisional merchandise managers presented a plan that has been favorably received by the store's executive team. They believe that if swimsuits (a seasonal offering except for a little resortwear during the winter) were alternated with furs (also seasonal), they could both use the same space, at different time periods. It was decided that swimsuits would take possession of the selling area from April until mid-August with furs taking over from late August until the beginning of April. Two small areas would always be functioning to cater to those customers who desire the out-of-season merchandise.

The visual merchandising department has been approached to suggest a new color scheme that would quickly and smoothly accommodate the transition from one type of merchandise to the other without requiring a major overhaul each time the merchandise offering is changed.

Questions

1. Is it feasible for such diverse merchandise groups to use the same selling area?
2. What approach would you suggest in terms of color to accomplish their goals?

Case 2

Ever since it opened, the Fashion Closet has concentrated on bringing its customers the best merchandise at affordable prices. The attraction has been a regular discount of 20 percent off department-store prices. Situated in an off-the-beaten-path location, its success is due to word-of-mouth advertising. With the profits realized, the owners sought a place in which to open a second unit. They recently found a vacant shop in a small center inhabited by fashion retailers who specialize in shoes, accessories, menswear, and children's wear, as well as another store that specializes in merchandise similar to the stock carried by the Fashion Closet.

Both partners believe the time is right for expansion and that the new center would be perfect. Their present operation is lackluster in terms of visual presentation, but this new location, amid stores that consider visual impression important, will require changes. A quick look at the other stores shows that care and attention are focused on window display. Although they are not ready to invest in professional trimming, the partners want to spruce up their windows. They want to achieve impact with color and have decided to do it with a monochromatic display signature against neutral backgrounds of white, tan, gray, or black. The neutral backgrounds will allow them to make frequent display changes without great cost. With carefully timed changes in the monochromatic schemes, their windows will signal to customers that new merchandise has arrived in the store.

The problem that confronts them is the monotony of monochromatic color schemes. They need advice on how to avoid the pitfalls of using a single color to attract attention.

Questions

1. Does the monochromatic approach seem appropriate?
2. Should they use only this color scheme?
3. How could monotony be avoided with such a color scheme?

NAME: _____ DATE: _____

EXERCISES

1. Photograph two window displays that feature any of the color harmonies derived from the color wheel. Mount the photographs on the form provided. In addition to mounting the photographs, fill in the requested information.

2. Prepare a color wheel that includes the primary, secondary, and tertiary colors. Apply the color with felt-tipped markers, with paint, by cutting up strips of Coloraid paper (available at any art store), or with chips of colored magazine paper.

3. Visit a paint shop or a department in a large home supplies store that sells housepaint such as Home Depot. It should have an extensive assortment of color chips from which customers may select any tint or shade of a particular hue. Select one primary color and one secondary color and a wide range of tints or shades of each and prepare a value scale ranging from the darkest shade or lightest tint. Cut the color chips and paste them on the form provided.

4. Photograph two window displays that use only neutrals. On the form provided, mount the photographs and evaluate each in terms of color effectiveness.

NAME: _____ DATE: _____

Exercise 1 DISPLAY WINDOWS WITH DIFFERENT COLOR HARMONIES

Color Harmony _____

Featured color (s) _____
_____

Neutral(s) _____
_____

Evaluation _____
_____
_____
_____

Color Harmony _____

Featured color(s) _____
_____

Neutral(s) _____
_____

Evaluation _____
_____
_____
_____

NAME: _____ DATE: _____

Exercise 2 COLOR WHEEL PREPARATION

NAME: _____ DATE: _____

Exercise 3 PRIMARY AND SECONDARY VALUE SCALES

Primary value scale

Secondary value scale

NAME: _____ DATE: _____

Exercise 4 NEUTRAL COLORED WINDOW DISPLAYS

Neutrals used _____

_____

How interest is achieved _____

_____

_____

Evaluation _____

_____

_____

_____

Neutrals used _____

_____

How interest is achieved _____

_____

_____

Evaluation _____

_____

_____

_____

Chapter 8
Lighting: Dramatizing the Selling Floor and Display Areas

LEARNING OBJECTIVES:

After completing this chapter, the student should be able to:

1. Discuss the importance of lighting to the selling floor and visual presentations.
2. Describe the various sources of light used by retailers, and visual merchandisers in particular, and the advantage of each type.
3. Differentiate between incandescent floodlights and spotlights.
4. Define the term *fiber optic lighting,* and explain the purposes it serves.
5. Explain why many retailers have added halogen or quartz lamps to their interiors and windows.
6. Give the reasons for the popularity of track lighting.
7. Contrast the results of using a PAR spotlight and a blown glass spotlight.
8. Describe two methods by which color can be achieved with lighting.

INTRODUCTION

The movie director's shout of "Lights, camera, action" is the signal that the film is about to be recorded. Imagine the result if the first of the three commands is eliminated. While the camera rolls and the actors go through their paces, inappropriate lighting could result in poor films. By changing nothing more than the intensity, direction, or color of the lights, shadows are altered, moods can be created, and the commonplace is transformed into the dramatic. Clever lighting can minimize unimportant areas and emphasize others.

Borrowing from the movie industry and the stage, visual merchandisers have turned lighting into a tool that does more than just illuminate a window or interior. No longer is lighting just a functional effort left to the whims of an architectural designer. After all, display is akin to theater in that it too requires dramatization to maximize the efforts of the director, or in the case of retailing, the visual merchandiser. In most companies, visual merchandisers play a significant role in the selection of lighting. While the decision is not theirs alone, they work in conjunction with the people in operations and with architects and lighting specialists to make certain that the chosen fixtures and systems will satisfy the needs of effective window presentation as well as interior illumination.

Smaller retail organizations that operate without an in-house visual merchandiser must rely on the expertise of an architect, interior designer, or lighting expert. In these situations, lighting decisions may fall short of what is necessary to provide distinctive display effects because of the absence of a visual merchandiser. In such cases, the freelance trimmer is called upon to augment the existing lighting by providing additional temporary lighting, such as floor spotlights, to enhance the store's visual presentations.

Whatever the situation, a knowledge of lighting is necessary to highlight the store's merchandise offerings, whether they be on the selling floor or in display windows.

In this chapter attention is focused on the different types of available light sources, lighting fixtures and systems, and the use of colored lighting.

LIGHT SOURCES

Other than natural daylight, which plays practically no part in store interior or window illumination, there are several sources of light employed by visual merchandisers. A knowledge of each will help you to make the appropriate choice in terms of both visual effect and economy of the operation. Each different type—fluorescent, incandescent, high intensity discharge lamps, neon, and halogen or quartz—is used for specific purposes.

Fluorescents

For cost-efficient, cool general lighting, fluorescent is the choice of many retailers. The bulbs come in many shapes, but the long, narrow cylindrical tubes that come in several lengths are used most frequently. A newer type is housed in fixtures that easily install on track systems. They are used by retailers for wall washing and display illumination. The advantage of this type of lighting is that it is visually

LIGHTING: DRAMATIZING THE SELLING FLOOR AND DISPLAY AREAS

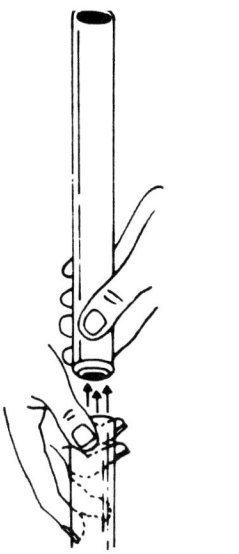

Figure 8-1. Color tubes for fluorescent bulbs come in 48" lengths and can be cut to fit any size bulb.

appealing and smaller than the typical fluorescents. Other advantages of fluorescent use in general are dramatic energy savings, as much as 75 percent when compared to incandescent lamps, long lamp life, and high light output.

The early fluorescent lights gave off a harsh, blue-like color that tended to wash out the shopper's complexion as well as the color of the merchandise. However, today's bulbs offer excellent color rendition and come in a variety of colors that can project coolness, warmth, or other desired effects. If color is needed for a particular temporary presentation, filters are available to encase the standard white tubes, as demonstrated in Figure 8-1.

The fluorescent bulb is most often used in interior ceiling, floor, and wall cases, in valances that frame windows and shadow boxes, and on lighting tracks. Although the bulbs are comparably inexpensive and long-lasting, the fixtures, especially those with pleasing surfaces, are expensive and in all cases except the track variety, are stationary, so they cannot be directed at specific targets. Without mixing fluorescents with incandescents or other types of lamps, the store's appearance will be stark, evenly illuminated, and devoid of any interesting or dramatic effects.

Many trimmers are using fluorescents over entire walls to create a dramatic effect. The fluorescent fixtures are recessed into a wall that is completely covered with a Plexiglas surface. In this way general lighting is achieved as well as a dramatic focal point for the department.

Incandescents

Although a general wash of light was regularly achieved by retailers with the standard incandescent bulbs, their maintenance was so costly that new breeds of this bulb are now being used. They are known as low voltage lamps. They provide more lumens per watt than standard incandescent bulbs, which come in spotlight or floodlight form, and are known as PAR bulbs and R bulbs, respectively. The low voltage lamps bring out the true colors of the merchandise, enhance textures, and create spectacular lighting effects. Whether highlighting a large area or spotlighting an object as shown in Figure 8-2, the precise beam pattern of low voltage lighting creates drama. There are many variations available in this type of lamp, ranging from those that accent items to those that throw very long beams. Another advantage of the low voltage incandescents is heat reduction. The heat thrown is actually two-thirds less than standard sources, which results in considerable savings for ventilation of the store. Finally, the lamps burn longer, which significantly reduces replacement and fixture relamping costs.

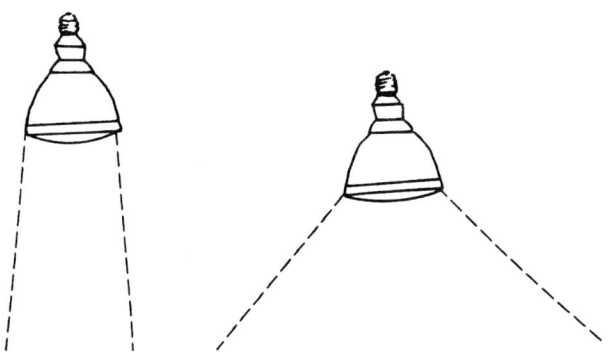

Figure 8-2. The beams of incandescents are either wide to highlight an area or narrow to spotlight or focus on a particular item.

Fiber Optic Lighting

Technically, fiber optic lighting is comprised of a remote light source carrying glass optical fibers. More important to the visual merchandiser are the benefits of the product. They include the elimination of ultraviolet and infrared wavelengths, directional spotlighting or floodlighting, simple maintenance, ease of concealment, and reduced power consumption. Because they give a cold light, heat-sensitive objects such as jewelry benefit from their use.

High Intensity Discharge

Commonly known as HIDs, these bulbs are very small, produce more light per watt than either the incandescents or fluorescents, and are energy savers. While they are readily available, visual merchandisers, for the most part, still ignore their usage in favor of fluorescents for general, overall lighting, and halogens and low voltage incandescents for accenting purposes. HIDs are making their mark in the home, however, where they are housed in unusual lighting fixtures.

Neon

Figure 8-3. The neon lighting adds interest to this dislay window. (*Courtesy of Ellen Diamond.*)

Once reserved for outdoor signs to identify the name of a store, neon lights are being used extensively in store interiors. A great advantage of neon, or cold cathode as it is technically known, is that it can easily be shaped to any form. These lights are relatively maintenance-free and cost little to operate. Available in a wide range of vivid colors, neon is used by visual merchandisers to build excitement. Neon quickly transforms a ho-hum junior department into a dance-floor environment with the flick of a light switch. Today's neon sculptors have broadened their scope of design to the creation of total environments that add immediate excitement to a department or window. Although neon is a source of light, it is relied on more for special effects than for total illumination, as seen in Figure 8-3.

Halogen

In their search for ways to improve the lighting of their wares, many retailers have turned to the halogen lamp for dramatic, intense lighting. The bulbs, which are housed in special fixtures, give off light that is unlike the light generated by the other bulb sources. Basically a whiter, brighter bulb, approximately one-quarter the size of a standard incandescent, it ideally enhances the visual image and totally washes a wall. Not only does it afford more light control, more efficiency, and a more intense light per watt, but the lamp has a longer life, about double that of incandescent bulbs.

LIGHTING FIXTURES AND SYSTEMS

In the past several decades there has been a drastic change in the lighting fixtures and systems available to retailers. The variety enables retailers to acquire distinctive lighting and decorative fixtures to complement any decor. So attractive are many lighting appliances that they become the focal points of some store interiors. Although the innovative lighting fixtures and systems are readily available, retailers don't constantly change their designs when a new one appears on the market. The investment is just too costly. These newer systems and fixtures are generally reserved for new branches and units that department stores and chain organizations open. For stores that have been in operation, visual merchandisers must be able to use what is available, adding fixtures and bulbs to existing systems.

RECESSED LIGHTING

Many stores have lighting systems that are recessed in the ceiling. A can or container holds floodlights that illuminate broad areas, and spotlights for narrow illumination or highlighting. Fluorescents are also often recessed and are used for overall, general lighting.

Figure 8-4 is an example of recessed incandescents being used for general illumination. It should be noted that a large number of incandescent floodlights are necessary to do the job. A few recessed fluorescents could serve the same purpose, but some retailers prefer both the visual effect projected by the continuous circles of lights and the shadows these bulbs play on the surrounding walls.

Incandescent spotlights can also be used in recessed fixtures. These fixtures swivel to enable the visual merchandiser to pinpoint a specific area. For even more flexibility, extension swivel rods can be attached to the cans, lowering the bulb below the ceiling surface and allowing light to be focused in any direction. Figure 8-5 shows an incandescent bulb that is recessed into a ceiling can, and a swivel extension rod adapter that not only lowers the light but permits it to be directed to another area.

Figure 8-4. Incandescent floodlights are used abundantly to illuminate this selling floor. (*Courtesy of FRCH Worldwide.*)

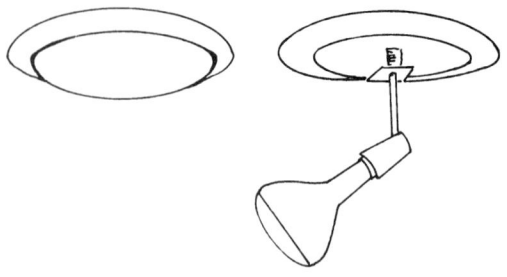

Figure 8-5. The extension rod adapter brings the light closer to the area of illumination.

In earlier recessed fluorescent fixtures, the bulbs were exposed, presenting a very unattractive appearance. Soon, egg crate casings were used to conceal the bulbs and later, Plexiglas panels. Today many casings are available that are used to conceal the bare fluorescent bulbs. It should be noted that while an aesthetic quality is achieved with these coverings, there is some reduction in the amount of projected light.

TRACK LIGHTING

While recessed lighting is often considered an attractive as well as functional method of lighting, the placement is stationary. In order to be able to adjust lights in the exact positions they are needed, many retailers use track lighting systems as seen in **Figure 8-6**. Track lighting is easy to install, does not involve complicated wiring, and can quickly transform an area into one that is attractive and perfectly illuminated. Tracks come in 2′, 4′, 6′, 8′, and 12′ lengths and can be arranged in many ways with the use of L, T, or flexible connectors, as featured in Figure 8-7.

To accent objects on a wall or to wash a wall with light, the track should be placed 3 feet from a wall that is 8 or 9 feet high, and 4 feet from walls that are 10 to 12 feet high. The proper positioning maximizes the effectiveness of the light thrown. The ability to swivel the containers allows items in a window

Figure 8-6. Used either on the ceiling or dropped down, track lights provide flexibility. (*Courtesy of Juno Lighting.*)

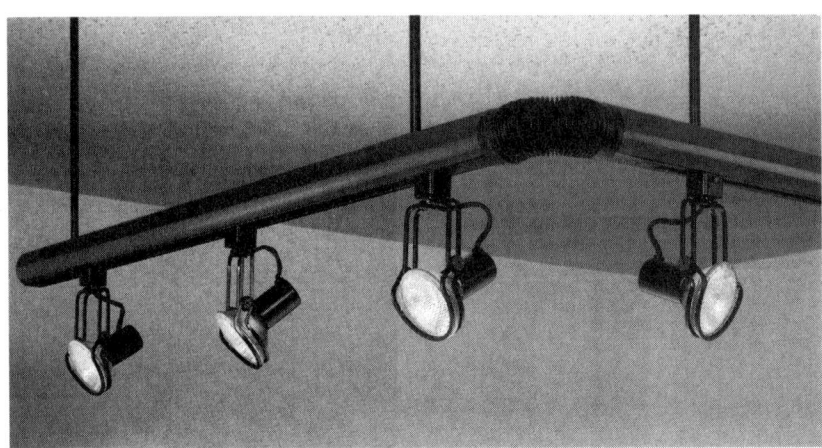

Figure 8-7. This flexible track light permits the turn of corners. (*Courtesy of Juno Lighting.*)

LIGHTING: DRAMATIZING THE SELLING FLOOR AND DISPLAY AREAS

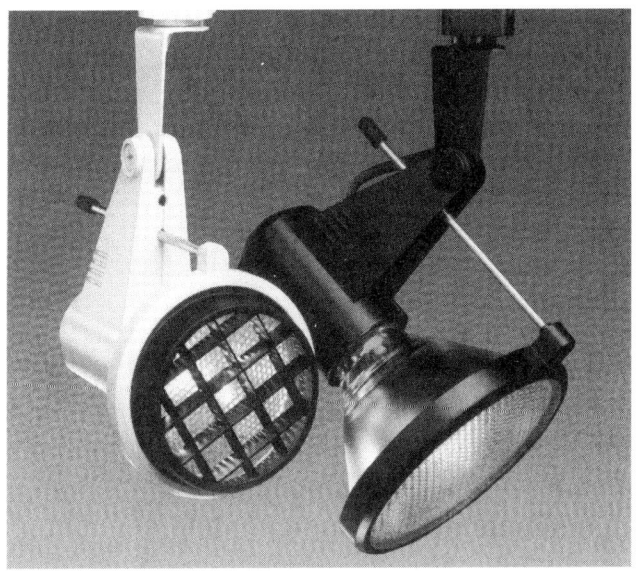

Figure 8-8. The open fixture exposes the bulb. (*Courtesy of Juno Lighting.*)

or on shelves to be perfectly highlighted. The proper choice of fixtures as well as the bulbs they house will give the effect desired by the store.

Today's offerings are very extensive, ranging from the simplest contemporary cans to those that fit any design decor. Figure 8-8 features one that totally exposes the bulb and is more functional than decorative. The majority of retailers, however, choose decorative types as featured in Figure 8-9. A popular type used by some merchants are the Wireforms by Juno as shown in Figure 8-10. When fluorescent lighting is the choice and flexibility is needed, compact fixtures that fit easily on tracks are the choice. One of the most versatile is the Mini-Biax by Juno Lighting, pictured in Figure 8-11, that enables the lamp to be rotated 358 degrees from a single mounting.

DECORATIVE LIGHTING

While the tracks and recessed fixtures provide the lighting necessary to generally light an area or spotlight a particular mannequin or item in a display, stores often use additional lighting to create a dramatic

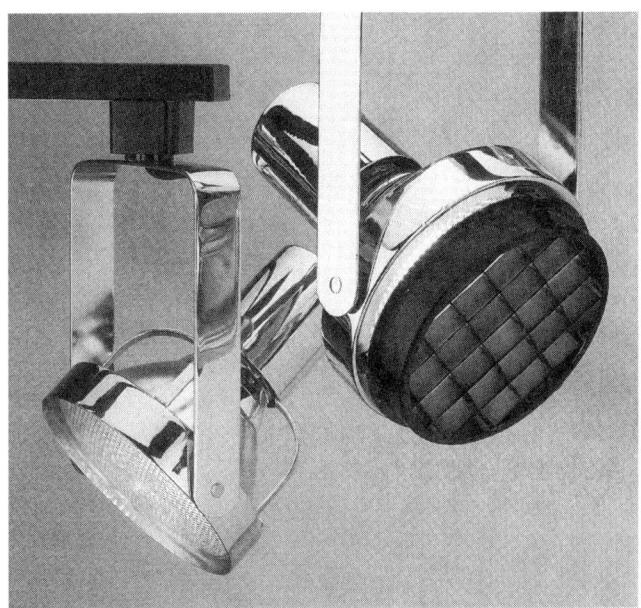

Figure 8-9. Decorative fixtures add interest to functionality. (*Courtesy of Juno Lighting.*)

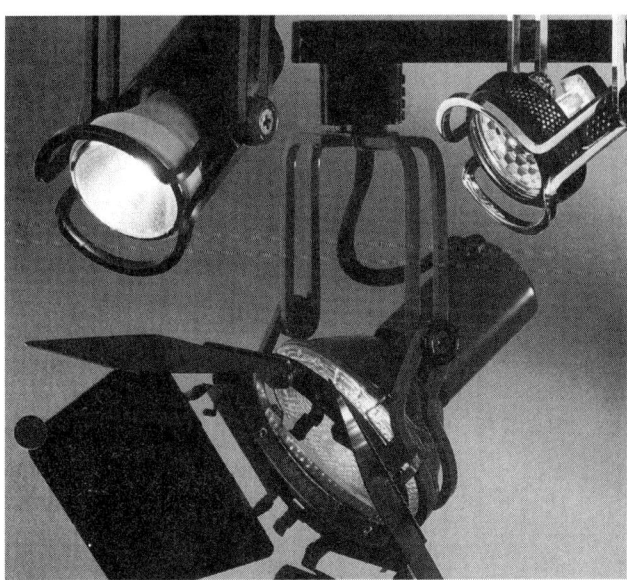

Figure 8-10. These Wireforms, popular with retailers, come with baffles to concentrate the light's beam. (*Courtesy of Juno Lighting.*)

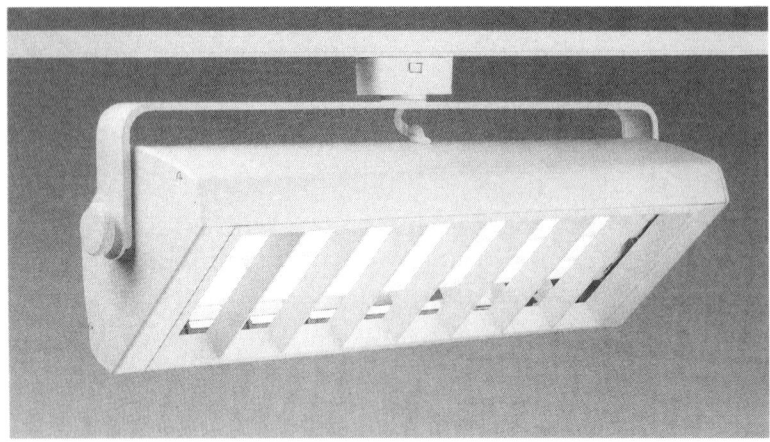

Figure 8-11. This track fixture rotates 358° for maximum flexibility. (Courtesy of Juno Lighting.)

effect. This lighting by itself will not generally be sufficient to illuminate an area but will help set a mood or create an impression or image to capture the shopper's attention. Figure 8-12 features a variety of decorative lighting used by retailers.

LIGHTING WITH COLOR

The application of colored lighting in a department or a window is risky business. The vast majority of visual merchandisers and store planners shy away from the use of colored lights because improper use can result in color change. If you have ever looked into a store window that is protected from the sun with amber transparent shades, you probably noticed that the color of the merchandise changed. The light streaming through the protective material has the same effect as if a colored light were used. Colored lighting should be used only for special effects or when it is necessary to intensify the color of the merchandise. The rule is to use the same color of light as the merchandise to be highlighted. Thus, a red light on a red dress is appropriate to intensify the color. A blue light on the same dress will drastically alter the color of the displayed dress and will confuse the shopper about the actual color of the dress.

If colored lighting is desired, there are two methods for achieving it. For short-term projects, colored acetate gels can be applied to the fixtures that house the bulbs. The gels come in a wide array of colors, are inexpensive, and are easy to use. However, extended use will result in cracking of the gels due to the heat from the light source. For periods of more than one week, it is best to use colored, round glass filters. They are long-lasting, fit easily into many spotlight cans, and are available in numerous colors.

Unless special lighting is necessary, white light should be the rule.

LIGHTING ACCESSORIES

In addition to the light fixtures and light sources that are used in visual merchandising, there are a number of accessories that assist in providing special effects for the trimmer. They include dimmers, flashers, fresnels, framing projectors, strobes, swivel sockets, and gels.

When a light is turned on, it automatically throws a specific amount of light according to the wattage of the bulb. In certain situa-

LIGHTING: DRAMATIZING THE SELLING FLOOR AND DISPLAY AREAS

Figure 8-12. Retailers use a variety of decorative lights such as an abundance of small twinkling lights for holiday displays, hanging fixtures to enhance a setting, and chandeliers for drama. (*Courtesy of Ellen Diamond and Nakatoa.*)

Figure 8-13. Templates projected with light add a variety of themes to visual presentations. (*Courtesy of Ellen Diamond.*)

tions, the trimmer wants to achieve a lower illuminated atmosphere without changing the bulbs. This is easily achieved with the use of a dimmer. The dimmer can be rotated until the desired amount of light is achieved.

A flasher is an attachment that fits into bulb sockets or onto electrical cords that causes lights to turn on and off. The end result is a twinkling, dramatic effect. At Christmastime, many visual installers make use of flashers.

The fresnel is a focusing lens that is used in front of a light to change the size of the beam. When the trimmer wants to make the adjustment from general lighting to spotlighting, a fresnel is used.

A pattern and framing projector is a light projector with built-in framing shutters for beam shaping; it also accepts patterned templates for image projection. They are used to simulate scenery, to create atmosphere, or to apply additional depth to any setting, as seen in Figure 8-13.

Strobes are bulbs that turn on and off. They are used to achieve dramatic effects.

A swivel socket is a versatile accessory item that fits into a light receptacle and swivels or rotates 360 degrees. It is used to direct the light bulb up or down or in any direction.

Gels, as discussed earlier, are colored acetate films that can be placed over a bulb. They provide short-term colored effects for the trimmer.

The table in Figure 8-14 lists and describes lighting terminology.

Figure 8-14. Common lighting terminology.

Common Lighting Terms

Term	Definition	Usage
Ballast	An electrical device that supplies the proper currency to the electric fixture.	Starts and operates a discharge lamp.
Chase Lights	10-watt cosmetic bulbs, set in a bar or flexible cord, that flash on and off.	For dramatic, theatrical effect.
Cove Lighting	Indirect lighting that is recessed in a cove or cornice and is reflected on the ceiling or a wall.	To softly light a wall or an area.
Dimmer	Mechanical device that changes the intensity of light.	For mood or dim lighting.
Filters	Colored, round glass disks that attach to spotlight fixtures.	To intensify a color present in a display.
Flashers	Attachments that fit into bulb sockets or onto electrical cords that cause lights to turn on and off.	For twinkling, dramatic effect.
Floodlight	Type of incandescent bulb available as PAR lamps or reflectors.	To throw a wide beam of light on an area.
Fresnel	Focusing lens in front of light to change size of beam.	To adjust from general floodlighting to spotlighting.
Gels	Colored acetate that may be placed over a bulb.	For short-term colored effect.
General Lighting	The basic or primary lighting of an area achieved with fluorescents or incandescent floodlights.	For an overall lighting effect that is to be supplemented with spotlights.
Halogen	A type of quartz lamp that offers longer-lasting, brighter, whiter light.	For more efficient and precise light control; for enhancing the visual image.
HID Lamp	High-intensity discharge bulbs; smaller in size and provide more light per watt than fluorescents and incandescents.	For concentrated lighting and shadow achievement.
Indirect Lighting	Light that is directed to the ceiling or walls and is concealed in cornices, cones, and valances.	For the lighting of general areas or for dramatic effect.
Neon	Cold cathode lighting that can be shaped easily to form designs.	For electric signs and decorative effects.
PAR Lamp	Hard surface floods or spots that throw bright, intense light and may be used indoors or outside.	For brighter, intense lighting.
Pattern and Framing Projector	Light projector with built-in framing shutters for beam shaping; it accepts pattern templates for image projection.	To project specific images, simulate scenery, create atmosphere, or supply additional depth to any setting.
Spotlight	Incandescent bulb that throws a narrow beam of light.	To highlight a particular object.
Strobes	Lights that flash on and off.	For dramatic effects.
Swivel Socket	A socket that fits into light receptacle and swivels or rotates 360°.	To direct light up or down or in any direction.
Track Lighting	A 4', 6', or 8' channel that attaches to a ceiling or any flat surface and is electrically wired. A variety of cans or containers, which house bulbs, can be easily fitted to track to achieve desired lighting.	For ease in adjusting lighting requirements as well as adding a decorative dimension to the setting.

LIGHT SYSTEM ACQUISITION

Lighting is a very technical aspect of visual merchandising and store design. Its proper use effectively illuminates selling areas and provides sufficient accenting for display installations.

Today's offerings are so diverse in terms of systems and light sources that careful selection is necessary to achieve the best results. While many visual merchandisers, as well as interior designers, are well versed in visual installations and fixture placement, some do not have the technical knowledge necessary to choose the most appropriate systems for their stores.

By visiting lighting professionals, one may learn about the benefits and disadvantages of what is available today. If visits to these professionals are difficult, many offer complete brochure packages that feature a host of products and describe their usage and costs. The names of these companies are available in the Yellow Pages directory or from organizations such as NADI (National Association of Display Industry) in New York City, IESNA (Illuminating Engineering Society of North America), and IALD (International Association of Lighting Designers), each of whose addresses may be obtained from *Visual Merchandising & Store Design* magazine. There are also many lighting trade expos across the country that feature a wealth of different lighting producers.

Any of these resources will help to familiarize the retailer with what's new and how the best possible system can be utilized. Since lighting installations are long-lasting, caution should be exercised before any purchases are made.

TOOLS OF THE TRADE

acetate gels
colored filters
dimmers
fiber optic lighting
flashers
fluorescents
framing projectors
fresnels
HIDs
incandescents
low voltage lamps
neon
patterned templates
recessed lighting
strobes
swivel sockets
tracks
wall washing

LIGHTING: DRAMATIZING THE SELLING FLOOR AND DISPLAY AREAS

CHAPTER REVIEW

KEY POINTS IN THE CHAPTER

1. Effective lighting in store interiors and windows is a result of what has been learned from lighting directors in the theater and movie industry.
2. Other than daylight, numerous sources of light are employed by visual merchandisers.
3. Fluorescents provide good general lighting at a comparatively low cost.
4. Fluorescent fixtures can be purchased that fit on tracks for more flexibility.
5. Incandescent bulbs come in a variety of shapes, sizes, and wattages and provide the retailer with good overall or general lighting as well as highlighting.
6. Low voltage lamps bring out the true color of merchandise, enhance textures, and have the advantage of heat reduction.
7. Fiber optic lighting benefits the visual merchandiser by eliminating ultraviolet and infrared wavelengths and reducing power consumption.
8. HIDs are very small bulbs that produce more light per bulb and are energy savers.
9. Track lighting enables the visual merchandiser to adjust the store's lighting easily by changing containers and bulbs to achieve the desired effect.
10. To add color, fluorescents can be encased with colored cylinders, and gels and filters can be placed over spotlights and floodlights.
11. Numerous lighting accessories such as dimmers, flashers, fresnels, strobes, and swivel sockets enable the visual merchandiser to achieve better results.
12. When setting out to acquire lighting systems, the visual merchandiser and store designer should learn about the advantages and disadvantages of the available products by visiting lighting manufacturers, attending trade expositions, and calling upon NADI and lighting associations for information.

DISCUSSION QUESTIONS

1. Which light source do most large retailers use to generally illuminate their store interiors?
2. What are the advantages of using fluorescent lighting?
3. How can standard fluorescent bulbs be adapted temporarily for presentations that require colored lighting?

4. What types of systems have made the use of fluorescents more versatile?
5. Why have the standard incandescents declined in popularity for general illumination?
6. Although floodlights and spotlights are both incandescents, what different purposes do they serve?
7. What advantage does the low voltage incandescent have over the older, traditional models?
8. How advantageous is the use of HIDs and halogens?
9. What purpose does fiber optic lighting play in retail environments?
10. Is neon a good general illuminator in visual presentations?
11. Discuss the advantage of track systems over recessed lighting systems.
12. How can spotlights be easily adapted for color usage?
13. Describe how improper use of color on merchandise can cause problems for the retailer.
14. In what simple way can the visual installer reduce the amount of light being projected from a bulb?
15. What purpose do framing projectors play?
16. What are strobe lights?
17. Describe the advantage of a swivel socket.
18. How should the visual merchandiser and interior designer prepare for the purchase of a lighting system?

CASE PROBLEMS

Case 1

Lackluster is perhaps the best way to describe the premises just vacated by a store in Dayton, Ohio and leased by a new retailer, Helen's Fashion Depot. The new tenant could change the layout by totally gutting the interior and windows and starting anew. Given the new company's limited budget, however, such an approach is out of the question.

The partners believe that a fresh coat of paint and shampooing the existing carpet would be a good beginning. The fixtures that will house the merchandise will be the inexpensive modular type that can be rearranged into a variety of configurations. The 950 square foot space, with a 20-foot frontage, doesn't really require an abundance of new, costly fixtures.

Except for the lighting, all of the problems seem to be solvable at modest expense. The previous tenant illuminated the store with two strips of fluorescent lighting down the center and sparsely spaced incandescent containers recessed into the ceiling. The two windows, parallel to sidewalk enclosed structures and located on either side of a center doorway, are outfitted with recessed fixtures. To say the least, the lighting leaves much to be desired.

Again, faced with limited capital, Helen's Fashion Depot would like to make as much lighting change as possible without totally changing the lighting arrangement. Complete renovation would cost much more than the new company could expend.

Questions

1. How would you enhance the existing interior lighting to accent the store and dramatize the featured merchandise without significant expense?
2. In what way can the two windows be outfitted with lighting that could simply, yet inexpensively, highlight the displays?

Case 2

Throughout the United States, shopping areas unlike the typical enclosed malls are being developed. For instance, the Boston area has its Quincy Market, a collection of sophisticated and unique shops, in an area that had been nearly abandoned. Other cities across the country are also revitalizing downtrodden areas, transforming them into the likes of New York City's South Street Seaport, Baltimore's Inner Harbor, and St. Louis' Union Station.

Unlike the suburban malls, these shopping facilities are anything but conventional. In keeping with the notion of innovation, the shopkeepers have generally chosen unique designs for their stores. The latest in fixturing, signage, and lighting is quickly apparent.

Peter and Paul have just leased a small unit, 600 square feet, with an open-back window that is 9 feet wide. The store interior is actually what the shoppers will see, because space is at a premium and nothing could really be used for a conventional window. In trying to devise a unique design to enhance their avant garde, unisex merchandise, the partners are willing to forego investing a great sum in merchandise fixtures and spend more on lighting.

They have visited many stores and lighting showrooms to develop a concept. They are interested in a designed lighting format that will not only illuminate the premises but will also establish a visual focal point.

Question

What lighting approach should Peter and Paul take in achieving their goal?

NAME: _____ DATE: _____

EXERCISES

1. Visit a major department store in a mall or downtown area and evaluate any department's lighting on the form provided.
2. Write or visit a lighting business that specializes in the illumination of retail interiors and windows. Get information on the following topics and prepare a report, complete with pictures and illustrations that they have supplied to you, to describe the state of the field.
   a. Trends in lighting
   b. Types of fixtures available
   c. Bulb classifications
   d. Use of colored light
   e. General illumination
   f. Highlighting
   g. Costs of lighting fixtures
   h. Low voltage lighting
   i. Dramatic lighting effects
   j. Innovative lighting

NAME: _____ DATE: _____

Exercise 1 STORE LIGHTING EVALUATION

STORE NAME: _____ DEPARTMENT: _____

<u>Type of Light Fixtures   Type of Bulb   Effectiveness</u>

General Lighting:

Highlighting:

General Comments:

Chapter 9
Themes and Settings for Windows and Interiors

LEARNING OBJECTIVES

After completing this chapter, the student should be able to:

1. Discuss the permanent total environment concept as it relates to visual merchandising.
2. Explain the fundamental principles associated with the introduction of each season's visual presentations.
3. Describe appropriate settings for the windows and interiors for each of the four seasons of the year.
4. List five holiday periods for which visual merchandisers must prepare and the types of installations they might produce for each.
5. Differentiate between presentations that are merchandise-oriented and those that are institutional.
6. Explain the role of the visual merchandising team in a store's special event.
7. Distinguish between unit and ensemble displays and discuss the emphasis of each type.
8. Give the rationale for using an abundance of one item in a presentation.

INTRODUCTION

When the curtain goes up in the theater or the opening scene flashes on the movie screen, the design of the set immediately creates a mood. Emotional responses to the mood begin to flow in the observers. This impact is largely the work of the director.

Windows and store interiors, too, can project a mood that can turn the shopper's head. Like the director of a theatrical endeavor, the visual merchandiser can create environments that are exciting and stimulating and significantly improve the appeal of the merchandise. Whether it is a permanent setting or one that changes entirely with the seasons or special holidays, the visual presentation is of the utmost importance.

Each company has a personality that can be enhanced by the manner in which the products are presented. A single mannequin in a window, elegantly presented, sends the message that exclusive merchandise is within, while a display of many items together puts the emphasis on price, appealing to the more cost-conscious shopper. Whatever the message, it can be conveyed easily by the windows and interior settings.

A major factor in the complexity of the presentations is the store's budget. Some companies rely heavily on visual installations to tempt the shopper and expend large sums throughout the year to achieve this goal. Others spend sparingly throughout the year and make the major expenditure at Christmas, when most retailers achieve their greatest profits. Still others make one major investment in visual presentation at the time of the company's opening, and use that setting as the attention-getter.

Whatever the situation, the visual effect can increase sales. Businesses that understand this fact are reaping the benefits from the visual merchandiser's expertise.

THE PERMANENT TOTAL ENVIRONMENT PHILOSOPHY

Theme parks such as Disney World, Universal Studios, and Epcot have captured the hearts and minds of visitors for many years. Borrowing from this concept, some retailers and restaurateurs have built premises based on a theme. These environments don't change with the seasons but remain constant. One of the early adherents to this philosophy was Banana Republic. Although its visual format has been replaced, it is worth mentioning because Banana Republic initiated the total environment philosophy that was eventually imitated by others. The company's original merchandising concept centered on safari-type clothing. In order to enhance the items displayed for sale, the visual merchandisers created an environment that immediately put the shopper in a setting that shouted safari. Every conceivable item, most of which were khaki-colored, was shown in wooden crates that were surrounded with bamboo poles, netting, jungle vegetation, and other safari elements. No matter what the time of year, the setting never changed. No special Christmas or Mother's Day displays were found at Banana Republic. Today, the company has reversed its merchandise philosophy and has totally refurbished its environments to complement the new styles. Again, no seasonal changes are made to depict a special time of the year, just a permanent setting that enhances the merchandise.

One of the companies that subscribes to the total environment philosophy is Rain Forest Cafe, A Wild Place to Shop and Eat, discussed in Chapter 3. Few companies today have captivated adults and children with their visual appearance as much as Rain Forest Cafe. A shopper who approaches the facility is greeted by a jungle-like atmosphere in which a bird trainer is sporting a colorful, live parrot. This is but one attention-getter that brings the crowds in to see more. Inside, a vast assortment of T-shirts, sweatshirts, shorts, etc., that depict animals and environmental settings are featured in a setting that is a reproduction of a rain forest complete with realistic, life-size and oversized animals. The result is magical. The eating area has the same environmental feeling, offering the patrons a startling visual experience.

Others that subscribe to the total environment philosophy include the Disney Stores, where a very large screen plays Disney animated movies and various famous characters such as Mickey Mouse and Donald Duck encircle the overhead of the store's display cases; Warner Bros., where the characters their movies made famous are featured throughout; the Fashion Cafe, where fashion-related photographs and costumes fill the interior; and Hard Rock Cafe, a restaurant and large retail area that initiated the concept in the dining industry.

Although the total environment philosophy is the rule for many businesses, the vast majority of retailers still believe in changing their atmosphere seasonally. At Christmas, their windows and interior spaces are transformed into arenas of tinsel, glitter, snow, animated figures, and Santa Claus; when the leaves are about to turn from green to russet, the stores take on the colors and textures of fall.

The shot in the arm that is needed to meet and hopefully beat last year's sales figures is supplied by the visual merchandiser. This holds true not only for the major department and specialty stores, but also for the independent retailer who employs the itinerant or freelance trimmer to adjust the store's message to whatever is appropriate for the time of year.

TYPES OF THEMES

The natural time to change an installation is when a new season is about to make its entrance, before a major holiday such as Christmas, and for special events such as the store's promotion of a particular designer. Whenever these seasons and events are about to show up on the store's calendar, the visual merchandisers are called upon to perform their special magic. There are also institutional themes such as a salute to the opening of the opera season in a major city or the recognition of a special week or month to alert citizens to the fight against a particular disease. No matter what the occasion, the task of the visual merchandiser is to produce inspiring displays.

Seasonal

Each season brings with it particular merchandise to feature, and nature suggests general settings in which to show it. The cold of winter, the budding and blooming of flowers in the spring, the warmth of summer, and the chill of fall each provide a unique opportunity to encourage customers to start thinking about what they need for the next season, and to buy it now. While the approach for introducing new seasons and the design of actual displays are up to the visual merchandiser, the length of time the display will occupy the windows and the specific merchandise to be featured are calculated by management to maximize sales.

Remember, too, that the total environment does not change with the same frequency as the windows in most retail operations. While the interior reflects the season or perhaps a major special storewide promotion, the windows may be changed as often as once a week to make timely statements about store image, special events, holidays, or other themes.

Summer. A splash of color or a display of merchandise such as swimsuits typifies the visual merchandiser's way of introducing this season. Summer is a time for fun, that long-awaited vacation, beach parties, summer camp, or just plain relaxation. Figure 9-1 features a typical summer theme. Merchants introduce summer items as early as the day after Easter and usually not later than May 1. If a store is fashion forward, the earlier time frame is best suited to its needs; if it is more promotionally oriented, the middle of May might be more appropriate. Each store must decide upon the pace that fits its merchandising concept and image. It should be understood that summer presentations don't exclusively center on fashion apparel and accessories. Stores like Crate & Barrel, for example, do a wealth of business in summertime items such as outdoor furniture, colorful picnicware, striking candle containers, etc.

Figure 9-1. The swimsuit theme signals it's summertime. (*Courtesy of Ellen Diamond.*)

Fall. With the winding down of summer sales, August is the month when retailers prepare for what is usually a big season. Prices in the fall are generally higher than those charged for summer goods, and the selling period is a long one. In order to capture the mood and motivate shoppers to spend, visual merchandisers often transform the store into one that smells of fall. Autumn leaves abound, as do the fruits of the season, such as pumpkins and gourds. No matter what time zone one is in, even as far south as Florida, an autumn look prevails in stores. While summer merchandising is limited to fewer departments, fall transcends all lines of merchandise. Back-to-school fashions, business clothing, activewear, accessories for apparel, and home furnishings all share the spotlight in fall themes. It is during this period that management of large and small stores alike spend major sums on visual merchandising in their windows and interiors.

Once an interior decor or motif has been chosen, the windows are targeted. The opening of the season might depict a back-to-school theme if children's clothing is sold, as seen in Figure 9-2, or an installation that features the latest in women's fashion, if the store is of a fashion orientation. In stores that feature linens for the home, a fresh look for fall might include darker colored or printed bedding. Whatever the emphasis, it is time to freshen up the display areas and make them produce as much business as possible.

Figure 9-2. These children's wear windows are typical of fall presentations. (*Courtesy of Ellen Diamond.*)

Winter. Although this calendar period includes the Christmas season, our discussion will intentionally exclude Christmas installations for separate examination in the next section on holidays.

It should be obvious by now that the store's seasonal displays do not coincide with the official calendar dates for the seasons. A store's season begins before the actual season. For example, although winter officially begins on December 21, winter merchandise displays usually overlap the fall ones. Some stores, in fact, do not differentiate between fall and winter, treating them as one season until Thanksgiving, the official beginning of the Christmas period.

It is in the windows and with specific merchandise that winter is best announced. Coat displays are a mainstay of the period in many major department stores, dominating windows and interior displays during October and November as seen in Figure 9-3. These months are also used to sell off the merchandise that didn't

Figure 9-3. Coat displays dominate window themes in many stores. (*Courtesy of Lord & Taylor.*)

meet the customer's expectations in the fall. With enormous shipments of Christmas merchandise arriving daily, the store must rid itself of older inventory. Sales windows abound. Merchants invest little money on visual merchandising at this time, saving their resources for Christmas. It is generally the interior displays that feature the marked-down items, with some retailers announcing sales in their windows.

While Christmas intersects the winter period and takes complete charge for six weeks, the second half of winter is still to be reckoned with. As in October and early November, sales dominate again in January and February. During this time, most companies aim to get rid of the season's slow movers or special purchases that were mixed to bolster the store's markup and profit picture.

Throughout the country there are many retailers that feature cruise or resort wear. It is not usually a big part of their business but offers them the chance to accomplish several things: to evaluate customer reaction to fashions earmarked for the summer season, to chase away the winter doldrums with fresh merchandise, and to serve the market of customers who vacation in the winter. During this period, some merchants build separate resort wear departments in areas that had housed other merchandise. Since stock levels are down, the store can afford to set aside space for this temporary sales area. Retailers call on the visual merchandisers to trot out fish netting, bright sunshine, seashells, and the like to complement the merchandise. If a store has several windows, some are usually earmarked for resort merchandise.

Spring. Following on the heels of the President's Day sales comes spring, a breath of fresh air for both retailers and customers. This season is typically short and low in sales volume but serves as a transition into summer. Stores introduce merchandise that is lighter in both color and fabric and feature them in settings like the one in Figure 9-4. They hope customers are so tired of the winter look and heavy fabrics that they will be enticed to purchase spring goods at regular prices. Stores that subscribe to a total interior change usually overflow with trees and flowers in large baskets or brightly painted pots. It is a time when live plants of all types are found throughout the store. The watering cans, gardening tools, and pails accent the freshness of the newly acquired merchandise for spring, as seen in Figure 9-5. Windows tend to display the same decor as the interiors with emphasis on airy environmental settings. Macy's, in their New York City flagship

Figure 9-4. The flowers in the wheelbarrow and the garden hose suggest that spring has arrived. (*Courtesy of Ellen Diamond.*)

store, ushers in spring with its annual Flower Show. It is a multimillion-dollar extravaganza that signals the coming of spring. The store is filled with exotic plantings of every type, and attracts scores of customers.

Holidays

While Christmas is unquestionably the major holiday of the year for the majority of the retailing world, other holidays play a vital role in the achievement of the year's total volume. Visit any fragrance department the week before Mother's Day and you will witness a special frenzy and an abundance of merchandise available. The selling period for each holiday varies, as does the number of departments served by the holiday promotions. Valentine's Day promotions require just a few days before the actual event, while the Christmas season lasts at least a full six weeks. Whatever the holiday, the visual merchandising team gives creative support to make it the most successful Valentine's Day or Father's Day ever.

Figure 9-5. Watering cans and garden tools announce that the doldrums of winter have passed. (*Courtesy of Ellen Diamond.*)

Christmas. There is no better time of the year than Christmas for those involved in visual merchandising to strut their stuff. Thanksgiving Day has come to signal the beginning of the Christmas shopping period, igniting a spark in many people's minds that the purchase of gifts should begin. If you've ever worked in retailing on the Friday after Thanksgiving or merely entered a store as a shopper on that day, you are aware that this is a time when serious purchasing is underway.

In order to maximize the sales volume for this time of the year, visual merchandisers begin planning months before Christmas. It is not the mere changing of one department's decor or the trimming of a particular window that is involved. This is the time for transformation of the store's interiors and windows into a magical wonderland that will capture the shopper's fancy. Many visual merchandisers begin their plans for Christmas by attending trade shows. The National Association of the Display Industry (NADI) sponsors ShopWest in California in July, which features a vast assortment of Christmas props and materials. Visual New York is another event that is held each May and December in New York City, with the May event featuring lines of Christmas ornamentation. In these expositions, every important producer of display-oriented materials is represented. Those responsible for the visual installations in their stores come away with a good foundation for their Christmas plans that are still months off.

The actual displays for Christmas generally are installed just prior to Thanksgiving, with some companies getting even an earlier start. While the interior Christmas decorations remain intact for the entire

Figure 9-6. Christmas ornaments, decorative fabrics, and an elegant doll depict Christmas in this window. (*Courtesy of Lord & Taylor.*)

holiday season, the windows will be changed frequently in most stores to give all of the departments a shot at the increased traffic. Each store's philosophy concerning Christmas windows is as different as its merchandising philosophy. Some believe that merchandise is what retailing is all about, so that is what should be featured, while an ever-growing number are investing in the institutional format that will be explored in a later section. Whatever the approach, planning is essential for success. Figure 9-6 shows a Christmas display.

President's Day. Retailers at one time celebrated both Washington's and Lincoln's birthdays by closing their stores. To commemorate these special days, visual merchandisers often used patriotic themes featuring likenesses of the presidents. It was a time of sentiment and pride, not a sales event. However, in the early 1960s, a few retailers opened their doors on these two days for final cleanup sales of winter merchandise. The practice has become universal, giving visual merchandisers a new theme on which to build. The week between Lincoln's and Washington's birthdays, President's Week, has become a remarkable sales period. Visual merchandisers must be terribly creative, however, because usually little money is earmarked for display during this period. The visual department usually prepares posters and signs and perhaps windows that combine both sales and institutional themes. The emphasis, however, is on the cleanup sales message.

Easter. Unlike Christmas with its extravagant presentations, in most stores Easter is not a major merchandising thrust. Some companies don't even bother to make a distinction between Easter finery and general spring finery, except in a few departments. Children's wear, if anything, gets the major share of the visual merchandising budget at Easter to buy the bunnies, baskets, and eggs that complement the bonnets and bows of the season. Some displays in women's wear feature the Easter theme, but more often than not there is just a freshening of the spring decor. Many shopping malls feature Easter settings with characters such as the Easter Bunny, as seen in Figure 9-7, to increase traffic.

Figure 9-7. Live characters, such as the Easter Bunny, attract shoppers to malls. (*Courtesy of Ellen Diamond.*)

Parents' Days. Mother's Day and Father's Day boost sales in some departments such as fragrances, clothing, and housewares, with Mother's Day the bigger retailing event. Merchants usually set aside about one week for windows devoted to these holidays. Interior presentations may last longer. The displays

Figure 9-8. A visual merchandiser prepares a Mother's Day presentation. (*Courtesy of Ellen Diamond.*)

are not usually complex, often relying on an abundance of gift boxes piled high to set the theme, as pictured in Figure 9-8.

Valentine's Day. Hearts, hearts, and more hearts are the mainstay for Valentine's Day installations. While an abundance of traffic occurs in the candy shop or department, many retailers successfully promote other items, such as jewelry and accessories for sweethearts to purchase. Purchasing usually peaks two or three days before Valentine's Day, although many retailers report a major thrust on the day itself. The holiday falls in a period in which most stores are more concerned with disposing of the merchandise from the previous season and looking forward to spring business.

Columbus Day. Much like President's Day, this holiday is an opportunity for stores to run special sales. The emphasis this time is usually on coats. Columbus Day has become the traditional day to purchase a winter coat at a reduced price. Some stores do use the institutional theme honoring Columbus and call on the visual department to create themes and execute displays that encourage fashion discovery. The emphasis, however, is on the sale, and not just on coats. The sign shop people keep busy creating the copy and producing the signs that motivate people to snap up the bargains.

Creative Themes

While the four seasons and major holidays provide a framework for planning merchandise presentations, much of the work visual merchandisers produce doesn't fall in either of these categories. These are the visual presentations that result from the ingenuity of the display persons and their inherent creativity.

Themes range from topics that deal with sporting events to extravagant grand ballroom festivities. There are no real guidelines, except that they must not overpower the merchandise. Of course, if the theme is institutional, the selling of the store's image is most important. For a merchandise-oriented display to be effective, the featured items must sell. A theatrically oriented window may have magnificent visual impact, only to leave the shopper puzzled about what the store is trying to promote.

Displays should be devoid of gimmicks and easy to understand. While the props may be clever and eye-appealing, the merchandise should take center stage. In Figures 9-9 through 9-11, the displays are the work of talented visual merchandisers.

Figure 9-9. An underwater theme enhances the water shoes. (*Courtesy of Niketowns.*)

Figure 9-10. Children playing on spray-painted tires set the scene for fall purchasing. (*Courtesy of Ellen Diamond.*)

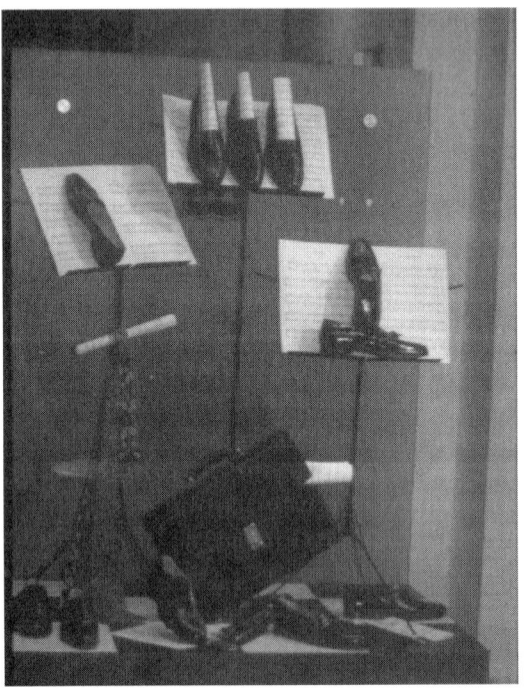

Figure 9-11. Music stands and sheet music provide a simple yet eye-appealing setting for the shoes. (*Courtesy of Ellen Diamond.*)

INSTITUTIONAL THEMES

A store may develop display themes that are based on the organization's interests, activities, and image rather than being built around certain merchandise. The concept of institutional display is more subtle than other concepts, concentrating on building an image for the store in the minds of the customers. Displays might tie in with celebrating the beginning of the next millennium or saluting a particular charity. Whatever the event, the store wants to say that here is a retailer with pride in its country and community, with interests beyond just making sales. In Figure 9-12 the Broadway musical, *Sunset Blvd.*, is the subject of an institutional display.

SPECIAL EVENTS AND PROMOTIONS

In order to increase customer traffic and boost sales volume, many major department stores plan special events. Some are storewide promotions that lend themselves to visual excitement, such as Marshall Field's lighting of the Christmas tree in the Chicago flagship's grand atrium and Macy's annual Flower Show in its New York City flagship.

The visual merchandising department plays a vital role in these promotions. Not only are the windows and interiors carefully trimmed for these events, but often an entire store is transformed to set the right mood for the spectacular.

Figure 9-12. Musical theater is just one of many institutional themes used by retailers. (*Courtesy of Ellen Diamond.*)

OTHER THEMES AND SETTINGS

In addition to the themes already discussed, retailers might have reason to use other themes such as ensemble displays and unit displays to sell their products.

Ensemble Displays

When the store wants to deliver a message that says, "I'm a complete outfit, buy me," it often chooses to feature the outfit or ensemble in a setting by itself. The intention is to entice the customer to buy a total package rather than one or two items. Most retailers direct their sales associates to suggestion sell, that is, to suggest other merchandise that complements the main item in the purchase. For example, a window or interior presentation might feature a tuxedo complete with shirt, bow tie, shoes, and socks. If properly presented, the shopper might easily be tempted to buy all of the accessories, not just the tuxedo.

Figure 9-13. The various elements of a merchandise group are featured in this ensemble display. (*Courtesy of Ellen Diamond.*)

Ensemble displays are not restricted to apparel. In home furnishings departments, for example, ensemble displays consisting of dinnerware, glassware, and flatware are often featured to tempt shoppers to buy the entire offering. Figures 9-13 and 9-14 feature ensemble displays.

Unit Displays

Some featured items, particularly small ones, may get lost in an installation. In order to boost their impact, the visual merchandiser may feature several of them in either a window or an interior presentation. Figure 9-15 features a unit display.

Figure 9-14. In this display, the goal is to show related pieces of merchandise that will motivate shopping. (*Courtesy of Ellen Diamond.*)

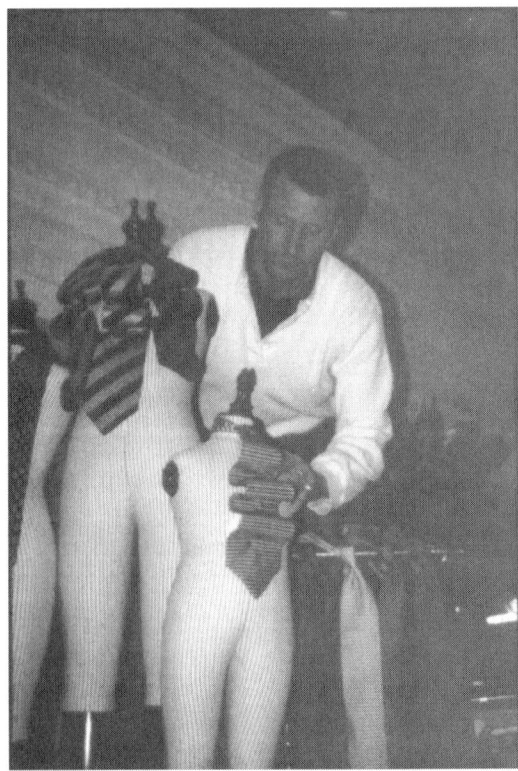

Figure 9-15. The trimmer is arranging the same ties, in different colors, to show their importance. (*Courtesy of Ellen Diamond.*)

THEMES AND SETTINGS FOR WINDOWS AND INTERIORS

TERMS OF THE TRADE

creative themes
ensemble displays
holiday displays
institutional themes
permanent total environment philosophy
seasonal display
unit displays
window calendar

CHAPTER REVIEW

KEY POINTS IN THE CHAPTER

1. It is the role of the visual merchandising department in many stores to develop themes and settings that best present the store's merchandise to the shopper.
2. Some stores subscribe to a permanent total environment philosophy and build their premises around a particular theme. Banana Republic was an originator of this concept.
3. Today, many restaurants subscribe to the permanent total environment philosophy. Most who use this concept, such as Rain Forest Cafe, carry an assortment of apparel to augment their dining facilities.
4. Each season is a natural unit of time around which to plan interior and window presentations.
5. The Christmas period generally requires more planning and development from the visual merchandising team than any other period.
6. In addition to Christmas, other holidays that provide themes for displays are Mother's Day, Father's Day, Easter, and Valentine's Day.
7. Much of the work done by visual merchandisers falls outside of seasonal themes and traditional holiday settings. The store depends on the creativity of the visual staff to come up with timely, motivating themes.
8. The institutional display route is taken by many stores to promote their image or to convey to the customer that they, the retailers, are aware of the many events that affect their customers.
9. More and more special events and promotions are dominating stores' interiors and windows in an attempt to increase customer interest in the company.

10. Many stores use ensemble displays to help motivate the customer to buy related items.
11. Unit displays feature an abundance of single items to magnify their importance.

DISCUSSION QUESTIONS

1. In what way may the visual merchandiser be compared to the theatrical director?
2. What name is given to the visual concept initiated by Banana Republic and now used by such companies as Rain Forest Cafe and the Disney stores? What purpose does it serve?
3. Discuss three factors to consider when planning a visual presentation for a window.
4. When is it generally advisable for the retailer to install the first summer display in a window?
5. Why do stores present their merchandise displays prior to the actual season for which the goods have been intended?
6. Is it appropriate to have a resort wear theme in a store's windows in the middle of the winter season? Why?
7. Which holiday provides the greatest opportunity for visual merchandisers to show their talents? Why?
8. At what types of industrial events can the visual merchandiser become familiar with the field's latest and most innovative products?
9. Which holiday signals the opening of the major purchasing period of the year for most retailers?
10. How has the visual staff's role changed since the early 1960s in regard to displays for Presidents' birthdays?
11. In addition to using the four seasons and major holidays for window settings, what other motifs can the visual merchandiser use to enhance the store's display presentations?
12. Sometimes window backgrounds are so overpowering that the merchandise is overlooked. Does this type of display serve a purpose?
13. For what reasons do the major stores use institutional visual merchandising?
14. How might a display be designed to promote the purchase of a total package rather than single items?
15. When is it appropriate to feature an abundance of a single item in a visual presentation?

CASE PROBLEMS

Case 1

Peter Flynn was an employee of the T. J. Sanders store when it opened 35 years ago. Originally hired as an apprentice in the visual merchandising department, Peter's responsibilities grew with the company's growth into an organization with a flagship store and eight branches. He achieved the plum position of vice president of visual merchandising before retiring last year.

His 35 years with the company coupled with their substantial success made Peter somewhat of a legend. Many believed his strongly held visual concepts played a major part in the store's emergence as a retailing leader. Now the search is on to find his replacement. Some of the more traditionally oriented members of management think Peter' successor should come from the ranks, specifically Peter's assistant for the past 15 years. Others believe that the time is ripe for new blood and that a departure from the store's typical displays would be most welcome. This group feels that creative themes, more dramatically oriented, would enhance the store's quest to capture segments of the market that weren't significantly served before. Although T. J. Sanders stocks its shelves and racks with fashion forward designs, this group thinks the visual presentations haven't matched the merchandiser's image.

Questions

1. Should the company continue the conceptual philosophy of Peter Flynn or embark on a more innovative course?
2. Would you promote the heir to the throne to the position of vice president of visual merchandising? Why?
3. What are the dangers of developing a new visual concept?
4. How would you safeguard against possible erosion of customer satisfaction while trying to appeal visually to another market segment?

Case 2

The institutional concept of visual merchandising has been a mainstay for Rockford's Department Store since it opened. While most of its competitors have favored purely promotional display, Rockford's always believed in a format that also included institutional presentations. Rockford's has its share of windows built around merchandise, but certain holidays are still thought worthy of an institutional approach. Little by little, as the store became more price and promotion oriented, the notion of institutional display became less important. While the Columbus Day and Presidents' Day windows once featured patriotic themes, the emphasis has now been placed on special sales. There are just a few obligatory signs to tie in the two historic events. Since the sale themes have helped to increase sales volume, there is little support for a return to the more traditional institutional approach for these holidays.

With these successes, however, top management feels it is time to dispense with nostalgic Christmas themes and use the windows exclusively to show off gift merchandise. The visual merchandising department feels that this approach will not only take the glamour and excitement out of the windows but will cause customers to feel the store's philosophy has become totally commercial. Management counters that customers have less time to spend shopping and would find it easier to make their purchases if more items were featured in the windows.

It is now four months before the Christmas season and plans must be made for visual presentations in the store's six main windows. Since the season traditionally runs from the day after Thanksgiving until Christmas Eve, it is time to formalize plans.

Questions

1. With whom do you agree? Defend your position with sound reasoning.
2. Present a plan that would accommodate both points of view.

EXERCISES

1. At a downtown retail area or shopping mall, photograph four different window or interior displays to illustrate themes and settings discussed in this chapter. Be sure to get permission to photograph from store management. Mount each photograph neatly on the forms provided, and complete the information on the forms.
2. Plan a three-dimensional display using an institutional theme of your choice. Construct a window out of foamboard or any other material, making certain to follow the fundamentals of design.
3. Write or call a member of a major store's visual merchandising department and make an appointment to interview the individual. Prepare a list of questions to be asked so that you will be able to present an oral report to the class on the following:
    a. Store's visual merchandising philosophy
    b. Theme sources
    c. Major display themes
    d. Special events
    e. Use of institutional displays

NAME: _____ DATE: _____

Exercise 1 PHOTOGRAPHS OF WINDOW OR INTERIOR DISPLAYS

Store Name _____ Theme _____
Overall Impression _____

Store Name _____ Theme _____
Overall Impression _____

NAME: _____ DATE: _____

Exercise 1 (continued)

Store Name _____ Theme _____
Overall Impression _____

Store Name _____ Theme _____
Overall Impression _____

Chapter 10
Signage and Graphics

LEARNING OBJECTIVES

Upon completing this chapter, the student should be able to:

1. List eight types of signs that are being used by today's retailers to motivate consumer purchasing.
2. Describe backlit transparencies and their importance on the selling floor.
3. Discuss how standing display fixtures are coordinated with signage to attract the customer's attention.
4. Explain the importance of manufacturer and designer logos in store signage.
5. Relate the importance of track signage in the retail environment.
6. Compile a list of the various materials used for construction, the characteristics of each, and their uses and advantages.
7. List the many materials used for sign lettering and discuss the applications for each type.
8. Compare conventional sign-making machines with computer sign printers.
9. Create a sign layout according to the principles of design.
10. Discuss the various sources of commercially made signs for use in visual merchandising.

INTRODUCTION

At no time in retailing history has the use of the written word been more important than it is today. Thirty years ago retailers were satisfied with identifying their stores by placing their names in a prominent space over the entrance to their premises. Neon signs were common for many merchants while others chose from an assortment of materials and letter styles, illuminated or not, to tell shoppers which store they were about to enter. The major retailers, in their multilevel units, used limited signage to identify their departments; nothing exceptionally artistic or inspirational, just simple words signifying Menswear, Juniors, or Home Furnishings.

In any major store today, one's eye is drawn to a variety of sign messages, each competing for the customer's attention. Not only are they informative, but they are often eye-catching formats, the work of graphic artists. No longer are the messages mere paper signs, but decorative, creative constructions that employ brass, wood, felt, Lucite, and other materials. Signage may be three-dimensional, screen-printed, illuminated light boxes, neon-oriented, or enhanced by geometric shapes and forms to deliver a powerful message that will motivate customer spending.

Retailers are enjoying vendor cooperation and involvement in their merchandising efforts. Recognizing the power of signage and graphics, many manufacturers participate in joint signage ventures with stores. By sharing the expense of creative signage and graphics, many suppliers guarantee that their names and logos will be evident inside the store and will direct the shopper to their own merchandise. In some instances, particularly in the case of cosmetics, the suppliers provide their own signage and graphics at no expense to the store.

Taking the signage and graphics provided by vendors one step further, many manufacturers provide stores with total selling fixtures, complete with signs, graphics, and logos, known as point of purchase displays. This concept is fully explored in Chapter 11.

With each passing day, the importance of signage and graphics becomes more apparent to the visual merchandiser and the retailer being served. Signs are the communicators of messages that move the shopper through the merchandise selection and purchasing stages. This chapter examines the types of signage, materials, and sign layout dominant in retailing today.

TYPES OF SIGNS

So powerful has the influence of signage become that most visual merchandisers are constantly searching for new signs and graphics to make merchandise presentations more exciting and provide better direction for the shopper. Stores might use a particular signage theme throughout the store, or might choose types that are specifically appropriate for one department or type of merchandise.

Banners

Made of fabric, plastic, or paper, banners are used extensively by retailers to spell out a theme, deliver a message, define a department, or just provide visual excitement and color in the store. They are particularly popular since their production and installation are comparatively inexpensive. Some banners come from the vendor and cost the retailer virtually nothing. Figure 10-1 features a banner supplied by the vendor.

Banners can be used in a number of ways, but the overhead variety, suspended from the ceiling by wire or chain, is the most popular. In order to keep the banner taut, it is often designed with top and bottom pockets or openings into which steel or wooden dowels are inserted.

Figure 10-1. The Lancome banners are used to capture attention. (*Courtesy of Ellen Diamond.*)

Wall Signs

The logical place to locate a sign is on a wall or a column. The message may denote a department, its entrance, a theme, or a specific informative message. The materials used depend on the expected permanency of the sign and its role in the visual presentation. Figure 10-2 features a typical wall sign.

Backlit Transparencies

The power of signage and graphics is most evident in photographic transparencies that are backlit with the aid of a lightbox. The color and vibrancy achieved through this medium have not been duplicated by any other form of signage. What makes this type of presentation even more exciting is its inexpensive cost and simplicity of production. Any slide, transparency, or color negative can be converted to a large transparency. The film is then placed in a lightbox, which is a fixture that houses fluorescent bulbs to uniformly light the transparency from behind.

The finished product is often supplied by vendors without cost to the retailer. These transparencies are easily mass produced, rolled, and shipped in cardboard cylinders. Some vendors, wishing to guarantee the most professional presentations, even provide retailers with the lightboxes at little or no cost. Since many stores report sales increases of 20

Figure 10-2. The wall signage denotes the department's merchandise emphasis. (*Courtesy of Ellen Diamond.*)

Figure 10-3. The backlit transparency is an effective way to attract shoppers. (*Courtesy of Ellen Diamond.*)

Figure 10-4. The combination of signage and fixtures is both functional and decorative. (*Courtesy of FRCH Worldwide.*)

percent or more when backlit transparencies are used, vendors believe the investment is well-founded.

Lightboxes are found in many different areas in stores and malls. In stores, they can easily be mounted on top of a show counter or on walls and columns, or incorporated directly into visual presentations that feature the merchandise. In malls, they are strategically placed in busy traffic areas and either promote a particular store and direct shoppers to it, or promote a particular product and indicate where it may be purchased. An example of a backlit transparency is presented in Figure 10-3.

Fixture-Contained Signage

Combining a permanent sign with a merchandise fixture is a method often used to publicize the name of the vendor whose merchandise is featured. The trend toward departmentalization by vendor or designer name necessitates that appropriate signage accompany the installations. This type of presentation is becoming increasingly popular, and is being designed and manufactured by point of purchase suppliers, explored in Chapter 11. Figure 10-4 features a sign and fixture combination.

Valance Signs

Particularly successful signage is often found adorning a valance. The valance, a structural piece used primarily to connect the upright panels of a case and to conceal light fixtures, is an excellent place to install a permanent sign. Most often signs give the name of the collection or name of the vendor's merchandise found in that area. With so much emphasis placed on designer or manufacturer labels or logos, many visual merchandisers use a replica of their logos on the valances. Figure 10-5 features this type of signage.

Signs on Glass

Some visual merchandisers feature a message directly on the glass of the store's windows. Adhesive letters can be applied easily to the glass as shown in Figure 10-6, and removed effortlessly when the presentation has outlived its usefulness. Designer names, catchy phrases, and timely themes are some possibilities.

SIGNAGE AND GRAPHICS

Figure 10-5. The Liz Claiborne sign and logo are permanently affixed to a valance. (*Courtesy of Ellen Diamond.*)

Pennants

Used to adorn merchandise or used by themselves, pennants are quickly and inexpensively created. Paper is least expensive and best suited to pennants because it may be curled or draped, but felt, vinyl, and other materials also work well for a pennant message.

Moving Message Signs

A device that is ideal for attracting attention inside stores and windows is the electronic moving message unit. The messages can be programmed easily and quickly with a variety of letter styles and symbols. The speed at which the words move can be adjusted to suit the store's needs. The units are generally used to notify shoppers of special sales or promotions and can be strategically placed at points of purchase for maximum exposure. Figure 10-7 shows a moving message sign that announces the next scheduled fashion show.

Track Signage

An excellent signage system is the type shown in Figure 10-8. A carrier beam is attached to the ceiling into which strips for signs are fitted. Each strip has a channel or track providing for the addition of another sign or panel. The system is perfect as a directory that can be seen from a great distance to tell the customer where specific merchandise may be found. If special sales or promotions are being featured, as is the case in most supermarkets and discount operations, the information can be attached quickly and conveniently to the system and just as easily removed when the events have been concluded.

Figure 10-6. Letters attached to windows bring the message to the shopper. (*Courtesy of Ellen Diamond.*)

Figure 10-7. Moving message units allow for frequent changes.

Neon Signs

Once relegated to storefronts announcing the name of the retailer, neon signage is making a great impact on visual merchandising. Its availability in a variety of shapes and designs makes it a perfect adjunct to brighten and highlight a department, product, or area. For many years, beer producers have been manufacturing such signage to promote their products. Borrowing from the beer industry, other vendors are jumping on the bandwagon. Many of the vendors supply these signs to their retail customers without charge. In this way they can guarantee that the illuminated message is exactly what is needed to best make the shopper aware of their merchandise. In keeping with the trend of other sign media, manufacturer and designer logos are being produced in neon, making them stand out even more to the shopper. For example, 9 West regularly places neon signs at the entrances to their in-store vendor shops. The motif they use is the one that is found on their shoe boxes and labels.

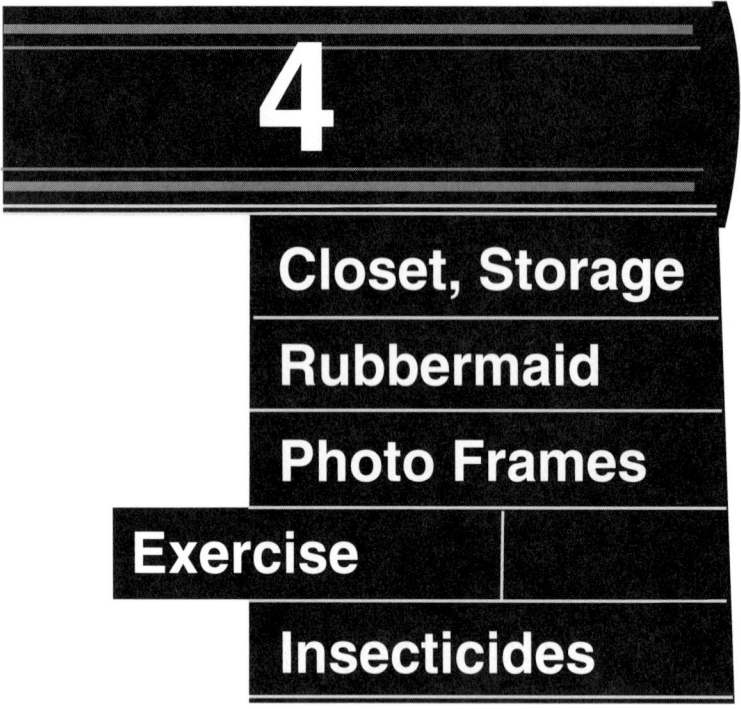

Figure 10-8. For directory signage, the track concept with interchangeable headlines is most versatile.

SIGN MATERIALS

In all types of signs, a variety of materials are used to achieve the specific appearance desired by the retailers. Aside from aesthetics, other factors such as durability, flexibility, and the cost of materials must be considered before the signage task is undertaken. If a sign is to be short-lived, it is economically unsound to construct it of costly materials. If it will be used for a long time, its construction must take into account factors that might cause the sign to lose its visual effectiveness. For example, paper might initially be an effective material but over time it could be damaged by the store's lighting or heating systems.

The list of materials used by today's signmakers continues to grow. Those that are used most frequently are described in Figure 10-9.

SIGNAGE AND GRAPHICS

Figure 10-9. Materials often used to make signs.

Materials Used in Signage

Material	Characteristics	Uses
Paper	Inexpensive; good color reproduction; quickly produced by sign machines, computers, transfer letters, and hand lettering.	Temporary or short-term for sales, special promotions, etc.
Cardboard	Relatively inexpensive; longer life than paper; may be produced quickly, in-house, by printing machines and hand lettering.	For insertion in freestanding fixtures or holders that attach to merchandise racks; for short-term usage.
Fabric	Long-lasting, available in many colors, may be draped, easily silk screened, hemmed for use in banners, modest cost.	Excellent for banners, long-lasting presentations; may be stretched on frames.
Lucite	Durable, available in transparent or translucent forms, retains shape, easily cut into variety of shapes, accepts paint easily.	For permanent signage on walls and columns or suspended from ceiling.
Wood	Very durable, may be stained or painted, easily cut into any shape.	For permanent or long-lasting displays, to add to a "natural" feeling.
Masonite	Excellent painting surface, thinness may cause warping or buckling, inexpensive.	In frames to prevent buckling; in semi-permanent situations.
Brass	Expensive, luxurious look, difficult to cut.	For permanent installations depicting luxury.

LETTER MATERIALS

The preceding section focused on the types of materials that are employed in the construction of signs. There is a wealth of material available today, for temporary or permanent installations, that enable the retailer to do more than just deliver a written message. The letter materials themselves, whether used to identify a department's name, highlight a designer collection, or announce special events in the store, help to make an impression on the shopper.

One of the most popular choices in dimensional signage is foam. Lightweight and inexpensive, it creates an illusion that belies its economy. It is available painted or unpainted and can be finished to resemble other materials such as wood or marble, both of which would be extremely costly. Application is simple, as it generally comes with a

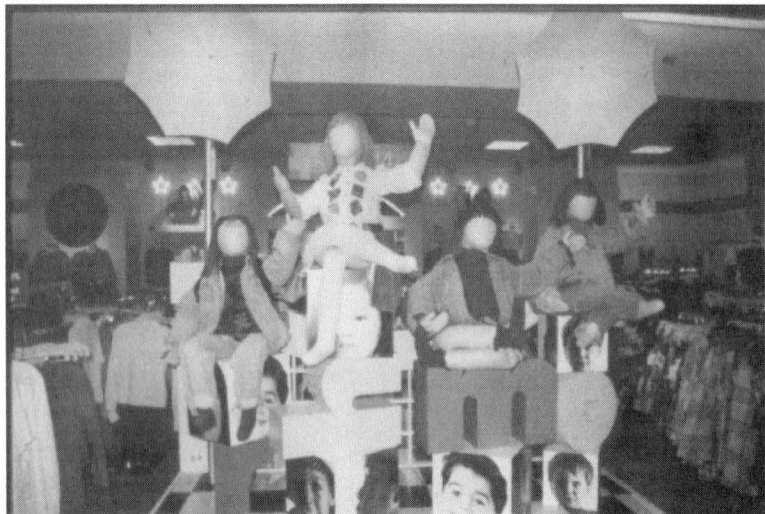

Figure 10-10. Dimensional letters, as used here, are important integral parts of the display design. (*Courtesy of Ellen Diamond.*)

self-stick backing of Velcro or pressure-sensitive tape or can be hung as part of the display design as seen in Figure 10-10.

More and more visual merchandisers are using metal letters for their presentations, mainly brass and aluminum. Each adds richness to the message. Figure 10-11 shows permanent brass letters used for the company's name. While brass is heavy and expensive and thus has limited use, aluminum is relatively inexpensive and lightweight and is used in many situations. Aluminum is often laminated to foam, in a variety of thicknesses, and mounted with double-face tape or Velcro.

Mirror is a material that is also being used extensively in visual merchandising. It is available in a variety of thicknesses and may be purchased in a form that is attached to foam, which gives extra dimension to the letter and makes it easy to mount with special tape or Velcro.

Wood and woodgrain laminates offer the retailer a look of richness and enhance a natural display. The letters come in a variety of styles and thicknesses and are easy to mount on any surface.

Plastic letters are used extensively by today's visual personnel. Made of injection-molded Plexiglas, they have a smooth surface and shiny appearance that is easy to maintain. They are readily available with adhesive backing for quick, simple mounting.

Vinyl, self-stick letters are excellent for quickly producing an informative sign or poster. They are available in a variety of typefaces and sizes and can be applied with little effort. The letters are adhesive-backed and the backing must be peeled off before they can be affixed to the sign's surface. Once in place, they cannot be adjusted or removed. Therefore, it is important for the sign creator to make certain that the layout is carefully planned and the individual letters are pressed into place correctly. If just one or two signs are required, this is an excellent, inexpensive method to

Figure 10-11. Brass letters add a sense of luxury to this retailer's name at the checkout counter. (*Courtesy of Juno Lighting.*)

achieve professional results. Figure 10-12 shows some of the type styles of vinyl lettering available to the visual merchandiser. The letters come in numerous colors as well as black and white and are available in most desired sizes.

For special presentations, when standard letters will not fit the bill, many visual merchandisers create their own. Using materials such as Foamcore and Sintra, letters are drawn and simply cut with the use of an X-acto knife. Of course, in order to create perfect letters, the visual merchandiser must be professionally trained. Once these letters are completed, they are often adhered to surfaces with the use of a hot glue gun. This adhesive material provides excellent durability.

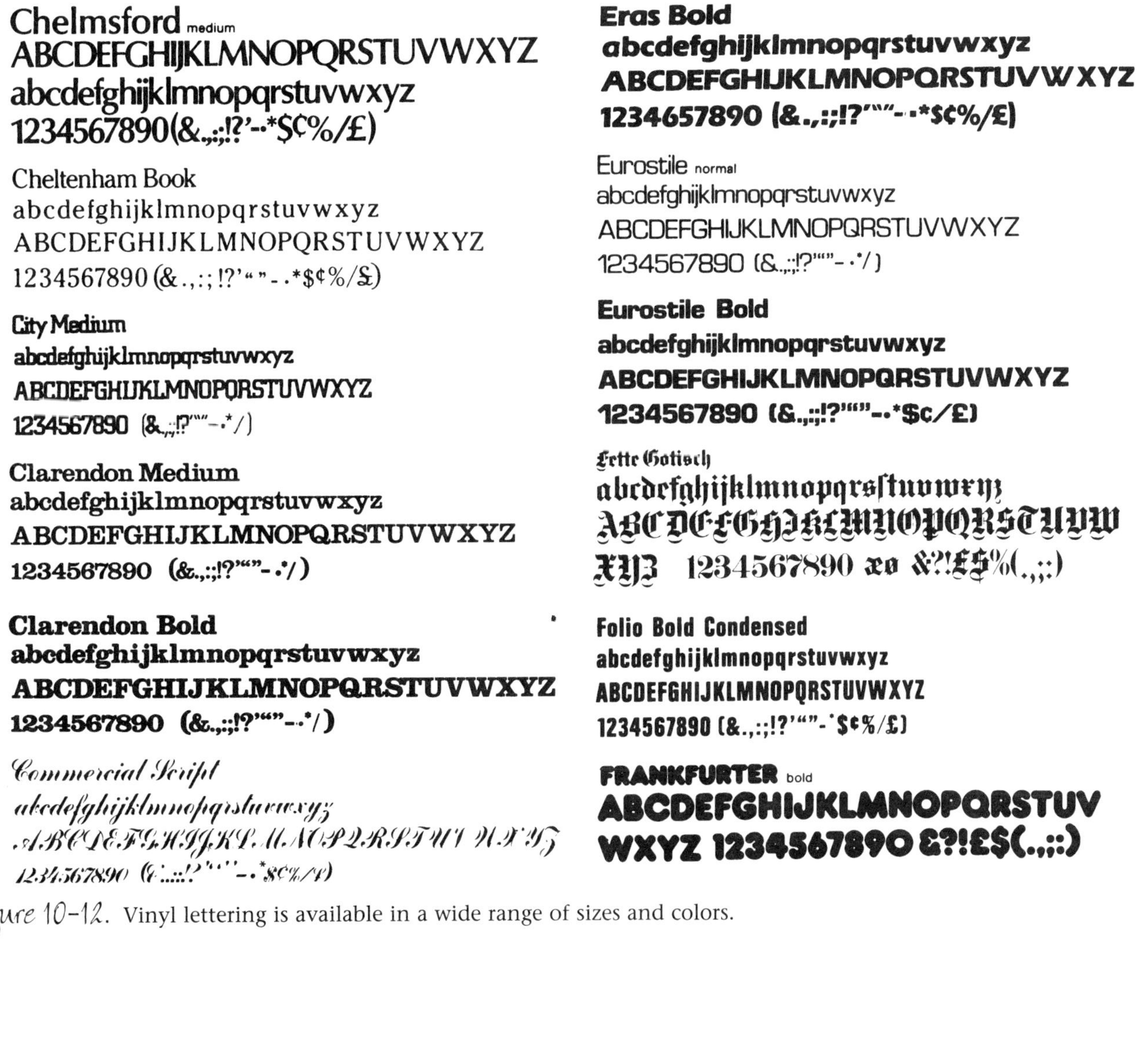

Chelmsford medium
ABCDEFGHIJKLMNOPQRSTUVWXYZ
abcdefghijklmnopqrstuvwxyz
1234567890(&.,:;!?'-*$¢%/£)

Cheltenham Book
abcdefghijklmnopqrstuvwxyz
ABCDEFGHIJKLMNOPQRSTUVWXYZ
1234567890 (&.,:; !?'" "-.*$¢%/£)

City Medium
abcdefghijklmnopqrstuvwxyz
ABCDEFGHIJKLMNOPQRSTUVWXYZ
1234567890 (&.,:;!?""-.*/)

Clarendon Medium
abcdefghijklmnopqrstuvwxyz
ABCDEFGHIJKLMNOPQRSTUVWXYZ
1234567890 (&.,:;!?""-.*/)

Clarendon Bold
abcdefghijklmnopqrstuvwxyz
ABCDEFGHIJKLMNOPQRSTUVWXYZ
1234567890 (&.,:;!?""-.*/)

Commercial Script
abcdefghijklmnopqrstuvwxyz
ABCDEFGHIJKLMNOPQRSTUVWXYZ
1234567890 (&.,:;!?""-.$¢%/£)*

Eras Bold
abcdefghijklmnopqrstuvwxyz
ABCDEFGHIJKLMNOPQRSTUVWXYZ
1234657890 (&.,:;!?""-.*$¢%/£)

Eurostile normal
abcdefghijklmnopqrstuvwxyz
ABCDEFGHIJKLMNOPQRSTUVWXYZ
1234567890 (&.,:;!?""-.*/)

Eurostile Bold
abcdefghijklmnopqrstuvwxyz
ABCDEFGHIJKLMNOPQRSTUVWXYZ
1234567890 (&.,:;!?""-.*$¢/£)

Fette Gotisch
abcdefghijklmnopqrsstuvwxyz
ABCDEFGHIJKLMNOPQRSTUVW
XYZ 1234567890 xo &?!£$%(.,;:)

Folio Bold Condensed
abcdefghijklmnopqrstuvwxyz
ABCDEFGHIJKLMNOPQRSTUVWXYZ
1234567890 (&.,:;!?""-.*$¢%/£)

FRANKFURTER bold
ABCDEFGHIJKLMNOPQRSTUV
WXYZ 1234567890 &?!£$(.,:;)

Figure 10-12. Vinyl lettering is available in a wide range of sizes and colors.

IN-HOUSE SIGN PRODUCTION

Having the right sign materials and letters is just one aspect of developing appropriate store signage. Knowing how to use these materials most effectively to motivate consumer purchasing is the real challenge. In order to create signs that have customer appeal and carry out the store's visual merchandising message, most major retailers maintain an in-house team to make certain that their signage has the desired impact.

Some signage is permanent and requires nothing more than the placement of purchased letters over department entrances. Other signs are temporary, such as those constructed for sales and special promotions. Usually these are paper or cardboard based, and the in-house staff must prepare copy and layouts to best fit the needs of the event.

Many retailers use sign-making machines to produce temporary signage. The metal or wood letters are arranged on the machine in the desired layout. After the letters are inked in the desired color, the machine is ready to produce an unlimited number of signs. The letters may need to be re-inked to guarantee a high-quality image of every letter on the sign.

While sign-making machines were once the standard technique used for sign production by in-house staffs, the vast majority of large retail organizations have turned to computers to produce their signs. A wide assortment of computer programs is available to fit every signmaker's needs. With a wealth of typefaces available and the user's creative abilities, it is possible to turn out signs of distinction. Since the signs are produced in large quantities to serve the needs of all the organization's units, the cost per sign is modest. While in-house computer signage has become commonplace in large organization retailing, it should be understood that some companies use computer sign services whereby the retailer initiates the process and, by means of a computer terminal that is tied into the service organization's mainframe, the sign is produced. The additional copies can be printed by the computer specialty company or on the retailer's own printer. The advancement of laser printers and color copiers has made in-house production a simple task. Figure 10-13 shows a computer-produced sign.

Templates, which are shapes and forms available in a wide assortment of type styles, are used to create a sign quickly and inexpensively. The user merely places the letter outline on a

Figure 10-13. Computer-produced signs featuring prices can be updated easily and quickly.

Figure 10-14. Calligraphy, produced by hand with either a dip or felt-tip marker, makes it easy to produce one-of-a-kind signs. (*Courtesy of Ellen Diamond.*)

board and fills in the entire letter or outline. Because each sign must be created individually, this method is generally used when only one sign is needed, as in the case of small retail operations. When many signs are needed, a sign-making machine is a better choice. Some stores use hand-lettered signs, although fewer and fewer artists are available to hand letter signs. Their cost is becoming prohibitive, and modern technology can produce quality signs more quickly. While the demand for hand-lettered signs is declining, there is still a need to produce price tickets for window displays. Since these are often produced on the job and needed quickly to complete a presentation, the use of a machine is not always practical. Independents or small chains have an even greater need for hand-lettered price tickets. They turn to freelancers or to the many small shops that produce their own visual presentations and do their own hand-lettering. Figure 10-14 shows a hand-lettering system that employs calligraphy. To make calligraphy even easier, there are many felt tip markers available that enable the user to complete the letters without the need to constantly dip a pen into ink. There is no problem with clogging, as in the case of the dip method. The felt tip provides an even flow until the ink runs dry.

SIGN LAYOUT

Whatever the choice of materials, the sign layout must conform to all the principles of good design. These are the same principles of balance, emphasis, harmony, proportion, and rhythm that were discussed in Chapter 6.

The message to be presented is not the decision of the signmaker but of those who planned the visual presentation in which the sign will play a part.

The following layout preparation, presented in stages, will be executed with press-on letters. Today, a great number of layout proposals are accomplished by computer, making it a speedier process. It should be understood, however, that no matter what materials are used, the task of preparing the layout from its inception to completion is the same.

Figure 10-15. Thumbnail sketches help the display staff visualize the best way to present information to the customer. (*Courtesy of Ellen Diamond.*)

Figure 10-16. The finished product, chosen from the thumbnail sketches. (*Courtesy of Ellen Diamond.*)

Stage one: The concept of the proposed sign is discussed with the individual responsible for the layout. This person is a member of the visual merchandising team. All of the elements such as the desired sign material, size of the finished product, informative points, price, etc., are presented at this time.

Stage two: The visual specialist develops several thumbnail sketches (small, roughly finished drawings) from which one will be selected to be made into the actual sign. Note that the same information is presented differently in each sketch in Figure 10-15.

Stage three: Each sketch is studied carefully by the visual merchandising team to determine the best one for reproduction with press-on letters. Figure 10-16 shows the finished product.

Stage four: If only one sign is needed, it is immediately delivered to the trimmers for installation in the visual presentation. When several copies of the same sign are required, they could be produced on a sign-making machine or an in-house computer, or sent to a professional printer.

COMMERCIAL SIGN SOURCES

The discussion so far has been about sign preparation by retail in-house staffs and the signage that is available from vendors at little or no cost. Many vendors opt to offer this signage so that it will provide a uniform message in all of the retail outlets they serve. However, not every store organization has these options. The large retailer

SIGNAGE AND GRAPHICS

Figure 10-17. A poster-size graphic, flanked by informative signage. (*Courtesy of Ellen Diamond.*)

might be bombarded with vendor-produced materials and be able to produce special signs in-house, but a small store lacks these resources.

Inspection of a small retailer's premises shows that while signs are not used abundantly, there are situations that warrant their use. Short on the dollars needed to advertise a sale in the print or broadcast media, small retailers generally notify shoppers with a sign in the window. The signs are relatively inexpensive and may be obtained from a signmaker who will hand letter any message, or from a company that can reproduce the message via computer. In either case, an attractive piece can be obtained quickly and efficiently.

Another source is the local photography store where a slide or print can be inexpensively transformed into a poster-size picture. Both black and white and color copies are quickly produced, with great clarity, on copiers. Especially with the use of bold graphics produced on color copiers, the small retailer can emulate the trends in visual merchandising that are central to major retailers' presentations. Figure 10-17 features a poster-size graphic used in conjunction with signage.

Although lithographic and silk-screening resources abound, these production techniques should be considered only if the retailer requires a large number of identical signs and graphics. The quality of such production is excellent and the presentations are generally outstanding. Artists prepare proofs or samples of the work for customer approval and then produce as many signs as needed. Since the per-sign cost decreases as the quantity ordered increases, this type of sign production is not very cost-effective for the smaller retailer whose quantity needs are not great.

TERMS OF THE TRADE

adhesive letters
artist's proof
backlit transparencies
banners
calligraphy
computer-designed signage
felt tip markers
fixture-contained signage

lightbox
moving message signs
neon
pennants
pressure-sensitive tape
silk screen signage
templates
thumbnail sketches
track signs
typefaces
valance signs
Velcro

CHAPTER REVIEW

KEY POINTS IN THE CHAPTER

1. Signage and graphics are making a greater impact on customers today than ever before in retailing history.
2. The list of signage types continues to grow as retailers discover new ways to motivate consumer purchasing.
3. Electric signage is becoming increasingly popular, with backlit transparencies a favorite of retailers.
4. Signs are no longer simple and routine but are now the creations of professional graphic artists.
5. Photography is playing a significant role in visual presentations because it is easily acquired at minimal cost.
6. Neon signs, once reserved for store identification, are now being used significantly in visual presentations.
7. Numerous materials are being used for signage, each offering a distinct advantage to the retailer.
8. An abundance of letter types enables the visual merchandiser to create signage that stimulates purchasing.
9. Many letters come with Velcro or pressure-sensitive tape backings for easy sign installation.
10. Most major retailers maintain in-house staffs to produce signs specifically for their stores' needs.
11. Signs can be quickly produced in-house and by outside sources using computers.
12. Although hand-lettered signs are disappearing from the retail scene, a knowledge of simple hand lettering is beneficial for the production of price tickets.

SIGNAGE AND GRAPHICS

13. With the availability of felt tip markers, calligraphy, a form of lettering, has become simpler to accomplish.
14. Sign layout generally involves four stages, each of which helps ensure the best possible final product.
15. Although free signage is often available from vendors and some sign production may be done on a store's premises, commercial sign houses are often used to produce computer and specialty signage such as silkscreened or lithographic types.

DISCUSSION QUESTIONS

1. What materials are used for signs to provide more permanency than paper?
2. What form of signage offers the greatest level of color and vibrancy?
3. Describe the backlit transparency type of signage.
4. Describe fixture-contained signage.
5. Discuss the different types of letter backings that enable the visual merchandiser to install a sign quickly.
6. For what major purpose is the moving message sign used by retailers?
7. Discuss the advantages of track signage.
8. Which industry led the way in neon signage?
9. How is computer technology being used in sign production?
10. In this era of mechanically lettered signage, why do some visual professionals use hand lettering?
11. What is the advantage of self-stick letters?
12. Briefly describe the four stages of sign layout and production.
13. What are the uses of lithography and silk screening in display?
14. How can slides, transparencies, or photographs be quickly and efficiently turned into attractive graphics?

CASE PROBLEMS

Case 1

David Neil is the trimmer for the Designing Woman, a small chain of ten specialty stores. The stores, all located within a radius of 150 miles, specialize in fashion forward dresses and sportswear. Recently, David was invited by management to participate in a planning session on the company's visual merchandising approach.

For its 30 years of operation the company has followed the traditional route of merchandise presentation. Dresses and other hanging merchandise have been housed on racks, with folded merchandise stacked in wall cases and on floor counters. The sales staff showed the items to the customers, rather than letting customers browse by themselves. While this format had worked well in the past, the company is noticing a new customer independence. The younger clientele seems to prefer the self-selection approach over the show and tell method. More and more, shoppers seem to be saying, "I'd rather look by myself."

Management is considering several changes to accommodate a more relaxed merchandising concept. Along with Mr. Neil, the company has decided on some fixture updating with show and sell counters replacing the older variety so that shoppers can handle the merchandise and serve themselves. Hanging merchandise will also be displayed to invite self-inspection by shoppers. The fixturing change should lend a new, relaxed environment to shopping.

While the stores' windows will remain intact, continuing to feature the types of presentations that always motivated lookers to come into the store, it is felt that something should be done to make the interior more exciting. The new fixturing isn't enough. David Neil suggested that a signage program would liven up an otherwise low-key interior. Although management thinks the suggestion is a good one, they want to make certain that the costs of exciting signage won't severely tax the store's visual merchandising budget.

Questions

1. What types of signage would be best suited for the Designing Woman?
2. How could you accomplish the goal with little money?
3. Should graphics be employed? If so, in what format?

Case 2

As the proprietor of a small boutique, Caryn Kelly has always had to deal with the challenge of visual merchandising on a shoestring. She trims her own windows and has generally received admiration for her efforts. Since the business was profitable, she felt that her visual presentations were on target.

In her store, as in any other retail business, there has been a continuous need for signage to announce sales and relate other messages to her customers. This was the one area that Caryn felt uncomfortable handling, but professionally produced signs were too expensive or the finished products were not to her liking. The typical paper sale sign affixed to the window just wasn't right. Still, she needed something to help her dispose of slow-selling merchandise.

She even tried her hand at lettering. The result was similar to the home-baked cake that might taste fine, but leaves much to be desired in terms of professionalism. Not only were her signs poorly executed, but her self-made price tickets looked equally dismal.

Caryn finally visited some professional signmakers who were a step above the typical paper sign producer. They offered many suggestions but each required a bigger investment than she could afford. The fabric banners and lightboxes that were suggested did not seem right for her limited usage. What she really wants is a system to produce professional-looking sales signage at minimum expense and on short notice.

Question

What approaches to sign preparation would you suggest for Caryn?

NAME: _____ DATE: _____

EXERCISES

1. Using the following information, produce four thumbnail sketches of a sign. Then produce a finished, full-size sign of the best sketch, using colored markers or press-on letters.

    Sale

    Imported Glassware

    Reductions 20-50%

    For President's Week Only

2. Visit a major department store or specialty store in your area to observe their signage and graphics. Complete the form provided, listing the types of signage and graphics and commenting on their effectiveness.

NAME: _____ DATE: _____

Exercise 2 SIGNAGE AND GRAPHICS ANALYSIS

STORE NAME _____

TYPE OF STORE _____

Type of Signage	Department	Effectiveness
1.		
2.		
3.		
4.		
5.		
6.		
7.		
8.		

Chapter 11
Point of Purchase Display

LEARNING OBJECTIVES

After completing this chapter, the student should be able to:

1. Define the term *point of purchase* as it relates to today's retail environments.
2. Discuss the reason for the wide cost variations in point of purchase fixturing.
3. Explain why vendors are anxious to provide retail clients with point of purchase units at little or no cost to them.
4. Tell about the various types of point of purchase fixtures that are used in today's retail establishments.
5. Discuss the various materials that go into the making of the point of purchase units.
6. List the various types of retailers who use point of purchase displays, and the types each use in their stores.

INTRODUCTION

For many years, manufacturers of small items such as hosiery, sunglasses, greeting cards, etc., were anxious for their products to make an impact on the selling floors of the retailers they sold to. Generally, most of these vendors found their merchandise mixed with offerings from other vendors, thus diminishing their presence in the overall merchandise mix. In an effort to separate and distinguish their items from the others, some of the vendors designed and produced inexpensive, self-contained stands and shelves that featured their lines exclusively. The units were generally constructed from corrugated materials and featured the brand's name, logo, or other identifying marks, and space on which to feature the merchandise. A visit to any supermarket, for example, would reveal a point of purchase display unit filled with hosiery or sunglasses, located somewhere near the checkout counters. Thus, when we thought of point of purchase displays, we concluded that there were inexpensively created display units, designed and produced by the vendors of consumer goods for use in retail operations. Today, the concept has been considerably expanded. While the early types of point of purchase units are still used successfully, others have joined them that are more costly and permanent.

The success of this type of display can be measured in a number of ways. First, as reported by the Point of Purchase Advertising Institute (POPAI), headquartered in Washington, D.C., the use of such devices increases sales by as much as 30 percent. Second, what was once a minor part of the display industry has now become a $12 billion industry. The significant advance in this type of merchandising has been attributed to the enormous increase in the number of in-store shops.

Figure 11-1. A self-contained point-of-purchase product unit. (*Courtesy of Kroy.*)

The early concept of point of purchase that used temporary, inexpensive display racks has now taken on a new definition. Today, POPAI defines point of purchase as "Displays, signs, structures and devices that are used to identify, advertise and/or merchandise an outlet, service or product and which serve as an aid to retail selling." An example of a typical point of purchase unit featuring the *label'r* product is shown in Figure 11-1.

In this chapter, the discussion focuses on the stores that use point of purchase units, the different types of units that are in today's marketplace, and the materials used in their construction.

RETAIL POINT OF PURCHASE USERS

It seems that no matter which store we enter today, there is some form of point of purchase display in evidence. Retailers such as mass merchandisers, supermarkets, warehouse clubs, pharmacies, greeting card stores, record shops, specialty organizations, and even department stores have moved into the point of purchase arena. Each utilizes the type of fixturing combined with signage that is best suited for its environment and will best motivate shoppers to buy.

Mass Merchandisers

Companies such as Wal-Mart, Kmart, and Target that deal with a vast assortment of merchandise that is value priced, are significant users of point of purchase units. The merchandise that these units feature are often items that the stores do not carry in abundant quantities but stock to round out their product lines. In order to emphasize items such as reading glasses, paperback books, records, and tapes, they are merely stacked on the holders supplied by vendors and feature the company name, logo, and a product assortment. The newer entries are interactive units, featured in the Target stores for music sales. Not only does the unit feature a variety of tapes and CDs, but there is a sound and sight monitor that, when started by the consumer, plays a sample of the tape or CD requested. Other interactive units are like the Nintendo unit featured in Figure 11-2 that enables the user to sample some products. The remainder of the units in these types of stores are the corrugated ones that are generally for temporary use, turning wire racks that can be quickly spun to see the entire offering, and wooden units that have more permanency.

If the items that are found on these units were mixed in with the remainder of the stores' merchandise mix, the stores would certainly lose the impulse purchases they generate.

Figure 11-2. This Nintendo unit allows the shopper to sample many offerings before making a selection. (*Courtesy of Ellen Diamond.*)

Supermarkets

When supermarkets originally opened their doors, their product assortment was primarily food oriented. Departments for produce, meats and poultry, canned goods, paper products, etc., were designed to satisfy the shopper's household needs and generate enough business to make the company profitable. As time went by, supermarkets became more and more price competitive, with markups and profits dwindling. One of the answers to this problem was the introduction of nonfood items. Merchants began to set aside shelf space for nontraditional supermarket items that carried higher markups than food, and thus brought greater revenue to the store.

Most supermarkets that want to feature unique or limited quantity items that they hope will appeal to the shoppers start by adding point of purchase units on their selling floors. Placed in high-traffic areas such as the checkout counters and endcaps, these units reap excellent rewards for the stores.

Warehouse Clubs

Throughout the country, a host of warehouse clubs have opened their doors to member shoppers. Major operators such as Sam's Club and Price-Cosco appeal to huge numbers of people seeking to save on purchases ranging from food items to household goods. Since these operations are totally devoid of service, the way many of their suppliers attract attention is through the use of point of purchase displays. Whether they are freestanding structures, which are generally of the corrugated type, or endcaps, they help to get the message across and sell goods.

Pharmacies

At one time, pharmacies were primarily designed to provide customers with prescription drugs and over-the-counter medicines, as well as other related items. Today, this type of retailing has significantly expanded to include a variety of other products. Whether the stores are individual proprietorships or large chains such as Walgreen's or Eckerd, items ranging from greeting cards to hosiery are successfully merchandised. In these operations, with medicine procurement the primary objective of patrons, the merchants must find ways to direct attention to the other products. For most, the key is to use point of purchase displays. The display units are strategically situated in such places as the prescription filling areas where people often wait for their prescriptions, at checkout counters, or for that matter, anywhere in the store. The units used in pharmacies include metallic wire stands that turn and feature items such as sunglasses; permanent fixtures that feature greeting cards and cosmetics, as seen in Figure 11-3; corrugated units that stock suntan lotion during the warm months; and glass-enclosed freestanding shelves that feature giftware.

Because competitive pricing limits the profits on pharmaceutical items, operators of these stores are merchandising more and more items that are less competitively priced and are often bought on impulse. What better way is there to alert shoppers to these items than with point of purchase displays?

Figure 11-3. Vendor cosmetics are often sold from units that feature their product lines. (*Courtesy of Ellen Diamond.*)

Greeting Card Stores

Primarily in business to sell greeting cards throughout the year, many of these stores are expanding their offerings to increase sales. As in the case of pharmacies, they

Figure 11-4. The Russell Stover display fixture houses a selection of boxed chocolates. (*Courtesy of Ellen Diamond.*)

utilize a host of point of purchase fixtures to feature their other merchandise. Products such as novelty toys, giftware, boxed chocolates as shown in Figure 11-4, and paperback books are found on special display units throughout the store to tempt the shoppers. Even special types of greeting cards that would be overlooked if merchandised along with the regular inventory are featured on point of purchase display units.

Specialty Organizations

The specialty shops, businesses that restrict their merchandise offerings to one major classification of goods, continue to grow in number. Whether the stores feature apparel, shoes, gourmet foods, recorded music, or anything else, the expansion rate is significant. In most of these shops, some extra items are featured. Since the assortments of these items are small and not part of the mainstream merchandise, these products are stacked on special shelf containers or racks called point of purchase fixtures. The apparel shop, for example, might stock a particular vendor's hosiery that is merchandised on a revolving rack supplied by the vendor. Generally placed near the store's checkout register, the display might remind a shopper to purchase hosiery to complete the outfit just purchased. The gourmet food store might have a special fixture that features a grower's wine of the month and alerts the shopper to its availability. The shoe store often features a special rack that offers a full line of shoelaces or shoe ornaments. If they were not prominently displayed on special fixturing, these items would sell in much smaller quantities.

Point of purchase fixtures in specialty stores range from those that have a temporary purpose to those that are sturdy, permanent fixtures.

Department Stores

A shopper entering a department store is not apt to find the point of purchase fixtures and displays that grace the premises of the mass merchandisers, supermarkets, warehouse clubs, and specialty stores. The department store is generally a service-oriented operation that is more upscale than most of these retailers. Thus, the point of purchase displays take on a different format and look.

One growing trend in the department store organization is the in-house vendor shop. Designers and well-known manufacturers such as Ralph Lauren, Donna Karan, Calvin Klein, and Chanel often

Figure 11-5. Elizabeth Arden's salon is typical of in-store shops. (*Courtesy of Ellen Diamond.*)

arrange to have separate shops inside the department store that are separate and apart from the regular departments. Figure 11-5 shows an in-store shop for Elizabeth Arden. These vendors often supply the fixturing, signage, special merchandise racks, identifiable logos, and anything else that is exclusive to their lines for the stores. Figure 11-6 shows a vendor-supplied rack complete with a manufacturer's logo. In this way, the shopper is shown the merchandise in a new light. Unlike the temporary corrugated fixtures found in other types of retail institutions, these point of purchase display fixtures and presentations are of the highest quality. Figure 11-7 features a display unit with product identification. The concept is good for both the vendor and the store. The vendor gains by having a special section devoted to its collection, and the store gains because the fixtures are often supplied by the vendors at no cost.

Figure 11-6. This Joe Boxer rack and logo, supplied by the vendor, attracts shopper attention. (*Courtesy of Ellen Diamond.*)

Figure 11-7. Ralph Lauren was one of the first designers to provide in-store display units, complete with signage, to retailers. (*Courtesy of Ellen Diamond.*)

TYPES OF POINT OF PURCHASE FIXTURES

As mentioned in the preceding section, there are different types of point of purchase displays and fixturing available to retailers. They range from the type that is designed to last for just a brief period of time to those that are more permanently installed.

Interactive Video

One of the newest formats provided for use in retail operations is known as interactive video. These screens entice the shopper to learn more about the specific products the display features. One major proponent of interactive video is Microsoft. In an area that is actually a shop within a shop, and that features unique signage and display racks, the interactive video has drawn significant attention. The prototype for this point of purchase display presentation is a 500-square-foot shop inside Nebraska Furniture Mart's Mega Mart. In this one area, an abundance of Microsoft's product line is featured. The interactive videos, encased in kiosks, allow customers to experiment with specific computer programs and learn about the benefits of their usage. Since the installation of this point of purchase store-within-a-store, Microsoft sales have increased 50 percent.

Gondolas

Constructed of materials such as wood, metal, and pegboard, gondolas are permanent fixtures that are on wheels and can be moved from one location to another. They house a variety of items including hosiery, computer software, foods, greeting cards, and so forth. They are equipped with signage that features the vendor's name and sometimes its logo and that gives immediate recognition to the products they house. They are found in all types of retail operations.

Closed-Circuit Video

Many apparel and women's accessories designers and manufacturers are developing special videos for use at the point of purchase. Designers like Donna Karan, for example, provide retailers with videotapes of runway shows of their latest collections. In this way, shoppers can stop, look, and listen to learn about the clothing. Figure 11-8 features monitors that

Figure 11-8. DKNY videos are featured in the DKNY department. (Courtesy of Ellen Diamond.)

show designer videos. If sufficiently motivated, the next step would be to examine the merchandise on the racks to see if something is found to be appealing.

Another very successful in-store video presentation was developed by Vera, a scarf manufacturer. The presentation shows the various ways scarves can be used to create interesting effects. Shown close to the counters where the scarves are available for sale, the video acts as a motivational device to examine the inventory.

In the Disney stores, there is a continuous showing on a large screen of the movies available on video. Young and old watch these features and are often tempted to buy those that catch their fancy. Adjacent to the viewing screen are shelves filled with the videos for easy purchase.

Motion Creations

Moving objects at the point of purchase are excellent tools to capture the attention of the shopper. One of the biggest users of these devices is the Disney Store. In both the windows and store interiors, a host of characters such as Mickey Mouse and Donald Duck can be seen in motion. They quickly capture the attention of the passersby, tempting them to come into the store where they are greeted by other motion creations, often resulting in a purchase.

In-Store Shops

The in-store shop is helping many vendors and retailers increase sales. While the fashion industry was the first to enter this market, many other industries have jumped on the bandwagon. The Nickelodeon brand, for example, enjoys a separate part of each Blockbuster Video store intended to attract parents and children. As the kids enter the area, they are automatically filmed and the results are played back on a video monitor. Also featured are play benches set in front of a television set that features Nickelodeon programming. Rounding out this point of purchase location are interactive terminals that allow the children to offer their opinions of Nickelodeon programming. Cutouts of the characters seen on the vendor's programs round out the presentation, making it a visually exciting presentation.

Others subscribing to the in-store shop concept include Wrangler, Reebok International, and the Bank of America, which now operates in-store facilities in supermarkets.

Countertop Cases

In order to attract shoppers to seek merchandise in the shelves, some vendors supply their retail clients with countertop glass enclosures that attractively highlight some items. One such company is Lantis

Corp., which uses the cases to spotlight its Killer Loop/Activ Sunglasses in department stores. The glasses are featured on a contemporary steel construction that allows for viewing from different sides. The products are targeted at skiers, surfers, and snowboarders and are separated from the traditional products on this construction, making them stand out.

Cardboard Fixtures

When temporary point of purchase fixturing is the goal, an inexpensive material is generally the choice. Often, some form of cardboard or corrugated material is used. Vendors have fixtures designed so they can be shipped in a folded state and easily assembled by the retailer. It might be a one-piece configuration that simply folds out along scored lines, with flaps quickly inserted into designated places for completion. Others involve several separate pieces that are quickly assembled.

Greeting cards for specific occasions such as graduation time, the latest best-seller paperback book, and seasonal decorations such as those used at Christmastime all make use of these temporary devices. When the period of selling has passed, the retailer generally disposes of these units and replaces them with others that are more timely.

Computer Stations

With the population becoming more and more computer literate, many vendors are now offering computer stations to their retail accounts that enable users to create their own products. One of the more popular types is the one that lets customers create their own greeting cards. Following simple computer instructions, customers choose the color of the paper, the design, the message, and any other detail to create personalized greeting cards. Personalized T-shirts are also created using the same technique.

While stores generally stock traditional T-shirts and greeting cards, the point of purchase computer station allows for originality and also acts as a motivational tool for the department.

TERMS OF THE TRADE

cardboard fixtures
closed-circuit video
computer stations
corrugated
endcaps
gondolas

in-store shops
interactive video
mass merchandisers
motion creations
point of purchase
POPAI
scored lines
shop within a shop
value-priced merchandise
warehouse clubs

CHAPTER REVIEW

KEY POINTS IN THE CHAPTER

1. The Point of Purchase Advertising Institute is the major organization that reports about the latest innovations in point of purchase displays.
2. Point of purchase is defined as "displays, signs, structures and devices that are used to identify, advertise and/or merchandise an outlet, service or product and which serve as an aid to retail selling."
3. While point of purchase displays are used throughout retailing, the types used by the various retailers differ according to their organizational types.
4. Mass merchandisers often use point of purchase units to feature merchandise that they do not carry in very large quantities, but stock nevertheless to round out their merchandise assortments.
5. Supermarkets, while primarily in business to sell food items, often use point of purchase units to feature nonfood items that are generally more profitable than their food lines. They usually place these items at endcaps and checkout counters.
6. Many pharmacies are adding nonpharmaceutical lines to their inventories as a means of expanding sales. These products are often featured on point of purchase display units and, if sufficiently eye-appealing, motivate shoppers to buy on impulse.
7. The department store was the first retailer to subscribe to the concept of in-store shops. Vendors such as designers and manufacturers provide the retailers with the fixtures and signage that form these shops and help to distinguish the merchandise found in them from the store's regular assortment.

8. Interactive video is one of the newest formats in point of purchase displays. The structures utilize screens that entice the shoppers to learn more about the products.
9. Gondolas are permanent fixtures on wheels that can be moved from one location to another. They hold merchandise as well as identifiable signage.
10. Closed-circuit video presents a vendor's complete line of merchandise, such as a designer's collection, and is intended to motivate the shopper to seek the merchandise on the selling floor.
11. Motion creations attract attention to specific products and are designed to convince the shopper to buy the store's items.
12. Cardboard fixtures are temporary and are utilized only for the period of time in which certain merchandise is salable. They are inexpensive, easy to assemble, and can be discarded after their usefulness has passed.
13. Computer stations enable shoppers to participate in the creation of their own products, such as personalized greeting cards and T-shirts.

DISCUSSION QUESTIONS

1. Define the term *point of purchase* according to the Point of Purchase Advertising Institute.
2. How do today's point of purchase displays differ from those that were popular when the concept was in its infancy?
3. By how much does POPAI report that point of purchase displays increase sales?
4. How large, in terms of dollars, is the point of purchase industry?
5. Which types of merchandise do the mass merchandisers such as Kmart generally sell through point of purchase units?
6. Why do supermarkets use point of purchase display fixtures to feature items other than food products?
7. Where do most supermarkets feature their point of purchase displays?
8. What types of products do pharmacies locate on point of purchase display units, and why do they choose to sell this merchandise?
9. What point of purchase concept has the department store embraced in which their vendors supply the fixturing?
10. What is meant by a shop within a shop?
11. How does interactive video work on the retail selling floor?
12. Describe the gondola fixture and the purpose that it serves for the retailer.

13. In what way do fashion designers utilize the retail operation's closed-circuit video installation?
14. Which major retailer employs motion creations as point of purchase motivators?
15. Why do some vendors supply their retail clients with cardboard fixturing instead of the more permanent varieties?
16. Why have computer stations become popular at the store's points of purchase?

CASE PROBLEMS

Case 1

The Gourmet Emporium is a specialty food chain that has been in business for 15 years. In the organization there are 20 units, with each carrying fresh produce, meats and poultry, imported and domestic cheeses, baked goods, and fully prepared meals that require no preparation before consumption. The company has been profitable since it opened its first store, always enjoying a steady clientele.

At the regular semiannual management meeting at company headquarters, the discussion turned to increasing volume and profits. Suggestions included expanding those stores that had available space adjacent to their existing premises so that new lines might be added, carrying greater depth in the products now featured, and perhaps reducing prices to gain an even greater market share.

Each of the suggestions met with both positive and negative reactions. For example, while expansion might be appropriate, not every unit had sufficient adjacent space to do so. Carrying greater inventories in the lines now featured might result in a lower stock turnover, which would hamper profits. Price reductions, while favored by some, would cut into profit margins if sales didn't increase appreciably.

At this point in time, management is still groping for a solution to bolster sales and profits.

Questions

1. What type of program could the Gourmet Emporium embark upon to carry out its desire to increase sales without undergoing major alterations?
2. Which products could they add to their existing lines, using the new format?

Case 2

Lansing's department store has been in business for 20 years and operates eight branches in addition to its flagship store. Business has generally been good, with steady gains in profit a regular trend.

The company is a full-service operation with sales associates and personal shoppers available to satisfy the customers' needs. The departments they offer include every aspect of clothing and accessories for men, women, and children, as well as home furnishings. The manner in which they merchandise the departments is to mix each category of merchandise together without any special attention to vendor names. Ladies' handbags, for example, features Coach, Gucci, Donna Karan, Liz Claiborne, etc., in one area. The other departments are similarly merchandised.

With more and more focus on designer labels, those carried at Lansing's often get lost among everything else offered for sale. A customer who is looking, for example, for a Calvin Klein suit, must browse all of the suit racks to find the desired label.

Pat Lane, senior vice president of merchandising, would like to see something new in terms of how special lines are featured. Other management people feel the same, but are reluctant to attempt any new approach because it would probably require a large outlay of capital to do so.

At this time, the company would like to find a way to differentiate among collections without having to expend significant dollars.

Questions

1. How could Lansing's solve its problem?
2. What approach should they take in order to make the change without incurring significant expense?

NAME: _____ DATE: _____

EXERCISES

1. Write to the Point of Purchase Advertising Institute in Washington, D.C. and ask for a list of the pamphlets, brochures, and publications they offer on the topic. After the list has been received, select one item and report about its use in point of purchase displays to the class.

2. Visit three supermarkets in your area for the purpose of reporting about their point of purchase display units. Using the form provided for your note-taking, prepare a report on the one that you believe makes the most significant use of point of purchase displays.

NAME: _____ DATE: _____

Exercise 2 SUPERMARKET POINT OF PURCHASE DISPLAYS

Name of Store _____

Types of Point of Purchase Units _____

_____

Point of Purchase Merchandise _____

Name of Store _____

Types of Point of Purchase Units _____

_____

Point of Purchase Merchandise _____

Name of Store _____

Types of Point of Purchase Units _____

_____

Point of Purchase Merchandise _____

NAME: _____ DATE: _____

Exercise 2 SUPERMARKET POINT OF PURCHASE DISPLAYS

Name of Store _____

Types of Point of Purchase Units _____

_____

Point of Purchase Merchandise _____

Name of Store _____

Types of Point of Purchase Units _____

_____

Point of Purchase Merchandise _____

Name of Store _____

Types of Point of Purchase Units _____

_____

Point of Purchase Merchandise _____

NAME: _____ DATE: _____

Exercise 2 SUPERMARKET POINT OF PURCHASE DISPLAYS

Name of Store _____

Types of Point of Purchase Units _____
_____

Point of Purchase Merchandise _____

Name of Store _____

Types of Point of Purchase Units _____
_____

Point of Purchase Merchandise _____

Name of Store _____

Types of Point of Purchase Units _____
_____

Point of Purchase Merchandise _____

Chapter 12
Execution of a Visual Presentation

LEARNING OBJECTIVES

After completing this chapter, the student should be able to:

1. Describe the stages in the execution of a visual merchandise presentation.
2. Discuss the relationship of background materials and props to the merchandise featured in the display.
3. List five ordinary props that are inexpensive, are easy to find, and make eye-catching installations.
4. Prepare a window space that is to house a new display theme.
5. From a variety of available mannequins, choose those that fit a specific theme or setting.
6. Explain the major steps involved in the installation of a window display.
7. Compare display sketches and graphic plans.
8. Draw a preliminary sketch for a window display.
9. Produce creative props and install them as exciting displays.

INTRODUCTION

Mastery of visual merchandising theory in such areas as design fundamentals, mannequin use, color comprehension, and copy preparation is vital to the execution of a presentation that has visual appeal and also motivates the shopper to purchase. However, an individual may know the concepts but lack the competence to actually assemble all of the elements into a good presentation. Compare this with someone who is knowledgeable in the terminology and schools of thought in the arts, but cannot produce his or her own artistic creations.

The installation of a display requires an approach that is carefully planned and executed with attention to every detail. A written outline or format is often helpful. This outline is similar to the sketch an artist does before beginning a painting. While this preparation is important to a novice, the seasoned professional in visual merchandising might not need to put every detail down on paper before executing the design. As more confidence is developed, some details will evolve naturally from a basic thumbnail sketch of a display. Of course, in companies that utilize the centralized approach to visual merchandising, as we explored in Chapter 2, detailed blueprints are prepared so that reproduction of the display is easily accomplished.

This chapter explores the various stages involved in the selection of the merchandise to be displayed, how the merchandise is prepared for the installation, the assembling of props and materials that will be used to enhance the merchandise, selection of mannequins and other forms, the preparation of the space that will be used, lighting preparation, the actual display installation, and the development of exciting and creative props for use in displays.

SELECTING THE MERCHANDISE

Several times throughout the text, this fundamental concept has been repeated: Unless an institutional concept is being developed, such as a store's commemoration of Columbus Day or a tie-in with National Health Week, *the emphasis for the presentation must be on the merchandise.* The background materials and props are merely enhancers. Selection of the merchandise for the display is the domain of the divisional merchandise manager or the buyer. If two departments' items are to be featured in one window, for example, both buyers should make selections that complement each other's merchandise. In branch stores, if directions do not come from the buyer in the flagship store, the department managers are called upon to select what's new.

Usually, and especially in department stores, only one classification of goods holds the spotlight. However, it is often necessary for the featured items to be properly accessorized. This not only enhances the main items but also helps to pre-sell other items, the end result being a larger purchase. When accessory items are required of secondary merchandise, such as shoes, handbags, and jewelry, the fashion director or coordinator is called upon to select the appropriate items.

In stores that specialize in furnishings and accessories for the home, such as Crate & Barrel and Williams-Sonoma, the merchandise to be featured is selected at the central visual merchandising

EXECUTION OF A VISUAL PRESENTATION

Figure 12-1. The use of accessories along with a main item often motivates an extra purchase. (*Courtesy of Ellen Diamond.*)

facilities by merchandisers. Since the displays generally include a variety of items, the decisions are made by several people. In this way, all of the stores in the respective chains will have a similar type of merchandise display running at the same time.

Figure 12-1 shows a display that features a main group of items along with accessories that not only act as display enhancers but might motivate shoppers to purchase more than just the main items. In addition to having the extras boost sales, the impact of the entire display is more effective than if only the main item were featured.

In order to make the greatest impact and increase sales, the merchandise chosen should be timely, have positive eye appeal, and make a statement. The message might be about a current popular style, a particular fabric, a trend that is developing, dinnerware and table accessories for the perfect Christmas dining table, or any theme that the store is trying to convey to its clientele.

It is imperative to have all of the merchandise and props ready when the trimmer is ready for the installation. Care should be taken to arrange the accessories so they will be featured with the appropriate outfit if the project is one featuring apparel. If items are not carefully organized, the wrong combinations might appear in the display.

PREPARING THE MERCHANDISE

Responsibility for preparing the merchandise varies, depending on the size of the store and whether it has its own visual merchandiser or retains a freelancer. When merchandise is on loan from a selling department in a large store for use in visual presentations, a specific procedure must be followed to make certain that the items are returned to the department from which they came. The visual merchandising department is responsible for preparing a merchandise loan form, as pictured on page 226. The procedure for the form's use is as follows:

1. The form is completed and signed by the borrower and the department manager, or in some situations by the assistant buyer of the lending department. Dates, quantities, merchandise descriptions, prices, etc., must be entered.
2. The department manager of the lending department keeps the original copy of the form and the borrower keeps a copy.
3. When the display has been dismantled and the merchandise is returned to the selling department, the lending manager completes the bottom of the form.
4. If some items are not returned, this is noted on the form.

Since each department is accountable for its inventory, it is very important that managers make certain that borrowed items are returned.

In large retail organizations the trimmers handle final touching up of the merchandise before the installation takes place. Clothing and soft accessories must be carefully ironed to eliminate wrinkles. Shoes should be polished, jewelry must be free of fingerprints, and all hang tags should be removed from garments. In smaller stores, where the freelancer's time is limited and the installation might take place during normal shopping hours, it is imperative that the merchandise be out of the customer's reach until it is needed by the trimmer.

ASSEMBLING PROPS AND MATERIALS

Once the merchandise leaves the hands of the assistant buyer or department manager and others responsible for its delivery to the place of installation, the visual merchandisers run the show. By this time the appropriate theme or setting has been established to best show off the merchandise. Unless the promotion is part of a major campaign, there isn't generally a great deal of money invested in new props for interior displays. Background equipment for such presentations is often chosen from the display storage area and freshened to fit the trimmer's needs. A new coat of paint, rearrangement of props into a new configuration, or using them exactly as they once were used are generally the routes taken for these installations. Pads, if used, are sometimes covered with new fabric to give the display a fresh look. Boxes, covered with colorful or seasonal papers, are redone to create new excitement.

Many stores use a variety of plants to complement their interior presentations. This is an effective way to cut costs. Care must be exercised in the use of plants, however, to make certain that low-light varieties are used and that they are watered regularly to maintain the plants' appearance. Dried flowers and artificial leaves are also excellent adjuncts to displays because they have eye appeal and are maintenance-free. At the conclusion of this chapter, step-by-step illustrations are presented for the development and use of artificial flower arrangements, complete with how-to instructions for their creation.

While more and more attention is paid to interior installations, windows are still the major attractions for the giant retailers. Especially involved in window preparation are the flagships of the large department stores. For the windows, the preparation and installation of the displays is another story. Stores that indulge in these pre-

EXECUTION OF A VISUAL PRESENTATION

Figure 12-2. By using simple props such as dryer vent tubing, the visual merchandiser achieves a design goal. (*Courtesy of Ellen Diamond.*)

sentations usually spend the bulk of their visual merchandising budgets on eye-catching windows that they hope will entice the shopper to enter the store. As we saw in Chapter 5, there is a multitude of props available from many sources. Using creative ability, the visual merchandiser selects just the right props and materials. Unless the presentation is institutionally oriented, inspiration must come from the merchandise. Does the item warrant a theatrical setting or does it stand on its own merits, shown against a simple background? These are but two of the questions that cross the display person's mind when deciding on materials and props. Another deals with the specifications and shape of the window structure. Some windows allow little in the way of props and materials, because of size or design. Figure 12-2 features a window that is actually part of the store. The trimmer had to prepare a window that captured the eye but didn't close off the shopper's view of the store. By using the right props and positioning them strategically, the visual merchandiser achieved the goal.

PREPARING THE DISPLAY SPACE

Too often, the space in which the design is to be presented is sorely neglected. Stains or cracks in the walls, fingerprints on the glass, stray pins on the floor, and burned-out lights can seriously mar the presentation's overall effectiveness. In order to produce a high-quality display, the trimmer must pay attention to environmental details as well as to the selection of merchandise. A retail organization that puts up with blemishes in the display areas may soon find its image suffering.

Windows and other display cases should be checked as follows:

Checklist

1. Make certain that the walls are freshly painted, all holes are filled in, and staples are removed. If pads that were used before are to be used again, check them for possible damage.
2. Examine valances and frames for blemishes. They might have to be repainted or covered with new material.
3. Vacuum the floor to remove fallen pins or staples.

Figure 12-3. A group of sophisticated mannequins successfully present fashion forward clothing. (*Courtesy of Ellen Diamond.*)

Figure 12-4. Mannequins in action poses add interest to merchandise. (*Courtesy of Carol Barnhart.*)

4. Clean window or display case glass to remove fingerprints and the film that often develops on enclosed windows.
5. Test all lights and replace burned-out bulbs.
6. Cut wires that were used to hold props and suspend merchandise from ceiling grills or other supports.
7. Clean the ventilation frame surrounding the glass.

SELECTING MANNEQUINS AND FORMS

In most situations a mannequin is the best way to feature apparel realistically. It enables the shopper to immediately appreciate the garment's silhouette and determine if it is appropriate for his or her needs. In Chapter 4, we learned about the enormous variety of mannequin types and materials and for what purposes each was best suited. Larger stores often have a storage area stacked with many types of mannequins ready to serve the purpose of the particular display. Smaller companies, with a limited budget and space, are less likely to have the opportunity to use different types of mannequins.

If a choice is available, study all of the mannequin styles and choose the ones most suited for the merchandise and the setting in which it will be featured. For example, if the design needs an air of sophistication, a good choice would be from fashion forward, elegant mannequins as featured in Figure 12-3.

Not only are style and image important to mannequin selection, but so are the mannequins' positions and the direction they face. A sitting model might be used to achieve interest and balance. Most visual merchandisers, however, learn early about the pitfalls and limitations of seated forms. They take up more space than standing mannequins and are more difficult to dress. Figure 12-4 shows a grouping of mannequins in a variety of positions. When properly coordinated, the effect is an interesting departure from the representational forms that are used abundantly by trimmers today.

Some windows don't lend themselves to full figures. Visual merchandisers are fortunate to have many other forms from which to choose. As with mannequins, some stores stock a variety of merchandise forms. These, too, should be chosen with care to display goods to their best advantage. Figure 12-5 shows some of these forms and how they are used effectively in installations.

Figure 12-9. In limited space, display torsos fit the bill. (*Courtesy of Ellen Diamond.*)

PREPARING THE LIGHTING

The last step before the actual installation of a display concerns lighting. Not only must each permanent light fixture be examined and tested for burned-out bulbs, but portable spotlights should be assembled in the right number. The bulbs for all of the fixtures should be examined to determine if they are housed with spotlights or floodlights, and changed if the required type is not present. Today's light offerings are so plentiful and diverse, as discussed in Chapter 8, that the trimmer has a wealth of products to choose from to make the installation most effective.

If colored lighting is essential to enhance the display, it will be necessary to prepare the right color of bulbs or gels to achieve the desired effect. Often trimmers who leave lighting requirements to chance find it difficult to come up with specific needs at the last moment. Without proper lighting, the presentation's effectiveness will suffer.

A final note on lighting concerns the use of time clocks to turn the lights on and off automatically in window displays. Most retailers recognize the fact that shoppers frequently examine their windows when the store is closed. The lights should remain on until they no longer serve a purpose. If lights are left on all day and night, power costs will increase and the bulbs will quickly burn out.

INSTALLING THE DISPLAY

When all of the preliminaries have been attended to, it is time to assemble and install the display's components. Since the windows play a vital role in motivating shoppers to purchase, it is best for them to be refurbished, if possible, early in the morning before the store opens for business or after closing time. Another consideration is the amount of disruption that takes place in trimming a window during regular hours. Some stores, especially the smaller independents, experience havoc if the installation occurs at a busy selling time. If an installation cannot be done when the store is closed, precision is of the utmost consideration. The less time for disruption, the better!

Follow this step-by-step procedure to install a display:

1. After the entire display area has been prepared as previously described, the background walls should be dressed. If the walls are permanently decorated for use in all displays, there is no further work in this step. Most visual merchandisers, however, rely on background walls to project a certain color, texture, or theme. Pads covered with fabric can adequately serve the needs of the display person. Although paper initially costs less than fabric, it has a short life and damages easily. Draped fabric walls also serve as background cover. Apply the background material quickly, making certain that neither staples nor other fasteners are visible to the viewer. It should be noted that pads can be prepared in advance in the store's visual merchandising facility, and can eliminate the time and fussing often associated with paper usage.

2. Position the props and fasten them securely. If they are installed carelessly in a window, vibration could cause the props to fall. This is particularly important when trimmers choose to fly props from the ceiling. Falling props could not only ruin the presentation, but could damage the mannequins, forms, and glass panels. In some cases, if window glass is broken, passers-by could be hurt, causing legal problems for the store.

3. Mannequins are handled next. There are two schools of thought on dressing them. One group prefers to dress the mannequins in an area adjacent to the window, and then place them, fully clothed, into the display. The other school chooses to fit the garments onto the mannequins inside the window. In the case of trimmer-made mannequins, the first choice is better since the operation could be time-consuming. Whatever the preference, place the mannequins without disturbing the flooring. Fabrics tend to shift, paper could tear, and wood could be scratched if care is not taken in the placement.

4. Apply the accessories to the mannequins next. Remove or conceal any merchandise tags.

5. Many windows, especially those of the case type, feature merchandise that is not shown on mannequins. Trimmers often fly some items or use various pedestals and props and a variety of stands for their presentation. These should be placed at this time. If both mannequins and merchandise on props are used, the mannequins should be placed first.

6. Direct the spotlights to the areas that are the highlights or focal points of the display.

7. Place showcards and price cards, if used, in the appropriate areas.

8. Examine the floors carefully for any marks left by the trimmer. Many installers remove their shoes during the installation, or use display socks over their shoes to minimize marks. However, if there are some blemishes, a handheld vacuum cleaner will remove them as well as stray pins and staples. The small vacuum cleaner is better than a full-size model at this point because it can fit easily into tight spots.

EXECUTION OF A VISUAL PRESENTATION

9. Survey the entire display to make certain that its appearance is exactly as planned and that every detail has been given consideration. The final check often requires moving a mannequin slightly, adjusting a spotlight, or replacing a sign. The job should not be considered finished until this step is completed.

DISPLAY SKETCHES

Many visual merchandisers prefer to complete a preliminary sketch of the upcoming display before it is actually executed. Not only does it graphically present the designer's thoughts, but it acts as a guide to those who will actually install the presentation. In major companies such as Lord & Taylor, where there is a large visual merchandising team, the director is often the individual totally responsible for theme designs, but the staff carries out the installations. It is certainly easier to convey design concepts with sketches or finished drawings than with words. In companies with distant branches that each have one or a few trimmers, with the director of visual merchandising located in the flagship store, the sketch is an excellent way to relate the display's concept. As with their merchandise offerings, most retailers want uniformity in their visual presentations to give the total company a unified image. Figure 12-6 features a Valentine's display sketch, complete with written instructions, to get the message across.

In some cases these sketches are accompanied by fabrics, paper, signs, etc., to ensure not only that the design is accomplished, but that the materials to best feature the merchandise are used.

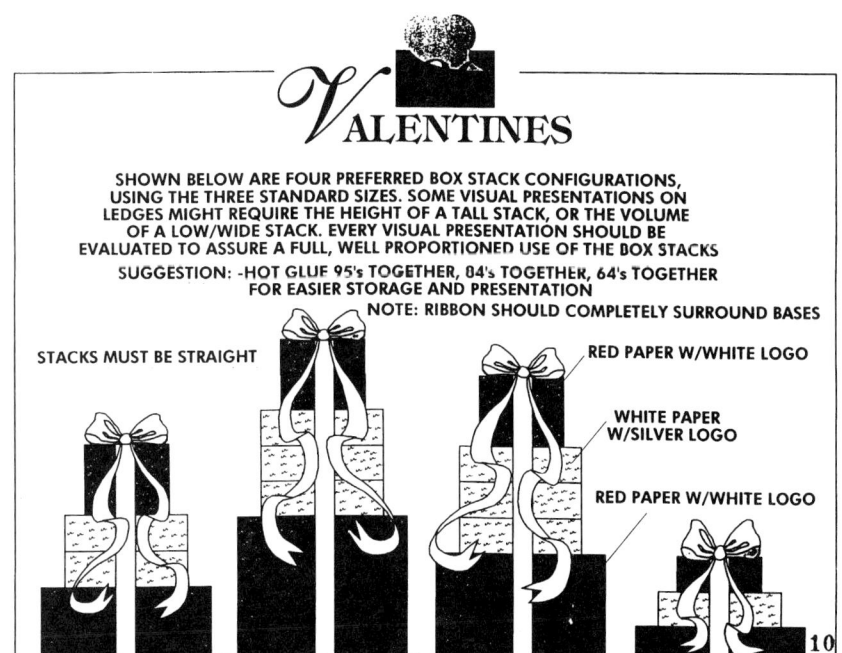

Figure 12-6. Sketches show the trimmer how the project should be achieved. (*Courtesy of Lord & Taylor.*)

GRAPHIC PLANS

Many chain organizations have hundreds of units across the country and do not employ professional trimmers to install their displays. In the preceding discussion, the sketches were meant for professional trimmers who could easily execute a quality display. Many companies, though, rely on a store manager or someone else whose principal duty is not display to dress a window or change an interior corner or niche. In order to make certain that the plan can be carried out easily, those companies might choose to set up a display in their home office or central headquarters, photograph it, and send the pictures along with a scaled graphic floor plan. These plans show the placement of mannequins, forms, props, floor lights, and signs. Nothing is left to the imagination of the installer, and even those less gifted in visual merchandising can carry out such a plan. In Figure 12-7, the finished display has been photographed, and the instructions for duplicating it have been sent to stores along with a graphic plan.

DEVELOPING SPECIFIC DISPLAYS

To help you fully visualize the actual creation of props and the process of setting them in displays, two illustrations are presented in step-by-step procedures, with some stages pictorially depicted. They are an underwater display and a spring display. In addition to these, the creation of three props that may be used in displays is featured: a large pot with flowers, ribbon-accented boxes, and the covering of a flower pot with fabric.

Underwater Shadow Box Display

Key stages of the installation are shown in Figures 12-8 through 12-13.

1. Foamcore should be cut to size and covered by stapling with moiré that runs horizontally to give a water effect. The moiré-covered boards can easily be attached to the wall with pins, whose heads are then snipped off.
2. Insert fiberglass rocks that are shaped by cutting with a small saw or knife and then sprayed the color of rocks. Those that are attached to the wall are secured with #32 pins. Remember to cut off pin heads.
3. Use asparagus ferns that have been dried, and set them into rocks.
4. Use rods to attach rocks to each other for security purposes.
5. Accent the setting with sea fans that have been sprayed white. (The sea fans and asparagus ferns are available in a florist shop.)
6. Accent the rest of the setting with pampas grass (also available from a florist shop), making certain that the grass hides the rods.
7. Add an odd number of fish on rods, sticking them into rocks.
8. Tiny shells might be strewn on the floor of the display for additional interest.
9. Merchandise such as jewelry, which is perfect for such a setting, is then added by placing some on the display floor, draping some over rocks, etc.

EXECUTION OF A VISUAL PRESENTATION

Signage Checklist

❑ 9x12 Fuzzy Rice Cooker

❑ 4x5 Jasmine Rice, Peanut & Thai Chili Sauce

NOTE:
- *Do NOT open or M.O.S. any bags of rice we sell. Purchase inexpensive rice from the grocery store.*
- *Use Classic bowls only. Replace onion bowls shown in photo.*
- *Place Henkel Knife sets to the back of feature.*

Jasmine Rice

DQ	Item Description	Sku	Display Comments
48	Classic Bowl	953562	
1	Fuzzy Rice Cooker	1184902	
18	Jade Jasmine Rice	595538	Light to set up; more arriving first week of packet
12	On Rice Book	1112150	
24	Jade Thai Chili Sauce	1137694	
36	Jade Peanut Sauce	342311	
12	Green Chopsticks	1186543	
4	Four Star Santuko	667311	
6	Asian Cutlery Flat Pack Set	1205178	
8	Wood Salad Plates	1138197	

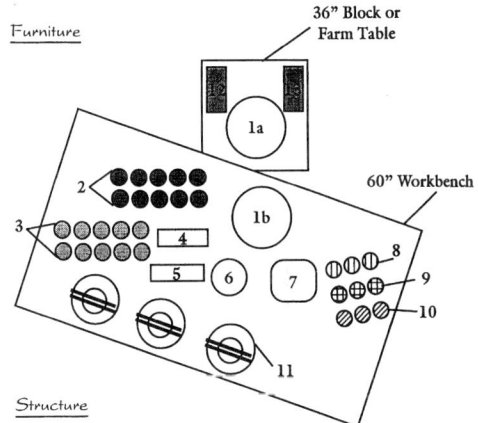

Structure

1a) Small oyster basket of Jade Rice is on an 8" riser on the back cube.
1b) Small oyster is on workbench.
2) Peanut Sauce is stacked 3 high, 5 across, 2 deep.
3) Thai Chili Sauce is stacked 2 high, 5 across, 2 deep.
4) *On Rice* book is on 4" riser.
5) *On Rice* book is on furniture.
6) Fill large biscotti jar with dunnage, pour store bought rice over dunnage.
7) Fuzzy rice cooker.
8) Classic rice bowls are stacked is 6 high, 3 across.
9) Classic rice bowls are stacked is 4 high, 3 across.
10) Classic rice bowls are stacked is 3 high, 3 across.
11) Wood plate with bowl, fill bowl with store bought rice.
12) Asian Knife, stack to the back on cube.
13) Oriental Knife, stack to the back on cube.

Figure 12-7. A display photograph, along with a graphic plan, instructs the trimmers how to reproduce the installation. (*Courtesy of Williams-Sonoma.*)

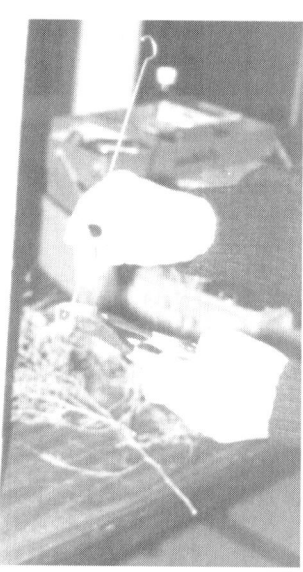

Figure 12-8. The foamcore has been cut to size and covered with moiré. (*Courtesy of Terry Perrine.*)

Figure 12-9. Fiberglass rocks are the first props to be inserted, followed by the asparagus ferns. (*Courtesy of Terry Perrine.*)

Figure 12-10. Rocks are attached to each other by means of steel rods. (*Courtesy of Terry Perrine.*)

Figure 12-11. Sprayed sea fans are then installed. (*Courtesy of Terry Perrine.*)

Figure 12-12. Pampas grass is the next material inserted. (*Courtesy of Terry Perrine.*)

Figure 12-13. Jewelry is then placed to complete the display. (*Courtesy of Terry Perrine.*)

EXECUTION OF A VISUAL PRESENTATION

Figure 12-14. Foamcore cut to size, covered with moiré, and placed in shadow box. (*Courtesy of Terry Perrine.*)

Figure 12-15. A lattice form has been embellished with leaves and flowers. (*Courtesy of Terry Perrine.*)

Spring Display

Figures 12-14 through 12-16 show some of the combined stages.

1. Buy a sheet of lattice (available in a lumber yard), cut to the size needed, and spray paint in the desired color.
2. Accent the lattice with leaves and butterflies.
3. Insert moiré-covered foamcore to fit the space, and then insert the lattice in front of the foamcore.
4. Paint flower pots in the color desired. Insert Styrofoam in pots, and cover the Styrofoam with moss.
5. Wire flowers together with floral tape to form clusters. Insert the floral arrangements into the pots.
6. Place the pots in an interesting manner, with one tipped over.
7. Use butterflies as accents.
8. This is an excellent setting for small items such as flatware and jewelry.

Figure 12-16. Flower pots, placed in an interesting manner, are inserted and the setting is ready to receive small items such as flatware and jewelry. (*Courtesy of Terry Perrine.*)

Props Created by Trimmer

Following are three props that can be easily created by the trimmer for use in a variety of displays.

Large Pot with Flowers

Figures 12-17 through 12-22 feature the construction of the prop.

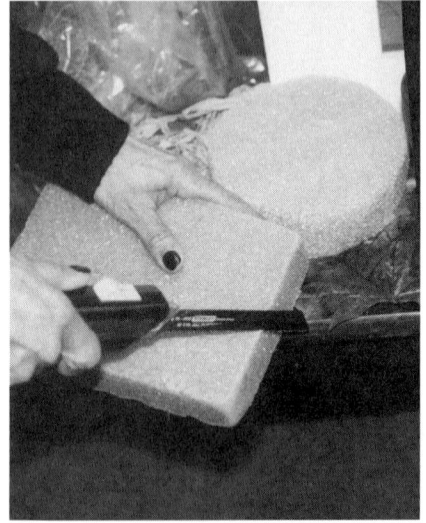

Figure 12-17. Styrofoam cut to size of pot opening. (*Courtesy of Terry Perrine.*)

Figure 12-18. Leaves are cut from branches for use as pot covering. (*Courtesy of Terry Perrine.*)

Figure 12-19. Pot is sprayed with glue and will be dressed to look like the finished one. (*Courtesy of Terry Perrine.*)

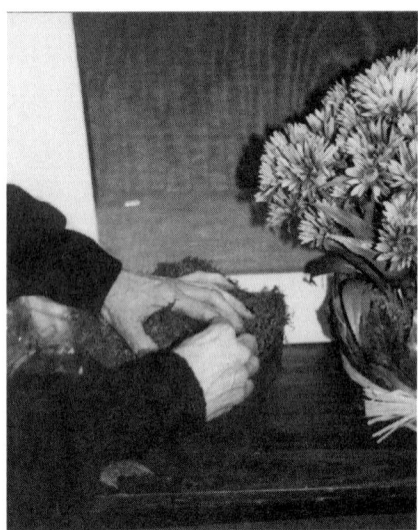

Figure 12-20. Moss is inserted in pot to camouflage Styrofoam. (*Courtesy of Terry Perrine.*)

Figure 12-21. Leaves are placed on pot's surface that has been sprayed with glue. (*Courtesy of Terry Perrine.*)

Figure 12-22. Raffia is tied around pot as a finishing touch. (*Courtesy of Terry Perrine.*)

1. Use a basic flower pot purchased at a nursery.
2. Cut out a Styrofoam circle to fit snugly into the pot's opening.
3. Cut leaves from branches.
4. Spray the pot with glue substance.
5. Use moss to cover the Styrofoam.
6. Affix the leaves to the pot.
7. Insert flowers into the pot.
8. Tie raffia around the pot.

Ribbon-Accented Boxes

Figures 12-23 through 12-26 illustrate how ribbon-accented boxes are created.

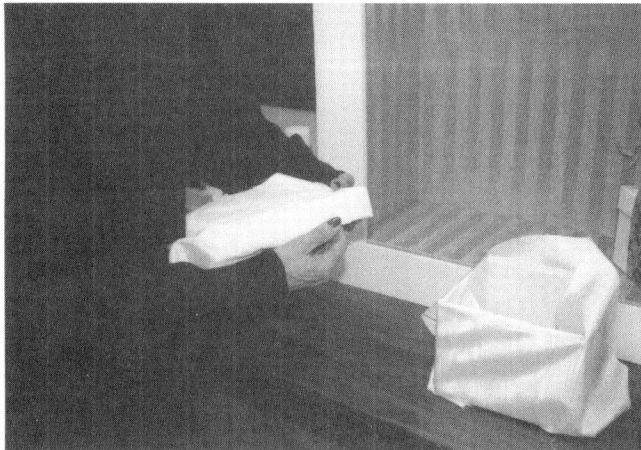

Figure 12-23. Jewelry boxes are covered with moiré. (*Courtesy of Terry Perrine.*)

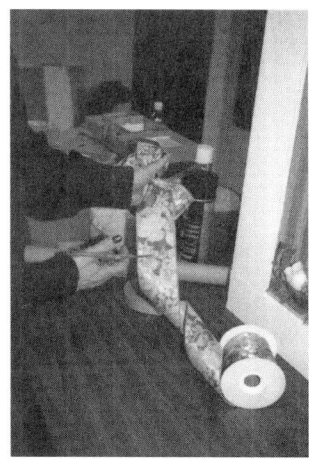

Figure 12-24. Ribbon is cut to size. (*Courtesy of Terry Perrine.*)

Figure 12-25. Large bow is created for attachment to boxes. (*Courtesy of Terry Perrine.*)

Figure 12-26. Decorated boxes used in display. (*Courtesy of Terry Perrine.*)

1. Cover boxes with moiré or other decorative fabric by using spray adhesive.
2. Add the ribbons in two directions, making certain the seams are in the back.
3. Make a large bow, measuring how much ribbon will be needed. A little extra should be left for tails. Bow is tied with wire and attached to ribbon box.

Fabric-Covered Flower Pot

1. Purchase a basic flower pot.
2. Cut fabric of choice large enough to cover the sides of pot and to tuck into pot.
3. Place transfer tape (available at supply shop) inside the lip of the pot and on base.
4. Pleat the fabric evenly until the pot is covered.

These are just a few of the props that are easy to create. With experience, there is no telling how many others you can create.

TERMS OF THE TRADE

asparagus ferns
display sketch
display socks
display time clock
flying props
garland
graphic plan
lattice
merchandise loan form
pampas grass
sea fans
Styrofoam
transfer tape
window and display case checklist
window valances

CHAPTER REVIEW

KEY POINTS IN THE CHAPTER

1. In the installation of a display, careful planning with attention to detail is a must to guarantee effectiveness.
2. The merchandise displayed in a visual presentation is the choice and responsibility of the store buyer, an assistant, or a department manager.
3. Before garments are positioned in the presentation, they must be carefully pressed, obvious merchandise tags must be removed, and the outfit should be accessorized for a total positive impact.
4. Accessorization is generally the responsibility of the store's fashion director or coordinator.
5. All props and materials should be selected and made ready for a specific installation time so as not to delay the presentation and leave display windows and cases undressed for longer periods than necessary.
6. To cut costs, most retailers require that props be reused as often as possible, being freshly painted and reassembled if necessary to convey a new look.
7. Display areas should be prepared carefully before an installation. This includes cleaning glass and floors and checking the lighting.
8. If an assortment of mannequins is available, the trimmer should carefully choose the most appropriate ones for the display.
9. Lighting should be arranged to guarantee the best visual effect. Floor spotlights should be placed properly to create the best lighting accents.
10. A step-by-step procedure should be followed in the installation of a display so that it will be carefully executed in the least amount of time.
11. Display sketches are often used, as well as graphic layouts, to convey the visual merchandise director's message to the trimmers.
12. Many props can be created by trimmers once they have mastered the knack of doing so.

DISCUSSION QUESTIONS

1. Why do some visual merchandisers intentionally minimize background props in a window?
2. Who is responsible for selecting the merchandise to be featured in a display?

3. Besides being shown as merchandise for sale, what role do accessories play when used in windows that focus on dresses or outfits?
4. How might a tired display prop be revitalized and reused?
5. What concerns are associated with the use of live plants in a display?
6. Does the store spend the bulk of its visual merchandising budget on window or interior display?
7. List five points to be checked before merchandise is installed in a window.
8. Which mannequin position is most difficult for the trimmer to dress?
9. Define the term *time clock*. What function does it serve in visual merchandising?
10. What is the best time of the day to trim a store's windows?
11. Why are fabric-covered pads favored by most trimmers over the use of paper?
12. Many visual merchandisers find felt to be especially useful. Why?
13. Where is the best place to dress a mannequin that is to be featured in a window?
14. Describe the purpose of a display sketch.
15. For what reasons are graphic scale drawings used in visual presentations?

CASE PROBLEMS

Case 1

Hartley's is a specialty chain that features junior sportswear and activewear. The company has been in business for 20 years and has experienced steady growth. Management operates from a centralized headquarters that is no more than 100 miles from any of the stores. The philosophy of the company has always been to keep its trading area confined to 150 miles so that the centralized staff can have personal contact with each unit. The 20 stores are close enough to headquarters that regular visits by top management and the merchandising team are possible.

Visual merchandising is accomplished with a manager and four trimmers who regularly visit each store to change the window and interior displays. Since the stores are within a manageable radius, the plan works perfectly. The presentations are professionally installed and seem to motivate shoppers to become customers.

Now Hartley's is embarking on an expansion program. It is in the process of acquiring a 12-store chain that is 300 miles from its base of operations. This is just the beginning of a program that calls for the acquisition of other small chains, some of which are even farther away than this current acquisition.

The only problem yet to be resolved concerns the visual merchandising function. It is not feasible to have the display team, which so successfully served the company when it was a smaller organization, trim all of the stores owned by Hartley's. Expansion of the visual staff would not only be expensive, but it would require another preparation point from which to service those stores that are too far from the company's original headquarters. Although the company recognizes effective display presentation as a necessity, it believes another solution must be found to maintain costs at a reasonable level.

Questions

1. How can the company maintain the quality level of its visual presentations?
2. Suggest an alternate solution that would maintain its present staff or even reduce the number while still providing effective visual merchandising.

Case 2

In approximately three months, Avidon's will open as a high-fashion specialty shop catering to affluent men and women. In addition to the typical designer merchandise usually associated with this type of retail operation, the company will feature an assortment of private label designs and accessories from all of the world's fashion centers.

The company plans a retail environment that is not typical of its contemporaries. The fixtures, lighting, and other interior elements will feature a decor oriented to antiques. No chrome, brass, or marble fittings will be used. The interior design will boast antique armoires, cupboards, tables, etc., to house the merchandise. Leaded glass will enhance the showcases.

In order to support this image of old-world elegance that the company wishes to project, it is formulating a new concept of visual merchandising and hiring a full-time visual merchandiser to handle all of the interior and window presentations. Although stores of this type often rely on freelancers, Avidon's is willing to hire a full-timer to keep the shop's visual presentations at a superior level. The individual will have overall responsibility for all visual merchandising, including installations in two windows and throughout the interior as well as the purchase of display equipment.

Since interviewing for the job is about to begin, management is preparing a list of questions to determine the candidates' eligibility for the job of visual merchandiser.

Questions

1. What type of experience should the successful candidate bring to the job?
2. How can management determine which individual holds the most promise?
3. Is there a test that can be used to determine the individual's ability to do a satisfactory job of visually merchandising Avidon's interior and windows?

NAME: _____ DATE: _____

EXERCISES

1. On the grid paper provided, prepare a graphic floor plan to scale for a closed-back window that measures 4 feet deep and 8 feet across. Each item, such as mannequins, forms, pedestals, props, etc., that occupies floor space should be indicated by its shape and floor placement. Make certain that the scale is noted and each form is marked to show what it represents.

2. From the types of window structures shown in Chapter 3, select one for a display that you will design. On the form provided, prepare a detailed sketch to show all of the component parts of your window. Mark each part of the drawing with a number that corresponds to the list of items that will accompany the sketch. For example, 1 for mannequins, 2 for pedestals, 3 for floor spotlights, 4 for background screen, 5 for display props, etc. Make certain that the information called for on the form is completed along with the sketch. Along with the directory of items, include color samples to be used for merchandise as well as the background materials and props.

NAME: _____ DATE: _____

Exercise 1 GRAPHIC FLOOR PLAN

NAME: _____ DATE: _____

Exercise 2 DISPLAY DESIGN SKETCH

Window Type: _____ Dimensions: _____
Display Theme: _____
_____

Directory of Items

Items	Number	Color

INDEX

Acetate gels, 154
Angled windows, 47
Analogous color scheme, 130
Arcade windows, 48
Awl, 98

Backlit transparencies, 187-188
Balance, 108-110
  asymmetrical, 110
  symmetrical, 109-110
Ballast, 157
Banners, 187
Budgeting, 10-11

Careers, 13-14
Carpet, 92
CAUS, 134
Ceiling grills, 12
Centralized visual merchandising, 6, 27-32
  alternate plan, 30-31
  total plan, 27-30
Chase lights, 157
Circular windows, 49
Claw hammer, 98
Color, 127-136
Color Association of America, 134
Color dimensions, 128-129
  hue, 128
  intensity, 129
  value, 128-129
Colored lighting, 154
  filters, 154
  gels, 154
Color harmonies, 129-132

analogous, 130
complementary, 130
double complementary, 131
monochromatic, 130
split complementary, 130
triad, 131
Color psychology, 134-136
  advancing colors, 134-135
  cool colors, 134
  emotional colors, 135-136
  receding colors, 134-135
  warm colors, 134
Color schemes, 133-134
Color tubes, 149
Color wheel, 129
Commercial sign sources, 196-197
Complementary color scheme, 130
Component parts of mannequins, 66-69
  arms, 68
  base attachments, 68
  hands, 68
  leg structure, 67
  torso, 67
Construction project, 29-30
Corner windows, 46-47
Cotton Incorporated, 134
Cove lighting, 157
Cutawl, 98

Decorative lighting, 153
Dimmers, 154
Directory signage, 190
Display accessories of the trade, 99
Display emphasis, 111-114

contrast, 112
directional, 114
lights and darks, 112-113
shape, 113
size, 112
textural, 113
unique placement, 114
Display fixturing, 11
Display house props, 96
Display installation, 227-229
Display materials, 88-92
  carpet, 92
  construction boards, 89-90
    foam boards, 89
    homosote, 90
    masonite, 89-90
    oaktag, 89
    plywood, 90
  fabric, 90
  wood, 92
    parquet, 92
Display tools, 97-99
Display walkthrough, 26-27
Dressing a mannequin, 69-71
Drill press, 98
Double complementary color scheme, 131

Elura, 72
Emotional effects of color, 135-136
Emphasis, principles of, 111-114
Ensemble display, 175-176

Fabric, 90-91
  bengaline, 91

INDEX

brocade, 91
burlap, 91
Jacquard, 91
lame, 91
mylar, 91
velvet, 91
Facilities rendering, 53-54
Fiber optic lighting, 150
Fixture-contained signage, 188
Fixturing, 50-54
    complete layout, 53-54
    floorcases, 50
    island cases, 51-52
    island tables, 51-52
    multipurpose merchandise systems, 51
    shadow boxes, 52
    show and sell fixtures, 52-53
    wall cases, 51
    vitrines, 52
Fixturing layouts, 53-54
Flagship stores, 4
Flashers, lighting, 156
Floorcases, 50
Fluorescent lighting, 148-149
Foamboard, 89
Focal point, 111
Feme-core, 89
Found display objects, 8, 93
Framing projector, 156
Freelance contract arrangements, 32-36
Freelancers, 6
Fresnels, 156
Furniture props, 93
Futuristic mannequins, 66

Gatorboard, 90
Gels, 156
Glass colored filters, 154
Graphic presentations, 28,32
Graphics, 186-197

Hacksaw, 98
Halogen bulbs, 150-151
Harmony in design, 118-19
IIIDs, 150
High intensity discharge, 150
Highlighting, 149
Homosote, 90
Hot glue gun, 98
Hue, 128

IALD, 158
IESNA, 158
Incandescent bulbs, 149
Indirect lighting, 157
In-house prop construction, 96
In-house sign production, 194-195
    computer generated, 194
    hand lettering, 195
        calligraphy, 195
    sign-making machines, 194
In-house staffs, 4

In-house visual departments, 22-27
Institutional visual themes, 175
Intensity, 129
Interiors, 49-50
Island display cases, 51-52
Island display tables, 51-52
Island windows, 48

Jacquard, 91

Kanekalon, 72
Kick-off seminar, 23

Labor costs, 12
Letter materials, 191-193
    foam, 191
    Fome-core, 193
    metal, 192
    mirror, 192
    plastic, 192
    Plexiglas, 192
    Sintra, 193
    wood, 192
    wood grain laminates, 192
    vinyl, 192-193
Light boxes, 187-188
Lighting, 147-158
Lighting accessories, 154, 156
    dimmers, 154
    flashers, 154, 156
    framing projectors, 154, 156
    fresnels, 154, 156
    gels, 154, 156
    strobes, 154, 156
    swivel sockets, 154, 156
    templates, 156
Lighting fixtures and systems, 151-153
    decorative, 153
    recessed, 151-152
    track, 152-153
Lighting terminology, 157
Lighting with color, 154
Light sources, 148-151
    fiber optic lighting, 150
    fluorescent, 148-149
    halogen, 150
    high intensity discharge, 150
    incandescent, 149
    neon, 150
Light system acquisition, 158

Makeup for mannequins, 72-73
Mannequins, 64-71
    types, 65-66
        futuristic human forms, 66
        representational forms, 66
        stylized forms, 65
        traditional human forms, 65
        trimmer constructed forms, 66
Masonite, 89-90
Materials, 11-12
Mat knife, 98

Merchandise loan form, 203,223
Merchandise preparation guidelines, 24-26
    overview, 26
    table of contents, 25
Merchandise props, 93-94
Mock windows, 6
Model windows, 27
Monochromatic color scheme, 130
Moving message signs, 189
Multipurpose merchandise systems, 51

NADI, 95, 158
National Association of Display Industries, 95
Neon, 150
Neon signs, 190
Neutral additions to color, 133

Oaktag, 89
Open-back windows, 47

Paint, 91-92
Paper, 91
    seamless, 91
Parallel-to-sidewalk windows, 46
PAR bulbs, 149
Pennant signs, 189
Phillips-head screwdriver, 98
Photographic transparencies, 187
Plywood, 90
Point of purchase, 10,205-215
    retail users, 206-210
        department stores, 209-210
        greeting card stores, 208-209
        mass merchandisers, 207
        pharmacies, 208
        specialty organizations, 209
        supermarkets, 207
        warehouse clubs, 208
Point of purchase fixtures, 211-213
    cardboard fixtures, 213
    closed circuit video, 211-212
    computer stations, 213
    countertop cases, 212-213
    gondolas, 211
    interactive video, 211
    motion creations, 212
POPAI, 10,206
Portfolio of work, 14
Primary colors, 129
Principles of design, 107-119
    balance, 108-109
        asymmetrical, 110
        symmetrical, 109-110
    emphasis, 111-114
        contrast, 112-114
        repetition, 112
        size, 111
        unique placement, 114
    harmony, 118-119
    proportion, 114-115
    rhythm, 116-118

Promostyl, 134
Promotional division, 5
Proportion, 114-115
Props, 11-12, 92-96
    display house props, 95
    found objects, 93
    furniture, 93
    in-house constructions, 96
    merchandise props, 93
Purchasing mannequins and forms, 74
PVC piping, 96

Recessed lighting, 151-152
Representational mannequins, 8, 66
Rhythm, 116-118
    alternation, 118
    continuous line, 116
    progression, 117
    radiation, 117
    repetition, 116

Sabre saw, 98
Safety factors, 12-13
Seamless paper, 91
Secondary colors, 129
Shades of color, 128-129
Shadow boxes, 52
Shadow box windows, 49
Show and sell fixtures, 52-53
Signage, 186-197
Sign layout 195-196
    thumbnail sketches, 196
Sign materials, 190-191
    brass, 191
    cardboard, 191
    fabric, 191
    lucite, 191
    masonite, 191
    paper, 191
    wood, 191
Signs on glass, 188
Sign types, 186-190
    backlit transparencies, 187-188
    banners, 187
    fixture-contained signage, 188
    moving message signs, 189
    neon signs 190
    pennants, 189
    signs on glass, 188
    track signage, 189
    valence signs, 188
    wall signs, 187

Sintra, 89
Six month visual plan, 23
Slatwall systems, 51
Special events, 175
Special promotions, 175
Spotlighting, 149
Split complementary color scheme, 130
Store front structures, 46-49
    angled windows, 47
    arcades, 48
    circular windows, 49
    corner windows, 46-47
    islands, 48
    open-back windows, 47
    parallel-to-sidewalk windows, 46
    shadow box windows, 49
    windowless windows, 48
Store of the Year Awards, 54-55
Store organizational structure, 5
Striking a mannequin, 13
Strobes, 156
Stylized mannequins, 65

Tack hammer, 98
Table saw, 98
Templates, 156
Thematic displays, 2
Tints, 128
Tools, 97-99
Tools of the trade, 98
    extras, 98
    minimum, 98
Torsos and other human forms, 73-74
Total environment philosophy, 2, 166-167
T pins, 99
Track lighting, 152
Track signage, 189
Traditional mannequins, 65
Triad color scheme, 131
Trimmer created mannequins, 66, 74-79
    children's forms,, 74-76
    men's forms, 76-78
    women's forms 78-79
T square, 98

Unit displays, 176

Valence signs, 188
Value, 128-129
Visual merchandiser responsibilities, 4
Visual merchandising definition,, 3
Visual merchandising trends, 6-10
    graphics, 9
    lighting,, 9
    mannequins, 8
    materials, 8
    point of purchase, 10
    props, 8
    signage, 9
    sound usage, 10
    store design, 7
Visual presentation execution, 221-236
    assembling materials, 224-225
    assembling props, 224-225
    display sketches, 229
    graphic plans, 229-230
    installing the display, 227-229
    preparing display space, 225-226
    preparing merchandise, 223-224
    selecting mannequins, 226
    selecting merchandise, 222-223
Visual themes,, 165-176
    Christmas, 171-172
    Columbus Day, 173
    creative types, 173
    Easter, 172
    fall, 168-169
    holidays, 171
    parent's days 172-173
    President's Days, 172
    seasons, 168
    spring, 170-171
    summer, 168
    Valentine's Day, 173
    winter, 169-170
Vitrines, 52

Wall cases, 51
Wall signs, 187
Wigs, 71-72
    horsehair, 71
    lacquered wigs, 71
    man-made fibers, 72
        Elura, 72
        Kanekalon, 72
        Luraflex, 72
    molded variety, 72
    novelty fibers, 72
Windowless windows, 48
Window schedule, 23-24
Window trimmer, 1-2
Wood, 92